GOD'S FIRE

MOSES AND THE MANAGEMENT
OF EXODUS

Alfred de Grazia

GOD'S FIRE

MOSES AND THE MANAGEMENT OF EXODUS

Metron Publications

Second edition
ISBN: 978-1-60377-085-9
LCCN: 2012923934
© Metron Publications, 1983, February 2013
All Rights Reserved

Metron Publications, P.O. Box 1213, PRINCETON N.J.
08542-1213
www.metron-publications.com

To Stephanie Neuman

*"It takes a chaos within oneself
to give birth to a shooting star."*

(FRIEDRICH NIETZSCHE)

COVER PICTURE: The cover of the First edition (1983) - *Moses,* by Klaud Sluter, "Puits de Moïse," Chartreuse de Champmol, Dijon, France (1403-1406)

FOREWORD

The Judaic, Christian, and Islamic religions go back to the Exodus from Egypt of the Hebrews under the leadership of Moses. They center upon this event and upon Moses. Ernst Sellin, a distinguished German authority on the Old Testament, once declared, "The ultimate and most important question for the investigation of Israelitic-Judaic religion must inevitably be: 'Who was Moses?'" [1] Despite his own reply and notwithstanding the hundreds of works on Moses that are catalogued by the Library of Congress, the question has remained unanswered.

I have found no book that deals adequately with the psychology of Moses, and therefore have portrayed fully the workings of his mind. No study has properly embraced Moses in his two great capacities as a manager and scientist, and so I have reconstructed these his qualities as well. Furthermore, the Exodus and Wanderings, those operations that Moses directed, are generally misunderstood, both in their particulars as Jewish history and in their representation of what was happening throughout the world in those days.

Part of the 3000-year misunderstanding stems from the strange environment in which Moses lived and worked. The Exodus was not a stroll through the desert by some truant slaves. The Exodus occurred in an extraordinary setting of great atmospheric and physical turbulence, a catastrophic world. Unless we comprehend precisely the natural and social upheavals of those days, we cannot grasp

Moses. Nor can we fathom the religion of Moses. I have introduced in every chapter new methods of viewing the environment of the Exodus. Meteorology and electricity are joined to chronology, archaeology and biblical study, and all of these with psychology, sociology and political analysis.

I have some confidence in this multidisciplinary approach, and I hope that others will capture from its results some of the exhilaration that I experienced in its conception and elaboration. The very first chapter tells how a comet passed by and the plagues struck. The second chapter describes the failed negotiations between Moses and the Pharaoh, and the subsequent pursuit and escape. Each subsequent chapter picks up a critical part of the story - to explain it, to add evidence, and to place it naturally, coherently and sympathetically into the general scheme. In the end, the reader will perhaps have derived the same conclusions as I have from the Old Testament account of the most human of all experiences, the birth and establishment of a great god.

Alfred de Grazia

Washington Square
New York City
21 June 1983

Table of Contents

FOREWORD _____ 9

I. PLAGUES AND COMETS _____ 15
Comets and Angels ... Cosmic Plagues ... The Destruction of Egypt,

II. THE SCENARIO OF EXODUS _____ 41
High-Level Negotiations ... Why Pharaoh pursued the Hebrews ... The Organized Move ... Opening and Closing the Waters ... Unforeseen Circumstances.

III. CATASTROPHE AND DIVINE FIRES _____ 71
Whose Angel?.,.The Censored Designs of Heaven ... The Gentile Exodus ... The Horror of Red ... The Electrostatic Age ... Yahweh's Electrical Fire Conglomerate ... The Celestial First Cause.

IV. THE ARK IN ACTION _____ 112
The Golden Box... Dangers of Electrocution ... The Ark at Work ... The Electric Oracle ... The Battle of Jericho ... The Ark's End ... God's Fire Gone,

V. LEGENDS AND MIRACLES _____ 167
Radiation Diseases ... The Electrochemical Factory... Manna... The Burnt Offering ... The Brazen Serpent and other Rods.... The Pouch of Judgement

VI. THE CHARISMA OF MOSES _____ 197
The Love Child.. A Disliking for Hebrews ... The Meek Killer ... The

Courtly Shepherd ... Circumcision and Speech Problems ... Scientist and Inventor ... Talking with Gods ... The Centralization of Hallucination ... An Israelite Opinion Survey ... Routinizing Charisma ... The Maniac Scientist.

VII. THE LEVITES AND THE REVOLTS _____ 259
Numbers Leaving Egypt ... Impedimenta ... Technicians and Security Police ... Blame the People ... Revolt of the Golden Calf ... Korah's Rebellion ... Freud and the Murder of Moses ... Beth Peor.

VIII. THE ELECTRIC GOD _____ 315
The Name of Yahweh ... The Character of Yahweh ... Sin vs. Science ... Immortality ... Monotheism.

CONCLUSION _____ 359

APPENDIX: TECHNIQUES FOR THE ASSESSMENT OF LEGENDARY HISTORY _____ 363
The Limits of Distortion ... Unbelieving Scholars ... The Ptagmatics of Legend

ENDNOTES _____ 396

INDEX _____ 435

LIST OF ILLUSTRATIONS

1. A Comet in Human Form ___ 20
2. The Plagues and Exodus ___ 30
3. Pharaoh's Army Drowned ___ 60
4. The Tidewaters Passage ___ 64
5. The Route of Exodus and Wanderings ___ 65
6. On Eagle's Wings ___ 72
7. Moses' Tablets and the Golden Calf Heretics ___ 83
8. Zeus Strikes Down Phaeton ___ 91
9. The Leyden jar ___ 117
10. Egyptian Ark in Procession ___ 120
11. Cherubim of Nimrud ___ 128
12. The Ark's Structure and Function ___ 130
13. Ground Plan and Design of the Tabernacle ___ 134
14. The Destruction of Jericho ___ 151
15. Moses with Horns, Veil and Mask ___ 172
16. The Brazen Serpent is Formed ___ 192
17. The Burning Bush ___ 213
18. Mass Electroshock ___ 293
19. Myth of the Death of Moses ___ 308
20. The Moses of Klaus Sluter ___ 362

LIST OF TABLES

I. Attitudes of Israelites Encamped at the Holy Mountain _____ 243
II. Affection and Aggression in the Books of Moses _____ 336
III. Sin, Blame, and Compulsion _____ 338

CHAPTER ONE

PLAGUES AND COMETS

Disbelief in the *Book of Exodus*, for the modern educated person, begins with the fantastic story of the infant Moses' survival and salvation in the bulrushes of the Nile, advances through Moses' encounter with the Burning Bush whence speaks Yahweh, ascends rapidly with the plagues of Egypt that follow his threats as Yahweh's messenger, and reaches a climax in the parting of the waters to let the Israelites escape and the closing of the waters upon the Egyptians.

Thereafter the incredulous reader can only sigh as one after another lesser miracle occurs - water from tapping a rock with a wand, manna from heaven, tablets engraved by Yahweh, a little Ark with a bench on which Yahweh perches when he pleases, and a tent in which he dwells. Overall is the panorama of the people wandering in the desert, observed closely by this same Yahweh, who calls them his chosen people, despite their giving every indication of not behaving as chosen people should, and indeed not wanting to behave as his chosen ones.

I doubt that we can make sense out of these or other events of the Exodus if we insist upon examining them as separate and distinct bits. If it were only a question of a man being addressed by a bush, we might reach into the mental asylums and locate thousands of hallucinators. And if it were only an earthquake that was shaking down the houses of Egypt, we could assert that hundreds of earthquakes occur annually. Of slave rebellions, there are a great many in history. Of stubborn pharaohs, how very many world leaders are stubborn. And so on, until every event is identified with its own kind, but the kinds do not mesh together.

There is, in every episode of this whole history, a mysterious factor "X", something that is common to all of the behavior and events. Rather than let a realization of this factor "X" dawn upon us gradually, I think that we may identify it now. It is not Yahweh, the God of Moses, at least not conventionally Himself. It is an uncomfortable idea at first, but it lends shape and meaning to all the parts. Let us call it only a hypothesis at the start, a large supposition, leaving it to the reader, as events progress and one's thoughts progress with them, to decide in the end whether the supposition helps pull the pieces of the story together, and furthermore whether it is the probable all-embracing influence that lends a very special character to those days and years.

COMETS AND ANGELS

Beginning with the famous plagues of Egypt, occurring just as Moses confronts the Pharaoh and beginning shortly before the day of the Exodus proper, we search for the common factor, "X". What were these plagues? A legendary account gives us a convenient summary of them

> Thus did God proceed against the Egyptians. First he cut off

Plagues and Comets

their water supply by turning their rivers into blood. They refused to let the Israelites go, and He sent the noisy, croaking frogs into their entrails. They refused to let the Israelites go, and He brought lice against them, which pierced their flesh like darts. They refused to let the Israelites go, and He sent barbarian legions against them, mixed hordes of wild beasts [1]. They refused to let the Israelites go, and he brought slaughter upon them, a very grievous pestilence. They refused to let the Israelites go, and He poured out naphtha over them, burning blains. They refused to let the Israelites go, and He caused His projectiles, the hail, to descend upon them. They refused to let the Israelites go, and He placed scaling-ladders against the walls for the locusts, which climbed them like men of war. They refused to let the Israelites go, and He cast them into dungeon darkness. They refused to let the Israelites go, and He slew their magnates, their first born sons [2].

All of the incredible plagues (including related phenomena that go beyond the magic number of ten) would come from a near passage of an awful celestial body; and nothing but the passage of such a large celestial body could cause the incredible plagues.

Many ancient writers known to us, who had something to say of the period of Exodus, mentioned a great sky-connected disturbance of the world. Among them are such well-known figures as Eusebius, Pliny, Plutarch, Ovid, Seneca, Varro, and Augustine [3]. Further, every modern archaeologist and geologist whose investigations can be indisputably fixed in the period have reported serious physical upheavals [4]. I use this insistent form to express the generality of agreement; contemporary egotism, we realize, fears and hates to believe that ancient times might have witnessed natural behavior of a scope and intensity not experienced today.

In 1602, Abraham Rockenbach, a German Professor at Frankfurt University, published a "Treatise on Comets according to a New Method," there offering the following conclusion:

> In the year of the world two thousand four hundred and fifty-three (1495 B.C.) - as many trustworthy authors, on the basis of many conjectures, have determined - a comet appeared which Pliny also mentioned in his second book. It was fiery, of irregular circular form, with a wrapped head; it was in the shape of a globe and was of terrible aspect. It is said that King Typhon ruled at that time in Egypt. (This king, assert reliable men, subjugated the kings of Egypt with the help of the giants.)[5] Certain (authorities) assert that the comet was seen in Syria, Babylonia, India, in the sign of Capricorn, in the form of a disc, at the time when the children of Israel advanced from Egypt toward the Promised Land, led on their way by the pillar of cloud during the day and by the pillar of fire at night [6].

Yahweh, says the Bible, led the people out of Egypt "with his face."[7] The comet joined the people when they began their march and provided their posterity with a familiar image: "And the Lord [Yahweh] went before them by day in a pillar of cloud to lead them along the way, and by night in a pillar of fire to give them light, that they might travel by day and by night; the pillar of cloud by day and the pillar of fire by night did not depart from the people."[8] When not Yahweh, the comet was an angel of Yahweh. The comet's head is the Angel of the Lord, its coma the wings, its tail the trailing gown. A recent compendium of cometary photographs and drawings displays several such images. Reproduced here, as Figure 1, is one of them.

A star with a rod is a cometary image. So we

understand Balaam the Prophet when he says: "A star shall advance from Jacob, and a staff shall rise from Israel" that will destroy Moab, Suthites, Edom and Seir [9]. Commenting upon this verse, B. Gemser explains why the word "staff" or "rod" here should actually be read as "comet." The Hebrew word is *shevet* and for comet is *shavit*. Jacob is Israel, and "father" of the tribes of Israel out of Egypt [10].

A variety of cometary shapes with the names given them, such as "horn-star," "goats," "daggers," "serpents" etc. is offered by Pliny. He reports also "a shining comet (called Zeus' comet) whose silvery tresses glow so brightly that it is scarcely possible to look at it, and which displays within it a shape in the likeness of a man's countenance."[11]

Since Yahweh watched out for them as Israel passed out of Egypt, "on this same night... all the Israelites must keep a vigil for the Lord throughout their generations."[12] There was a physical presence in the sky, else they would have nothing to watch for. With the retirement of the original body, the anniversary merged with and strengthened the rites of spring, for the time was near the Spring equinox.

One more quotation can suffice here to suggest the cometary presence: "By a mighty hand and an outstretched arm, and by great terrors the Lord has snatched your nation from the midst of another. Out of heaven he let you hear his voice... and on Earth he let you see his great fire, and you heard his words out of the midst of the fire."[13]

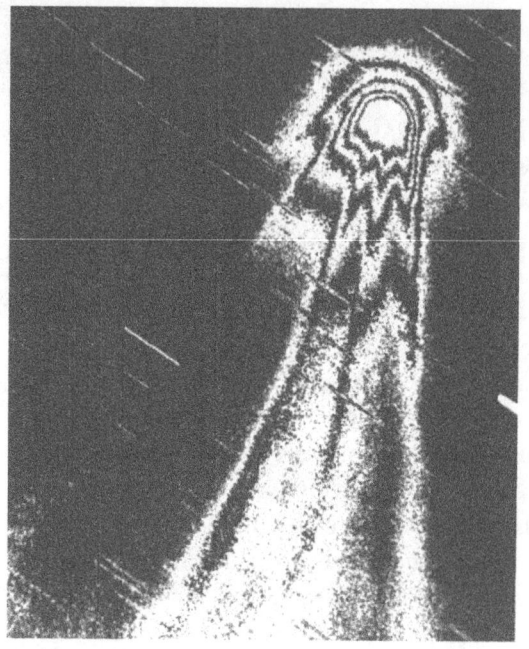

Figure 1. A Comet in Human Form. Source: *Atlas of Cometary Forms,* J. Rahe et al., NASA, Washington, D.C., Sp-198 (1969). Isodensitometer tracing of Greenwich photograph of Oct. 3, 1908, 30 min. exposure, Comet Morehouse 1908III.

The Bible dates the Exodus 480 years prior to the beginning of the construction of the Temple to Yahweh at Jerusalem, about 960 B.C., some twelve generations having passed.[14] This provides a date of 1440 B.C. for the Exodus, not too far from Rockenbach's date, allowing for calenderizing discrepancies. Cyril of Alexandria assigns both the great fire of Phaeton and the deluge of Deucalion to the sixty-seventh year of Moses; Kugler regards the idea as plausible. Velikovsky's reconstruction of Egyptian-Judaic chronology, partially supported by Bimson, permits the retention of the Biblical date, and we shall use it in this book.[15]

Whether we are or are not descended from that fraction of humanity whose story is told here or from that larger fraction - called Christian or Moslem - whose story has assimilated this particular story, our lives are spent under the lingering effects of the great comet. Our minds, religious attitudes, social institutions, wars, sex behavior, eating habits and even the sciences are pervaded by its influence. Human memories and consequently human histories have not yet fully recovered from the shocks of the event. We bury, distort, and sublimate the memories in many ways.[16]

The Bible itself is a case in point. There myth is cozy with history. And the combination has been fiercely, obsessively retained, as if a purely historical recollection would be unbearably painful. Although the second of the five Books of Moses, the *Exodus,* is the best account that we have of that year, its most ancient lines were written down under stressful circumstances; to these lines, perhaps of Moses himself, a full oral tradition was added in the course of several centuries. The materials were sometimes lost; they were copied, rewritten, amended, translated and retranslated, time and time again.

A similar history befell the other *Books of Moses*. The basic document which we use was given its penultimate form some 2500 years ago and its study today depends largely upon this canonization plus some volumes of legends and commentaries of the Jews, some old writings that are based upon writings no longer extant, and many modern archaeological discoveries in Egypt and the "Lands of the Bible."

Further involved in the study of *Exodus* are the social sciences, such as the anthropology and psychology of religion, the history of science, and the sociology of organization, and even the natural sciences, especially geology, the atmospheric sciences and astronomy. All are usable at various stages of investigation. When the facts are few, and their reference, the *Exodus,* is still only a few pages long, then we must admit of every imaginable intellectual and scientific contrivance to extract from and add meaning to those few facts. Withal, the reader will be astonished when he comes to see how rich and unequivocal are the sources in the Bible itself for the main theses of this work.

Not to be passed over is an obvious fact of a stubborn significant type: the Jews have always claimed the inseparability of catastrophe from the foundation of their religion. Thus when the medieval publicist and commentator Judah Halevi argued the merits of Judaism over Islam and Christianity, he fixed its superiority upon its unique origins in divine revelation amidst catastrophe [17]. Despite their philosophical defense, both of these religions had to remain in effect branches of Judaism because they had to claim a

Plagues and Comets

part in Moses and the Exodus.

We return now to the Comet of that winter as it approaches ominously the Earth. It is on a stretched solar orbit, counterclockwise like the Earth, and of similar speed. It is producing a number of effects, although it is months away from its apparent target. When it finally closes in for a near pass at the globe, it gives rise to the famous plagues of Egypt. These effects could occur, since the comet was very large and radiant, so long as it was within a million miles of Earth, and would be heavily experienced on both its approach and recession.

Generality cannot be avoided here. We wish, as Aristotle phrased it once, to be as precise as the facts will allow. Data would be needed on a number of motions, speeds, volumes, densities, and charges in order to calculate the pattern, timing, and effects of the Earth-Comet encounter. Given ever more intensive research and repeated calculations, I think that the scenario could come much closer to the reality of the encounter.

Its mass may have been smaller than the Moon's or even larger than that of planet Venus, as Velikovsky thought. Part of the mass would be contained in the far reaching cometary tail or train. N. Bobromikov ascribes to several modern comets an original mass, taken together before explosion, of the Moon [18]. Astronomers are most reluctant to conjecture a comet of such size or greater, lacking an historical experience, and it is true that, at a close distance or in collision, a very much smaller body would do the same damage.[19]

The comet called by many "Typhon," brought "destructive, diseased and disorderly" changes with "abnormal seasons and temperatures," wrote Plutarch [20]. We shall have more to say about it in the next chapter.

COSMIC PLAGUES

The fateful encounters between ex-Prince Moses and Pharaoh Thoum took place at the Egyptian capital city, of 'Itj-towy, near the Delta [21]. They occurred amidst cosmic and mundane turmoil. Moses had returned from exile abroad ahead of the events. After dealing with his followers, he felt secure enough of his backing and certain enough of the emergent unsettling natural forces to approach the king of Egypt as the chief spokesman for the Hebrews. Estimates of the period occupied by the plagues and the negotiations between Hebrews and Egyptians range from a few weeks to years. A tradition gives one year for the plagues. Pliny, writing in the first century A.D., reports that the briefest comet was visible seven days, the longest for 180 days (following Seneca).[22] A few weeks may be presumed necessary and sufficient. More would be inconsistent with the phenomena of a cometary encounter; less would not allow time for the goings to and fro, the shocks of experience, the communication of rumors and reports.

Early "Eloist" editors named four plagues: blood, hail, locusts, and darkness [23]. The number of plagues is an abstract of reality, a literary device for the editors of the Bible on the one hand (because they liked decimals) and a scientific abstraction for those who were and are trying to divide the turbulent natural unity into types of effects. The variation in the "number" of plagues is, in itself, an indication of an

Plagues and Comets

underlying complex and catastrophic reality.

Philo Judaeus, in his 2000-year-old *Life of Moses*, reaches close to reality in a seemingly naive comment that all four basic elements of the universe - earth, air, fire and water - were involved in the plagues of Exodus [24]. Legend points out that the plagues proceeding from air and fire were entrusted to Moses whereas the others were reserved for God with the solid parts assigned to Aaron [25]. There are ten listed here. To these ten, traditionally denominated as plagues, we may add two logically and causally connected phenomena, the serpent-rod contest between Aaron and the Pharaoh's magicians, which preceded the first plague, and the opening and closing of the sea waters that let the Israelites safely out of Egypt.

Moses had already gained experience with a lively, twisting rod at the instigation of his mentor, Yahweh. This was when he encountered Yahweh at the Burning Bush, of which more will be said later. (Yahweh will often be spoken of as if he existed; it is a convenience of reference to be clarified as the book moves on; care will be taken not to lead the reader astray by creating a special figure, distinct from Moses, who acts independently of Moses or freed from a priestly or editorial formula.)

Moses would not have gained access to the Pharaoh and his advisers if he were not already known and respected and if they had not been uneasy. Moses and Aaron would not have introduced their rod into the conference with Pharaoh unless they were convinced of its superiority. It was perhaps heavily magnetized; it would behave strangely in the presence of metal objects, whether on the robes of persons, or on furnishings, or perhaps unobtrusively carried by Moses and

Aaron, who might have borne other magnetized or electrified objects as well [26]. A tendency to draw to one end of itself the rods of the Egyptian scientists, as they were cast down near it, would give rise to the story that it had swallowed them.

Moses was already quite aware of the enhanced electrical excitement of the Earth in anticipation of the comet, and might well have played upon static charges on gilded draperies or clothing to let Aaron's rod cling, and climb and spark. That Moses would have been able to produce a rod and perform such tricks better than the Egyptian scientists has to do with who Moses was. Again, we will defer this matter.

Now came the reddening and poisoning of all the waters. Both should indicate a heavy fall-out of some combination of radioactive red phosphorous, cinnabar, ammonia, sulphur, and ferrous oxides. Since the population was not reported dying in large numbers yet, the fall-out may be presumed to have not been heavily radioactive, except that one must decide whether the radiation disease soon to come was part of this fall, or of a later one.

Radiation came probably with the later plague of dust that caused sores and boils on all exposed animals and people, for this latter is so specific. But meanwhile there were other troubles. There were frogs, then lice or gnats, then beasts or flies. So far as troubles go, these are all of a kind, pests, all, they agitate and multiply and emerge into the human habitat in response to a warming of the earth, and enhanced electrical currents flowing though the earth, and an increase in the food supply occasioned by the death of water animals and organic life generally.

Plagues and Comets

Their great numbers present no problem. An isolated, luminous cloud in a clear sky in Hutchinson, Minn. USA, dropped 50-100 insects of the non-luminous species *hemiptera* per square foot [27]. A Dutch woman, fleeing with her babies through the woods near her house from the explosions of the volcano Krakatoa, Java, in 1883, found herself covered with leeches when she halted. All kinds of animals were fleeing from above and below the ground [28]. So the dust crawled with vermin and swarms of flies were everywhere, proliferating on the dead fish and frogs. But, as yet, no great number of persons had succumbed to the evil conditions.

The water supply was the worst problem. Unlike fairy tale plots, there was here no neat progression from bad to worse, such as would be concocted to bring increasing pressure upon the Pharaoh. For a poisoned water supply is worse than a plague of insects and frogs. It stank, of course, from the death of its organic life and a combination of the gases and putrefaction and perhaps the causes of its pollution, sulphur and phosphates.

Daiches thinks that he finds an inconsistency in the Bible between a verse that tells of all the water turning to blood and another that describes the Egyptians as digging round about the river Nile for water to drink [29]. In fact, the contradiction is a confirmation of what is said here: new wells bring in filtered, unreddened water. With invisible radioactivity (which he did not of course consider) a shelf of ground water could be contaminated, but would be unnoticeable at that time and for years afterwards, if at all, there being the vague word "leprosy" to cover the symptoms.

We wonder whether something could be made of the

magicians predicting the plague of frogs but not that of lice. (A legend calls this "prediction" to our attention.) There is some ambiguity in Velikovsky's conjectures about vermin, since he wondered whether they might be underground productions or would descend with the train of the comet. If from below ground, the vermin, we guess, would have been predicted; if extra-terrestrial in origin, there would have been no precedent for the prediction.

It has become scientifically permissible recently to suppose plagues to descend from space via dust, comets, or meteorites, and the search for evidence of organic evolution on meteorites is an acceptable scientific issue [30]. I doubt that the comet had to inject the atmosphere with vermin in order to explain them; there have been ample cases of local fall-outs of fast-breeding and erupting insects. An Italian observer of the Neapolitan earthquake of 1805 had much to say of unusual animal behavior, of which I quote a few lines:

> Rabbits and moles were seen to leave their holes; birds rose, as if scared, from the places on which they had alighted; and fish left the bottom of the sea and approached the shores, where at some places great numbers of them were taken. Even ants and reptiles abandoned, in clear daylight, their subterranean holes in great disorder, many hours before the shocks were felt. Large flights of locusts were seen creeping though the streets of Naples toward the sea the night before the earthquake. Winged ants took refuge during the darkness in the rooms of the houses [31].

A legend calls "the fourth plague"... "a mixed horde of wild animals, lions, bears, wolves and panthers, and so many birds of prey of different kinds that the light of the sun and the moon was darkened as they circled through the

Plagues and Comets

air."[32] In great natural disasters - earthquakes, floods, volcanism - the beasts, both wild and domestic, are driven by their psychological and physiological needs to invade the haunts of humans. If the Bible does not include this, one must conjecture it; it is a logical event, not exaggerated in the startled eyes of the people experiencing it.

But perhaps we are leaping ahead of ourselves, for other things happened before the Egyptian earthquake, to wit, electrical fires running along the ground, a plague of boils and sores, and a hail of burning naphtha and meteoritic stones. After these came a plague of locusts (we presume these to be belated arrivals from outside the centers of population, awakened from dormancy by electrical and thermal currents in the ground), then afterwards only came the earthquake.

The plague of boils and sores on flocks and people came in connection with a fall of hot ash, as from a furnace. Moses, it is said, casts a handful of furnace ashes into the air before the Pharaoh to demonstrate his point (reminding one of some of the more popular college instructors of elementary physics and chemistry). Sure enough, shortly after his announcement, the ash fell and plague or infection spread. One wishes the Bible supplied more dates. If the ash were radioactive, within a few days sores would appear. The ashes "produced leprosy upon the skins of the Egyptians, and blains of a peculiar kind, soft within and dry on top."[33] The boils were burning blains and blisters [34]. Centuries later, Solomon reminds Yahweh of "the people... which thou didst bring out of Egypt, from the midst of the iron furnace."[35]

Figure 2. Pestilence, locusts, fire and hail are shown to obdurate pharaoh. then comes the slaughter of the first born (which the Hebrews avoided by marking their door with sheep's blood). Finally the Hebrews are bidden to leave Egypt. Source: reproduced with the permission of the trustees of the Pierpont Morgan Library, New York

Fine dust was failing, but quick death was contained in the fall of *barad* (the Hebrew word for "meteorites"). This hailstorm not only inflicted a heavy death toll upon people and animals - it fell in heaps - but carried fire with it. Fire can fall with stones when a volcano is vigorously erupting near at hand. Volcanoes were erupting everywhere but seemingly not near at hand. Fires running on the ground were probably electrical. They were probably running up the taller buildings of the government and of the official class, and, too, the pyramids. People were burned in the palace, even the King's son, according to legend. The indications of a mixed fire and stone downpour are logically associated with a cosmic fall-out from a cometary tail [36]. The fires were of naphtha (hydrocarbons) and simultaneously electrical.

> A fire rested in the hailstones as the burning wick swims in the oil of a lamp. The Egyptians were smitten either by the hail or by the fire. In one case as the other their flesh was seared, and the bodies of the many that were slain by the hail were consumed by the fire. The hailstones heaped themselves up like a wall, so that the carcasses of the slain beasts could not be removed [37].

The legend tells how the Pharaoh, in refusing permission to the Israelites to go, following the hailstorm and fire, declared that his god Baal-Zephon would block them, and that truly the Israelites were in desperate straits when they came before the sanctuary of Baal-Zephon [38]. This may have been when they discovered their passage blocked by the rushing tidal waters. Possibly the Pharaoh saw in Baal-Zephon the celestial source of the hail and fire.

Hordes of locusts emerged prematurely from the

ground and were blown in from other parts by furious winds, which just as quickly swept them away. "I will bring locusts into your country and they shall cover the face of the lands." Thus speaks Yahweh, implying a foreign terrestrial invasion [39]. But why did the locusts then quickly move on, after what must have been a brief respite and repast? Probably the heavy winds as explained drove them on; but also they might have been impelled by the sense of worse things to come.

The darkness that came next was unearthly, says the legend; it came from hell and it could be felt. The winds blew out the fires or else the density of the dark swallowed up the fires that could be lit. The winds were carrying in the dense clouds of dust from everywhere, obscuring all natural light. Local, and even world-wide obscuration from natural disasters is not unknown in recent times, sometimes with long-lasting effects as with Krakatoa. But this was only the beginning of a dimmed world destined to endure for many years.

  The profound darkness lasted for seven days, or perhaps nine. It became worse: people moved about for the first three days. It was still dark, on the seventh (ninth?) day, when the Egyptian army launched its pursuit of the Hebrews, who had been on the road for three days from the morning after the slaughter of the first-born of Egypt by Yahweh [40]. Did this earthshaking event occur in full darkness, then? If so, how could Moses find his way to the Pharaoh's palace for the final permission to leave? I am inclined to think that the great upheaval had come before the full darkness, and that Moses met with the Pharaoh for the last time amidst the gathering gloom. Then it was that he received permission for the Hebrews to depart with all their worldly possessions.

  A strong implication rests in Moses' words to the

Pharaoh on being refused as the darkness of the third day continued to grow. Pharaoh says angrily: "...Never see my face again; for in the day you see my face you shall die." Replies Moses: "As you say. I will not see your face again."[41] The next and last meeting in the middle of the night after the passover and smiting of the first-born would have been in even greater darkness, and Moses' face would be obscured.

Many terrible things happened in the gloom. Although the Bible says that "all the people of Israel had light where they dwelt,"[42] some of the Hebrews lived in dark zones, according to legend. The great light of the comet did not break through the clouds until the night before they departed. According to legend, "the infliction of darkness served another purpose. Among the Israelites there were many wicked men, who refused to leave Egypt, and god determined to put them out of the way. But that the Egyptians might not say they had succumbed to the plague like themselves, God slew them under cover of the darkness, and in the darkness they were buried by their fellow-Israelites, and the Egyptians knew nothing of what had happened. But the number of these wicked men had been very great, and the children of Israel spared to leave Egypt were but a small fraction of the original Israelitish population."[43]

A legend has the Pharaoh complaining: "Thou didst say yesterday, 'All the first-born in the land of Egypt will die.' but now as many as nine-tenth of the inhabitants have perished."[44]

What are the facts of the first-born, we must ask? Gressmann tried to solve the riddle anthropologically.

Yahweh wanted the Hebrews to go out to the desert to sacrifice their first-born to him. The Pharaoh was frustrating this appetite of the god and hence Yahweh turned upon him to kill his first-born. This story, ways Gressmann, can be composed from the most ancient sources of the Old Testament [45].

Velikovsky sought to solve the riddle linguistically. Thus, Yahweh decrees that he shall kill the first-born of all of Egypt, from the Pharaoh to the maidservant, not excepting the cattle. Moses passes the word along; Pharaoh again refuses; the event occurs as predicted; the Pharaoh accedes to the departure from Egypt. Velikovsky finds a link between the almost indistinguishable Hebrew words, "first-born" and "well-born," and explains that the latter was intended, and that the earthquake was especially severe on the Egyptian upper classes who lived in stone houses, whereas the Hebrews and others, less smitten, lived in mud or thatch houses. This ignores the fate of the other "first-born" of maids, prisoners, and cattle - "I will smite all the first-born in the land of Egypt both man and beast"[46] - and is doubtful, given the history of earthquakes, which strike crowded quarters of the poors and let the rich flee to their courtyards.

It may be more logical to give partial exemption to the people of Goshen from all the plagues simply because of the erratic nature of the disasters. Enough truth may rest in this geophysical separation to justify a later tale of a special dispensation for being Hebrew. So far as concerns the first-born, Moses had already proclaimed to the Pharaoh:

> Thus says the Lord, Israel is my first-born son, and I say to you, 'Let my son go that he may serve me'; if you refuse to let him go, behold, I will slay your first-born son [47].

The analogy is clear: Israel is first-born son, i.e. the chosen ones, to Yahweh; Egypt is first-born, the chosen ones, to the divine Pharaoh. Let mine go, else I will kill yours. Afterwards, references to first-born are to be interpreted in the light of this analogy.

Further, if the Pharaoh's first-born son happens to have been killed, there will have arisen a general rumor to the effect that the "cream of Egypt was destroyed." Hereditary elites are notoriously self-centered.

The lintels of Hebrew houses were marked with sheep's blood to inform Yahweh not to destroy his people dwelling within, particularly the first-born. Many Arabs continue this custom. Yahweh would "pass over" them. Prof. Beer finds in the word "passah" the original meaning "Jumping of the ram." Several images now occur: the original spring sacrifices, the identification of Yahweh with the ram of Egyptian Thoth (Hermes) and thus a clue to Moses' religious origins, the passing over of the god in a cometary form, the awesome destruction of most homes and buildings by violent earthquake, and the passover into the desert from Egypt.

Moses and his Hebrew cohorts knew beforehand much of what happened, and understood the interconnections, and therefore the succession, of many of the events. The Egyptian leaders knew, too, although perhaps not so clearly as Moses, but they had to stay put. They had no "promised land" towards which to flee.

THE DESTRUCTION OF EGYPT

An immense gravitational-electric strain interrupted the Earth's rotation. Earthquakes faulted the ground and fires broke out, mingling with the electrical fires. In many areas most houses were shattered. The pyramids stood the strains well. They were an excellent solution in stone for shock-proof structures. They must have been ablaze with Saint-Elmo's fire with great eyes of the gods alight at their peaks. The eye at the peak of the pyramid is of this age. (Thanks to the Masonic order, it may be found today on the American dollar bill.)

Now the Earth prepared to tilt, in order to decelerate less. A tilt of the axis wreaks less strain upon it than a sudden slowdown of rotation or revolution [48]. An oblique approach of the comet would also have contributed to the choice of the tilt over the abrupt slowdown, since its electrical-gravitational pull was at a sharp angle to the rotation.

Whether it actually tilted is a highly debatable question, to which we address only a few remarks in this book. We say here merely that the strain to tilt must have occurred and had consequences. The question is not beyond the capabilities of geophysics to resolve. A research team would obtain a set of measurements showing the angles of stress of disturbed monuments and geological features; it would postulate several chronological settings; it would calculate a number of possible movements of the crust resulting from combinations of decelerating and tilting forces; and significant statistical correlations would be computed.

Tidal waves swept the coastal areas, and whenever the land was flat, raged inland for many miles. If the Delta area of Goshen was spared some of the disaster until some of the Hebrews had left, it was a miracle, perhaps related to the preventive measures that Moses and the leaders ordered. But Goshen may have been overturned as the Hebrews were crossing the Sea of Passage; a Jewish legend says that the cities they had built for the Pharaoh collapsed.

Here again is what happened, told, now, from the Egyptian viewpoint. It is taken from the papyrus of Ipuwer, an Egyptian writing shortly after the Exodus [49]. Velikovsky located it in its true historical context, and independent sources have fixed the same time for it [50].

> *Forsooth, great and small say: I wish I might die....*
> *Would that there might be an end of men, no conception, no birth!*
> *He who places his brother in the ground is everywhere,*
> *There is not a house where there was not one dead.*
>
> *The children of princes are dashed against the wall;*
> *The children of princes are cast out in the streets.*
> *It is groaning that is throughout the land, mingled with lamentations.*
>
> *O that the earth would cease from noise, and tumult be no more!*
> *Years of noise. There is no end to noise.*
> *The land turns round as does a potter's wheel.*

The towns are destroyed. Upper Egypt has become dry.
All is ruin.
The land is not light

Gates, columns and walls are consumed by fire
 The fire has mounted up on high.

Plague is throughout the land. Blood is everywhere.
The river is blood. Men shrink from tasting and thirst after
            water.
Hair has fallen out for everybody.
Women are barren; none can conceive.
Trees are destroyed. No fruit nor herbs are found.
Grain has perished on every side.
Cattle are left to stray.
The laws of the judgement-hall are cast forth.
The storehouse of the king is the common property of everyone.
Behold no craftsmen work.
A man strikes his brother.
One uses violence against another.
If three men journey upon a road, they are found to be two
         men; the greater number slay the less.
Noble ladies go hungry.
She who looked at her face in water is possessor of a mirror.
Serfs become lords of serfs.

The Desert is throughout the land
A foreign tribe from abroad has come to Egypt
There are none found to stand and protect themselves
Enemies enter into the temples - weep.
Woe is me because of the misery of this time.

Plagues and Comets

We note here, in addition to the other plague evidence of the Bible, complete social breakdown of a type never observable in modern disasters, even at Hiroshima (where outside help came); prolonged chaos, for Ipuwer has experienced weeks and months of it; a foreign desert tribe has taken over the country and its temples; death is everywhere; wobbling of the Earth, possibly the tilting axis slowly coming to rest; fires mounting to the sky, consuming stone; radiation disease (falling hair, women barren); all Upper Egypt affected as well as Lower Egypt. Ipuwer mentions the baffling death of his Pharaoh, but much more detail is supplied, again from the Egyptian side, particularly as to the manner of death of King Thoum. This is from the inscribed stone of el-Arish [51]:

> The land was in great affliction... It was great upheaval in the residence... Nobody left the palace during nine days, and during these nine days of upheaval there was such a tempest that neither the men nor the gods could see the faces of their next.... His majesty... went to battle against the companions of Apopi [fierce god of darkness]. His majesty [the culprits] finds on this place called Pi-Kharoti. Now even the majesty of Ra-Harmachis fought with the evil-doers in this pool, the Place of the Whirlpool, the evil-doers prevailed not over his majesty. His majesty leapt into the so-called Place of the Whirlpool.

The el-Arish inscription reports that the King's son led a search party that heard "all that happened... the combats of the King Thoum" and that the prince was badly burned and his companions killed by a "blast." "The children of Apopi... fell upon Egypt at the fall of darkness. They conquered only to destroy." The prince fled the land in the face of the invading Hyksos. Later "the air cooled off, and the countries dried."

CHAPTER TWO

THE SCENARIO OF EXODUS

Amidst the escalating terrors of the plagues, the Egyptian government struggled to control the total situation. Boldly exploiting the disasters, Moses and his followers hastened to organize the Exodus. Negotiations proceeded in an ever more tense setting. The antagonist of the God-King, Pharaoh Thaoi Thoum, was the man Moses. What Moses was really like and what his background was will be portrayed later. In anticipation, here one may consider that Moses was a Hebraic Egyptian raised in a royal household, on the princely level of an adopted son of a princess. He had a named father whom he never saw. He was exiled by his pharaoh-father, and was now back on the scene of his earlier life, dealing with a pharaoh who, considering Egyptian royal incest practices, could have been his step-brother, his step-uncle, or his step-father, or even a combination thereof, and whom he had once known well.

Much that the Bible contains about the behavior of the Egyptian elite seems to come from an inside view. Professional journalists assigned to world capitals would probably agree that the exchanges between the Hebrew and the Egyptian leaders sound true. The general format could hardly have been corrupted, although Moses' reports must have been extensively rewritten. Whoever was writing the scene originally (and it was probably Moses) dealt familiarly with their conduct. Moses "knew his way around."

HIGH-LEVEL NEGOTIATIONS

When it came time to deal with the Pharaoh, there appears to have been no trouble in gaining access to the greatest ruler on earth. Moses, if an ordinary agitator, would have been jailed or executed offhand. His background, scientific reputation, and government connections prevented this fate. And that is precisely what Aaron and the Jews had counted on in seeking him out as their leader (not to mention Yahweh, who insisted that Moses be his spokesman and that of Israel.)

Moses had found an ethnic connection; very well. The Pharaoh's government wanted to solve the problem of growing unrest in Goshen and elsewhere. "That the Levites, who promote the state of unrest, are not interfered with is apparently due to the uncanny air of power which the Egyptians scent as emanating from Moses." So writes Buber [1]. "Ben David has asserted that Moses possessed some knowledge of electricity," reported Salverte.[2] "Some knowledge" is an understatement; we shall see him as the world's best electrical scientist until Benjamin Franklin. Actually, I think, the Egyptians wanted Moses to help them not only to settle the unrest, but also because he came out of exile already known to them as one of their top-ranking scientist-magicians, and his predictions, noisomely ethnic as they were, gave them another input on what was happening

The Scenario of Exodus 43

in the natural world.

The negotiations over the permit for the Jews to leave their homes in Goshen, Egypt, were based upon conditions and motives clear to both sides. The Hebrews were primarily interested in economic freedom, not religious freedom; Yahweh wanted to help them, but it is always "Let My people go, that they may serve Me." Moses, that is, was interested in theocratic power.

Moses did not plead the economic cause. It would be useless to do so: no ruler in the world would let a useful subject people resign from the nation where they had resided for centuries. Imagine, for instance, the response of the Habsburg Emperor of the old Austro-Hungarian Empire in the face of such a demand. He would laugh and be pleased to hear that so much work was being exacted, especially considering that the same complaining people had houses, flocks, and lambs to slaughter in most homes when sacrifices were called for.

Furthermore, the Hebrews had religious freedom. They were not being denied their God (significantly, the Egyptians refer to the Hebrew god as "Elohim".) True, at one point in the negotiations Moses actually made his strongest argument: that some Egyptians would stone the Jews if they conducted large public religious celebrations. The Pharaoh does not object to this argument; he is in fact sympathetic (and mind you, the Hebrew Bible is saying this!). But he feels that this problem of free public worship can be overcome by means other than letting the Jews move out of Egypt with all of their worldly goods, and without compensation.

The Pharaoh Thoum is not quoted in support of his

father's policy, but it must have still remained the official policy: the Jews were to be suppressed and mistrusted, lest, as the Bible itself quotes the father: "If war befall us, they join our enemies and fight against us and escape from the land."[3]

Were the negotiations conducted in good faith? No, not on the Pharaoh's side nor on Moses. Moses intended all along to take his following out of Egypt forever, but he let the Pharaoh believe it would only be a brief trip to conduct sacrifices in the wide-open spaces. The Pharaoh never did believe this and made Moses appear insincere by counter-offers that would have let the Hebrews sacrifice freely within Egypt. Then again he said he would let the men alone go forth to sacrifice; only the men, after all, conducted sacrifices. Then again, later, all the people might go, but without their herds. He says bluntly, well along in the negotiations: "You have evil purposes in mind."

Moses never believed the Pharaoh, either; all along the voice of Yahweh dinned in his ears that the Pharaoh would be impossibly obdurate. Pharaoh Thoum guaranteed on three separate occasions the permit, only to rescind it after the occasion for the permit - a plague had passed.

So far as the script reads, there were fourteen encounters between Moses and Pharaoh, plus three unsuccessful attempts by Moses to see him. The initiative was taken by Moses on seven occasions and by Pharaoh on seven. The scenario is plausible; an expert on labor bargaining or diplomacy would readily grant this. Most of the initiatives of Moses occurred in the early part and middle of the series, when Pharaoh was apparently incensed and confused. The calls by Pharaoh came mostly later. And in the

The Scenario of Exodus

last stages both parties responded to the events unpretentiously, for matters were quite out of control. When the final permission to leave came, the Hebrews were already in motion.

So Moses pleaded what he knew best and what the Egyptians knew that he knew best. And he played upon the foreknowledge of disaster that he possessed, and here again the Pharaoh and his staff knew that Moses could advance evidence in his favor. Moses identified the agent of these forces of impending disaster as the Israelite god. The Egyptians were wondering whose god was agitating the world.

The largest lessons in anthropology and theology are sometimes forgotten in the haste of students to address the details of Exodus. No rulers would ever conduct any kind of discussions in which plagues were the topic, without watching the sky; they were talking of gods and the gods had one true home and one main realm - the sky. This had been true since the days of creation, thousands of years before, by ancient reckoning in many cultures.

The Pharaoh did not dispute the existence of Yahweh, indeed he reasoned and behaved as a typical sceptical and sophisticated ruler: "Maybe their god, which is not unlike our gods, Amen, Thoth, and Horus, has gotten something going for them." His obduracy, of which the Bible makes much, is to a certain degree rational and prompted by his knowing full well that the Hebrew complaint was almost entirely political and economic.

It was Moses' scientific renown, coupled with the increasingly terrible natural manifestations, that prompted the Pharaoh to conduct the negotiations on Moses' religious grounds. He wanted any information (and so did his advisers) that would help cope with the deteriorating general situation caused by a raging great god. He begged Moses, not on one occasion alone, but twice, to intercede with the Lord on his behalf and to ask the Lord to bless him. One would say that the ruler was converted, not so much to Judaism, as to Moses as a verified expert and predictor.

This came later with the breaking down of the hard heart of Pharaoh. Most commentators on *Exodus* and indeed most careful readers of the Bible are baffled by a large problem. It has incited theologians and philosophers to perform remarkable feats of rationalization ever since the mosaic tradition came to be reassembled and committed to writing 3000 years ago.

Why did Yahweh, time after time, harden the Pharaoh's heart? Why did Yahweh predict repeatedly, beginning with his first appearance at the Burning Bush, that Pharaoh would not let the Hebrews go, and that he, Yahweh, would not let the Pharaoh let the people go? Why was it necessary to visit every single plague upon the helpless country? Why is everyone concerned - Moses, Yahweh, the Pharaoh and all others who participated in or reported the events - willing and ready to let the plagues run their full course?

Childs, for example speaks of the "strange atmosphere which surrounds the plague stories," of "the extravagant length of the stories," and of "a pervading quality of historical distance" not characterizing miracles such as that of Elijah on Carmel [4]. He wonders at the "mystery of Pharaoh's resistance" and "the ultimate strangeness of the plague narrative."[5] Childs then demonstrates that the

The Scenario of Exodus

narrative was edited to impose the idea of Moses as a prophet upon the events, but that Moses was not behaving like a true prophet; rather, Moses, too, was watching the events.

That is, the Bible was assembled to portray the history of the world as the working of divine will. Its editors took up Moses as a prophet of the divine will. It therefore had to shape the account of the plagues to incorporate Moses as their prophet. This procedure later led many, including scholars such as Gressmann, to see Moses as the miracle worker and magician. But, in fact, the narrative is independent of Moses.

The narrative is independent of Pharaoh, too. "Repeated efforts to illuminate the concept of hardness" [6] of Pharaoh have failed. And Yahweh moves inexorably, while insisting that these humans play out their pathetic roles.

There can be only one reason for these behaviors, and theologians, not knowing it, have labored vainly to explain otherwise: the great natural force - the body in the sky - that was operative would hear no plea, see no reason to cease, change not its course until it had completed its approach, destruction and departure in its own time, inevitably, remorselessly, heartlessly.

Further, the Bible is reporting after the fact; it had to give meaning to the fact; it had therefore to implant free will where there was no free will, call for solutions when there was only resolution, and present history in the catastrophic model of Greek tragedy, where the characters are set into motion as if they were free, while affirming in the end that there was no alternative to what they did or what happened to them.

Loudly, clearly, and predictably, the Bible sends forth the signals of desperate creatures from a world in distress. Under such circumstances, the hardness of Pharaoh is understandable, just as it is understandable why in the end he surrenders permission for the Exodus to occur.

Buber asks: "Why does Pharaoh permit himself to be convinced? We find ourselves face to face with a historical mystery."[7] Nor does Buber try to answer his own question. It is just as well. He has already destroyed, in his impeccable unbelieving theological style, the grounds for its solution. "The negotiations between Moses and Pharaoh and the associated plagues, can scarcely... be fitted into historical reality."[8] How could a king negotiate with "a representative of the slaves," he asks. He proceeds farther, with what he - and most other scholars - regards as the only way to demystify the plagues, to diminish them: "masses of small frogs which come out of the river (it is summer, and the season for the flood);" a winter hailstorm; next year a swarm of locusts; one spring a sandstorm of hitherto unknown fury bringing darkness for days; a children's epidemic which cuts down the king's own son: "Go forth! he cries" to the "hated one standing before him."[9]

If, by contrast, our version of the events is accepted, we may give credence to Jewish legends that other nations besides the Hebrews were mutinying [10]. Moreover, riots had broken out prior to the final earthquake and passover, a riot of the "first-born." Was a group of highly-placed Egyptians in incipient rebellion [11] ?

The final night of the Passover may refer to the passover from Egypt into Sinai, or the passover of the Lord's Angel to destroy Egypt, or the Yahweh's passover of the

The Scenario of Exodus

protected Hebrew area "on his way" to the Egyptian concentrations, but certainly not merely to a traditional shepherd's festival to usher in spring (Buber, sic!).

It was on this night before they departed from Egypt, incidentally, that the Hebrews baked bread for the feast. The haste before the departure, say many biblical authorities, prompted instructions to take unleavened bread, whence has come the matzos of ages since and today. Folklore, however, has long told us that bread dough will not rise in a thunderstorm. The Hebrews could not get their dough to rise, owing to intense electrostatic disturbances, but baked the flat dough into bread anyhow. The earth heaved and, as with the greatest earthquakes, electrical storms broke out in the darkness. The two are interconnected. Yahweh "appeared in Egypt, attended by nine thousand myriads of the Angels of Destruction who are fashioned some of hail and some of flames, and whose glances drive terror and trembling to the heart of the beholder;" but Yahweh took the main task of destruction upon himself [12].

A rabbinical source [13] maintains that 49 out of 50 Hebrews perished in the plague of darkness, and a legend declares that the faction readying for the flight slew their fellow Hebrews who would not go along [14]. Eusebius quotes a passage ascribed to Artapanus about the last night before Exodus: there was "hail and earthquakes by night, so that those who fled from the earthquakes were killed by the hail, and those who sought shelter from the hail were destroyed by the earthquakes. And at that time all the houses fell in, and most of the temples."[15]

Velikovsky adds, too, a source from the midrashim: "The seventh plague, the plague of barad (meteorites):

earthquake, fire, meteorites." He points out that the Egyptians have always regarded this night, the 13th of the month, and the number 13, as unlucky, a superstition the Jews did not share, and that the Aztecs, across the seas in Mexico, marked the 13th day of the month as "Earthquake day" when the sun began a new age [16], and all work ceased on this day, that was passed in a kind of catatonic fear.

WHY PHARAOH PURSUED THE HEBREWS

Given the chaos and the final consent to the inevitable, it may seem surprising that the Hebrews should be pursued. Yet "when the king of Egypt was told that the people had fled, the mind of Pharaoh and his servants was changed towards the people, and they said: "What is this we have done, that we have let Israel go from serving us."[17] Or, as a Jewish legend has it: "Now that the children of Israel had gone from them, the Egyptians recognized how valuable an element they had been in their country." [18] It was not the whole Jewish people as a working force that they pursued; it could not have been; it would have been unreasonable, impolitic, rash, and inconsequential, given the sad circumstances of the country. The target of the pursuit was Moses, the Levites, and the knowledge, designs, metals, jewels, and equipment with which they were absconding.

Political science is largely a study of non-rational behavior; still, a fear of loss of secret knowledge in the Exodus cannot be deemed non-rational, even if the chase was doomed. A parallel may be drawn. According to Heilbron [19], in the "world's greatest collections" there are

The Scenario of Exodus 51

some 315 electricians of the period between 1600 and 1790 whose publications are noticed. Calculating with 40 years as the average duration of a scholarly career, the average of published producers per generation for Euro-America, which had an average population of perhaps fifty millions over the whole period, was then 67. In any year, that is, one might expect one or two active electricians per million people. In Egypt and the Near East, before the Exodus catastrophe, there lived perhaps twelve million people. Supposing a higher electrification of the environment and a greater theocratic interest in electricity, the ratio of experts to population was probably greater. The Egyptian government might reasonably view with alarm and suspicion the subversive activities of Moses and his Levite followers, even if there were only a dozen of them. The Soviet and American governments strenuously sought to seize and employ a small group of German scientists at the end of World War II.

Also, the Egyptian leadership wanted to prevent a junction of the Jews with foreign enemies. The Egyptians would have just learned of the movements of the Hyksos tribesmen towards Egypt. "Putting two and two together " and, as sometimes happens in military intelligence, coming out with five as the answer, the Egyptian high command would have reported to the Pharaoh at this very moment that the Jews were heading for a rendez-vous with these forces out of Arabia, and together they would turn upon Egypt. Moses, it would appear obvious, had been in touch with them while in exile [20]. Little did Egyptian intelligence realize that the Jews themselves were soon to enter into desperate battles with elements of the same Hyksos who, in the Bible, are called Amalekites [21].

In the midst of the chaos, the idea finally possessed the top elite of Egypt that they were losing some of the best applied scientific talents of the country all at once, at the moment when they were most critically needed, together with some of the most advanced technical apparatus in Egypt. Whether the Egyptians knew that the lands of their foreign enemies were also stricken is immaterial; they would have behaved in the same way. They must have felt a fearful loss of power, already experienced from the natural and "divine" forces. But now, as politicians often feel when otherwise powerless, "'Here is a matter we can do something about."

We shall go deeply into the matter, but might presently declare what lay behind the changed mind of the Egyptians. In Egypt during the Middle Empire, electricity was a central concern of the government. Among many functions ascribed to the pyramids, one stands out as the most plausible: they were electrical guidance and control equipment. The great gods Horus, Thoth, and Amon, the nearest to Israel's Yahweh, were thunderbolting and cosmic fire gods. The word "pyramid" is Greek and "pyr" means "fire" as in "funeral pyre."

Especially later on, the distinction among fires lessened and electrical fire and combustion are given the same word. The Great Pyramid compound at Giza was called *Khuti*, "the Lights". Egypt was flat and the best way to observe and utilize electricity was by the pyramidal design; the pyramid was a superior artificial mountain from whose peak (a metallic cap), St. Elmo's fire would frequently be discharged skywards. At times, a whole pyramid would light up, miraculously without signs of burning afterwards.

The Scenario of Exodus

The pyramids had long been the rock and strength of the Pharaohs and Egyptian elite, too. They were of the Old and Middle Kingdoms, of the age of thunderbolting electric gods, and must have been centers of atmospheric science and of electrical phenomena. Religion and science were tied to the pyramids, and the genealogy, traditions, and faith of the royal family and elite.

Even today, thousands of miles and thousands of years away, more people belong to the "pyramid cult" than, say, to the Episcopalian Church. Millions of people believe in pyramid electricity. Associations with roots in secret pyramid knowledge number their members by the millions. Books on pyramids are continually being published. Hundreds of general stores in America have recently carried pyramid devices, which are said to prolong life, to sharpen razor blades, and perform other marvels.

These facts should suffice to stress the obstacles facing someone like Moses who did not deny the religious and scientific phenomena that are observed by means of the pyramids, such as the voice of the gods and the electrical "temperature" of the environment, but who argued that they might also be observed by means of a small electrical device of the type of the Leyden jar, which could even be portable. The great pyramid compared with the tiny electric device was like the early giant computers compared with the miniature computer of today.

So, his argument would go, when the peak of the pyramid lit up, a compactly constructed arc (ark) would also activate, and when a lower pyramid would light up, the ark would signal faster, and that "eyes" would appear on both) and that when the pyramid edges began to light up from the top edge and run down, the ark would talk "a blue streak"' and its surroundings would become dangerous. And in the end, in both cases, fire would leap down and run around the premises [22]. The Ark, then, must be defined in a preliminary way here; very much is made of it later on, as the secrets of Moses' science took concrete form in the Ark of the Covenant, among other things.

The ground ark, unlike the pyramid or mountain altar, makes its own divine fire. It does not depend upon a single point high up to provide the electrical discharge. In a small machine, grounded by one pole and pointed to the sky at the opposing pole, the two being insulated from each other, an opposing charge is accumulated at the poles and, when sufficiently charged, the poles exchange a spark, a light, a divine fire. Unlike the pyramid, or mountain, the Ark can be moved to where its sources of strength are greatest and its effects can be most effective for psychological or other purposes.

The Ark is not weak. Set up properly, and given the electrical conditions of today, a sparking machine, a large Leyden jar, can accumulate and discharge tens of thousands of volts. It was something, both in actuality and potentiality, that would indeed interest the rulers of an empire. We may recall that it was only the awareness that a nuclear chain reaction might be created and fashioned into a bomb that prompted the American President and his closest advisers to launch the huge and top secret Manhattan project.

In this chapter, I will provide only a single indication of the Ark at work, for the weapon is treated heavily later on. This is a passage from a legend of the Jews, and has some of the typical markings of a fairytale:

The Scenario of Exodus

> It was through the Ark that all the miracles on the way through the desert had been wrought. Two sparks issued from the Cherubim that shaded the Ark, and these killed all the serpents and scorpions that crossed the path of the Israelites, and furthermore burned all thorns that threatened to injure the wanderers on their march through the desert. The smoke rising from these scorched thorns, moreover, rose straight as a column, and shed a fragrance that perfumed all the world, so that nations exclaimed: 'Who is it that cometh out of the wilderness like pillars of smoke, perfumed with myrrh and frankincense, with all powders of the merchant [23] ?

It may be useful to continue in this fanciful vein. Probably the Egyptian leaders knew about the Leyden jar effect. They seem to have had an interest in studying such phenomena. But they were probably "isolationists," disinclined to making new weapons for foreign adventures and also without inclination to change the established order and rites. There were probably budgetary priorities involved. A new temple or pyramid would have the same effect on defense spending as a large aircraft carrier does now, Moses was perhaps a "hawk" in foreign affairs, coming from an internationalist Near East background, and would have been keen on weapons systems that could be carried abroad.

Thus, if for some time Moses and some fellow-scientists, mostly Hebrew and Thoth religious pragmatists, had been experimenting with ark devices, and urging applications of the devices for military expeditions, domestic propaganda operations, and even "home-made altars" for middle-class funeral parks, the Egyptian conservatives would be deeply concerned and hostile. And they would exile Moses for this kind of trouble-making far quicker than for the accidental homicide of a labor foreman (which is the reason the Bible gives for his being condemned to death by the Pharaoh and forced into exile). And, too, it is typical of human behavior that when Moses had gotten his own electrical system going, he had the same obsessions about its being duplicated in other forms, about its falling into the hands of the enemy, or regarding even its being understood by ordinary people.

THE ORGANIZED MOVE

The instant that Moses heard the voice of Yahweh at the Burning Bush, two deep motives in his ambitious character joined. One was to act upon the knowledge of the tremendous changes about to occur to the world. The other was to tie in his actions, not with an Egyptian bureaucracy of which he had been heartily sick and disenchanted, but with a restless people with whom he was also connected. This kind of switch is common, witness George Washington.

Furthermore, Moses was in a unique position. He knew the sources of technical support personnel that others did not. These were the Levites. He was a Levi himself. They were assimilated Egyptian Hebrews. "Levites don't work like other Israelites," goes the legend [24]. They knew the Egyptian technology. They had probably flourished in Egypt since the time of Joseph, not a tribe but a skill echelon; skills are housed in families and clans, not in tribes which are more like nations. Many Levites had Egyptian names. The ill-fated Levite, Korah, was reported to have been Treasurer to the Pharaoh. Maccoby calls them a "leader and liaison class."[26]

The Scenario of Exodus

The idea of a Hebrew sub-proletarian mass is nonsense. How could the descendents of Joseph be mere slaves? (Unless, indeed, they were like the generally competent Greek slaves whom the Roman took.) Recalling the earlier quotation of the Pharaoh's father, how could the Jews as a nation "Join our enemies and fight against us and escape" without their having in the first place a potential social organization? Look only at the preparations for departure. Give the scheme, as detailed in the Bible - including even the elaborate instructions for stripping the awed Egyptians of their jewelry and roasting the last dinner before moving out to a logistical expert, and ask his opinion.

There are several references to the Egyptians who were neighbors. The Hebrews were not in ghettos. Many did not want to leave, and probably many that did leave, and their Egyptian friends, were leaving in fear of being enveloped by the successive disasters.

Israel, the core element, that is to say, was organized down to the last battle ration and, indeed, so says the Bible, moved out girdled for battle. Slaves are never permitted weapons. The Hebrews, says a legend, bore swords and "five sorts of arms."[27] Moses knew long before Machiavelli "why unarmed prophets fail." Further, slaves are not permitted genealogies, but a legend about the first battle of the Jews in the desert, with the Amalekites, the Hyksos, has the enemy luring unsuspecting Jews out of the camp by calling out their family names that they uncovered among the captured Egyptian archives [28].

Compare them with the Huns, the Tartars, the Teutons, the American wagon trains, the Sud-Afrikaaners of the Great Trek and say whether the popular imagination of a throng of fleeing people could be correct. We note, too, that a "mixed multitude" accompanied the Hebrews. Apparently many friends and gentile relatives thought that they would be better off leaving with the resolute and well organized Hebrews than to remain in Egypt.

It is conceivable, then, that a people moving out under such duress, with such immense natural and human forces pressing in upon them, would have among its leaders men who would seek to seize amidst the confusion the most valuable technological devices that they knew about and could possible use in the journey and battles ahead of them.

Legend has it that Moses was a poor man in the desert. For, many Jews were carrying jewels and metal that were .. given" them by the Egyptians, out of superstitious hope promoted by the Jews themselves, that their departure would end the plagues. But Moses was burdened down with the remains of the great Joseph. It is well, however, that the charismatic leader think not of material dross. Carrying the dust of Joseph was possession of legitimate authority. The Bible uses the same word for the coffin of Joseph as for the Ark. And Joseph's coffin, like the later Ark, may well have carried Mose's most closely guarded secrets.

Indeed as one re-examines the relation between Moses and the people, one gets an impression of a kind of expeditionary contract that is subordinated to the Lord's covenant with Israel, of which Moses is executor. It is glued by a common resolve and a professed religious unity, but nevertheless a kind of agreement which we can imagine to have been worded: We have heard of you, Moses, and you've heard of us. You say that you can do this for us? We can do this for you. Now let's get going.

The Scenario of Exodus

The people are continuously recalling Moses to his promises: "Is not this what we said to you in Egypt, 'Let us alone and let us serve the Egyptians'? For it would have been better for us to serve the Egyptians than to die in the wilderness."[29] Some Bible-editors, totally committed to Yahweh and the leaders, berate the people continually for "complaining". Moses in turn is saying: You must follow me because I speak for God. You cannot turn back on God (me, Moses). At the Sea of Reeds, with the Egyptian force fast advancing upon them, they say to Moses in effect, the whole thing was your idea! (And with a Yiddish humor, the first in history: "Is it because there are no graves in Egypt that you have taken us away to die in the wilderness?"[30] Evidently, from a kind of well-qualified expedition manager, Moses was quickly transformed by events into a charismatic leader.

OPENING AND CLOSING THE WATERS

> "And the waters of the Red Sea divided, and not they alone, but all the water in heaven and on earth, in whatever vessel it was, in cisterns, in wells, in caves, in casks, in pitchers, in drinking cups, and in glasses, and none of these waters returned to their former estate until Israel had passed through the sea on dry land."[31]

The legend makes a point. The earth tilted in its attraction to the passing comet. The Almagest sky map of the astronomer Ptolemy shows a bit of sky to the south unseen today and fails to show a bit of sky to the north; the map was probably copied from maps drawn before the Exodus [32].

Figure 3: Pharaoh's army drowned
XVI Century enameled plate, France

The Scenario of Exodus   61

Probably all Egyptian temples shifted several degrees North to catch the sun in a new position on the winter solstice following the Exodus [33].

In Upper Egypt, at 32°34'E/21°46'N, at Ovadi es Sebova (South), excavators discovered three temple foundations; one, the original, rested against the hillside from before Exodus; two were constructed later on. A shift of 5°01' between temple I and the temples II-III is evident. When the temple by Amenhotep III was built, the innermost target of the solstitial sun of winter had to be shifted to catch the sunrise on the eastern horizon farther north. One may reason that the axis of the Earth shifted, carrying Egypt further North by 5°01' or that a great earthquake moved the hill and its attached temple counterclockwise [34].

The waters that confronted the Israelites were unexpected. Else the Exodus would not have gone in that direction; they would have known that they would be trapped. But the Red Sea sent a tidal wave north that ran through the belt of lakes between it and the Mediterranean. (Today it is the route of the Suez Canal.) The Israelites watched with distress the oncoming Egyptian army. The light in the sky never faded on that gloomy night before the sea [35].

"Then the Angel of God who went before the host of Israel moved and went behind them; and the pillar of cloud moved from before them and stood behind them, coming between the host of Egypt and the host of Israel. And there was the cloud and the darkness; and the night passed without one coming near the other all night." The Hebrew version carries "and the night disappeared in light..."[36]

"God caused the sea to go back by a strong east wind, the wind He always makes use of when he chastises the nations," as in the Deluge, the Destruction of the Tower of Babel, of Samaria, of Jerusalem, of Tyre [37]. Battles of Egyptian and Israelite Angels waged in the skies. The Egyptian soldiers were met by strong winds, fiery darts, lightning flashes, thunder, hailstones and coals of fire [38]. The chariot wheels and the hooves of the horses were burned by divine fire and got stuck in a boiling mud [39]. (America's worst earthquake was around New Madrid in Missouri, in 1811, and an observer tells of his horses suddenly sinking up to their bellies in new black mud.)[40] It would appear that, even while all the aspects of the plague of the first-born repeated themselves, a tidal motion was added because here waters were involved. The accompanying Figure 4 displays several possible movements of the waters and of the two masses of human beings.

  The plan of march of the Israelites was southeastward through a known gap in the shallow lakes that stretched between the Mediterranean and Red Seas. When they arrived at the jump-off point at Pi-ha-khiroth, they were met by a wall of water. It was the tidal wave moving north from the Red Sea, following the comet and the tilt of the earth.

  They waited out the night in sight of the pursuing Egyptian force. The earth's tilt paused. The tilted waters continued to rise [41] and rush north. But gaps opened. The Israelites passed through, Moses and his Levite troops in the vanguard. The Egyptians perceived the gaps, too, and headed somewhat south of the Israelite passageway, intending to gain time.

The Scenario of Exodus

Then the tidal flood drops from its heights and reverses to the south. It catches some of the Israelites and the main body of the Egyptians and their leaders, including the Pharaoh. Even before the flood engulfs them, the Egyptian forces are deep in mire - perhaps in the old bed of a lake, perhaps in a new earthquake fissure eruption. The Israelites who remain alive continue southeastwards (Figure 5) leaving Egypt behind. They learn then something of what would have happened if they had taken the northern route by the Great Sea.

> The peoples have heard, they tremble:
> Pangs have seized upon the inhabitants of Philistia.
> Now are the chiefs of Edom dismayed;
> The leaders of Moab, trembling seizes them;
> all the inhabitants of Canaan have melted away.
> Terror and dreadfall upon them;
> because of the greatness of Thy arm,
> they are as still as a stone.
> Till Thy people, o Lord, pass by,
> Till the people pass by whom Thou hast purchased.[42]

I have chosen Mt. Horeb at the Eastern end of the Gulf of Aqaba as the "Holy Mountain" of Moses, instead of Mt. Sinai, following Winnett's arguments. (*The Mosaic Tradition,* p. 86 et passim.) This would be the Midianite (and Kenite) territory, where Moses passed his exile. Gressmann (*Mose,* 414) agrees and sees the Exodus moving along the Egyptian "Highway of Reeds," which continues, after Horeb, down to Arabia. Bimson places the capital of the XIII Dynasty at Itj-towy, near the Delta ("Israel in Egypt," p. 15, citing Hayes 12 *JNES,* 1953, 33-8).

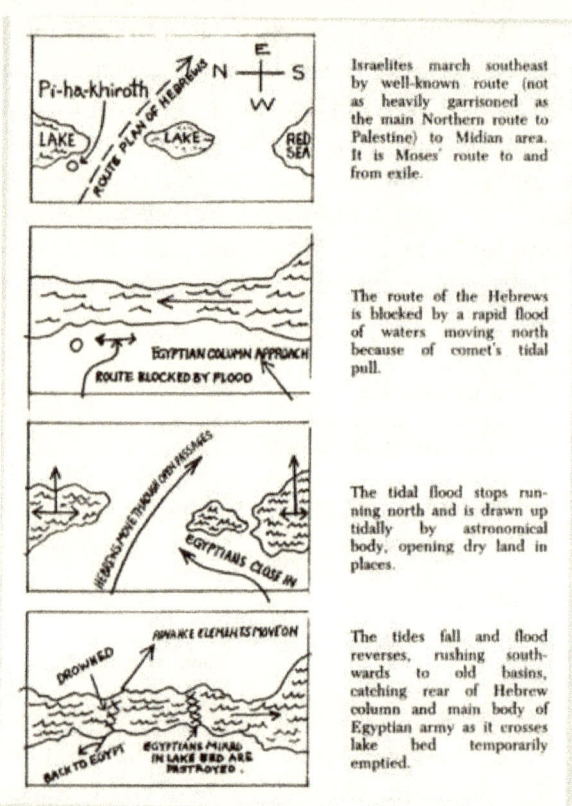

Fig 4. The Tidewaters Passage
(Present-day maps of these waters may not be helpful, although a careful hydrological study might reveal ancient basins and flood channels.)

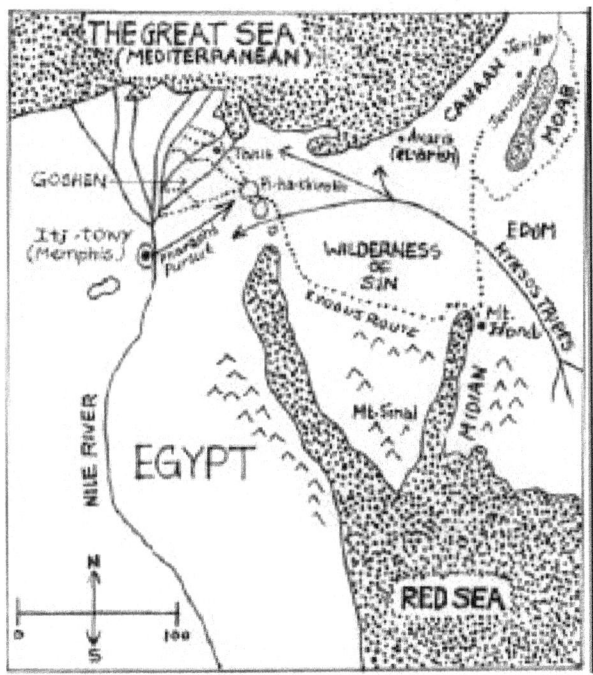

Figure 5. The route of Exodus and wandering

UNFORESEEN CIRCUMSTANCES

It is doubtful that even Moses, when he first conceived of returning to Egypt and exploiting his connections, knowledge, and daring - an event that can be fixed from his sight of the Burning Bush from which Yahweh addressed him - had any idea of how bad conditions would really become. And if, at the beginning, in the typical psychology of the great but frustrated man, thinking in the lonely wilds of his life's purpose, he began to hear from a superhuman being, and only half-believed in what he had heard, but was nevertheless seized by the idea of uniting his return to Egyptian affairs with the need of the Hebrews for a spokesman, then by the middle of the series of disastrous events, he could well be fully convinced that Yahweh was personally guiding all, and that even Egypt's best scientist-politician could do little without a god.

Although the Jews were compelled by coastal tidal waves and hostile terrified nations to head southwards on the Sinai peninsula, they may also have chosen that direction upon the instigation of Moses. Moses may have believed that "the Promised Land" was where he had already been. For, after all, if the Jews had come from Palestine, and were to return there, it would be a returning home to the old condition, not a discovery of the Promised Land. Biblical scholar Auerbach believes that the goal of Exodus was to settle down at the oasis of Kadesh where Moses saw the Burning Bush.

Although Moses had in mind Kadesh or Midian as the terminus of the Exodus, it is possible, even probable, that he thought of this location as an organization and staging area for the ultimate descent upon Canaan. His great ambitiousness and the dreams and wishful thinking of his officers would point to Canaan; also, he would have foreseen the need to consolidate his forces, to integrate their diverse elements, to train and discipline the people, and to gather resources for the second phase of the movement.

Moses could hardly have imagined the horrible immensity of the natural catastrophe. A legend recites that the plague of hail in Egypt had brought great famine to Jethro's Midianites [43]. Upon arriving in his "promised land" there was little left there but parched earth, dry water holes, flaming mountains, and, Thank God, Yahweh. By now Moses and the leaders must have known that they could go nowhere until they were in better shape all-around and the natural forces had become subdued.

The Bible says, as things get better and then bad again, "Moses spoke thus to the people of Israel, but they did not listen to Moses, because of their broken spirit and their cruel bondage."[44] The words read like a modern sociology textbook: their "slave psychology" couldn't stand up to the idealistic behavior that they had promised. But noone could have foreseen the catastrophe visited upon gentile and Jew alike. Even princes despaired.

So Moses promised too much, and the people of Israel expected too much. And they paid for promises unperformed and conditions unforeseen. The Bible says that some 2.5 millions plus a great number of outsiders, "a mixed multitude," set out from Egypt. The general view is that this was a greatly exaggerated figure for "how could the desert into which they were moving support such a mass of people?"

The desert did not, unfortunately, support them. Jewish tradition, more believable, says that the vast majority of the people perished in the passage out of Egypt. If the Biblical figure is used, perhaps only one out of a hundred survived. The waters that closed upon the princes of Egypt and their only "strike-force in readiness" washed over most of the pursued as well. A great number may have turned back immediately. Nor did the desert support even the remainder, though well-organized and led.

By that time, Moses must have been as fanatically possessed as any man could be, insane with the problems of a people clinging only to hope and staring wild-eyed and worshipfully at alternative hopes. Whatever he did had to be quite mad. But what he did was rational unto the occasion. He insisted upon his obsessions. He exercised his talents, and those of the Levites and Aaron, and all the capabilities of his instruments.

He worked Yahweh, "the Lord," furiously, wrenching from this Great Father Figure concession after concession, arrangement after arrangement, law upon law, giving up in the end only his right to cross the Jordan River into the Promised Land. And it is said by some, such as Sigmund Freud, that he did not give up this right. Rather, he was put to death in a final revolt against his rule, possibly on the grounds that he, Moses, was impossibly intolerant and unfit for a new society - a leader of a long march that had now to end.

And, with the understanding of Moses' behavior, the parts of the Exodus pursuit come together. In the dire national emergency, the Pharaoh and his national security

The Scenario of Exodus 69

council had to do what any modern high command would have done: turn their backs on a country in turmoil and disaster in order to regain control of the men and apparatus, which were needed to control nature (the gods), and to prevent them from being used by foreign enemies.

What followed spelled the ruination of Egypt for centuries. "In the morning watch the Lord in the pillar of fire and of cloud looked down upon the host of the Egyptians, and discomfited them so they turned to flee." But then Yahweh gave the word to Moses to wave his hand, and the sea closed down [45].

Not only were the weaponry and Hebrews now beyond recapture, but the only organized striking force of Egypt perished, with its Commander-in-Chief, in the whirlpools of immense crosstides near Pi-ha-khiroth just as the forward elements of the Jewish column passed beyond the waters. Then it was, as Egypt lay helpless and in ruins, that the furious and equally distressed "King-Shepherds" Hyksos of Arabia, the Biblical Amalekites, fleeing from their own ruined lands, swept into Egypt and subjected the country to their rule. The XIIth Dynasty that had endured over centuries and that had extended Egyptian sovereignty as far north as Byblos (Syria) was ended in this year of Exodus [46]. For hundreds of years to come, the Bible speaks only rarely of Egypt and then merely of the popular nostalgia for the great land. The silence is awesome: we see it in the catastrophe and the Hyksos take-over. And also the actuality of the disaster of the pursuing army. Else we should have had repeated expeditions to recapture these slaves. The American army was quick to pursue the Sioux Indians after the massacre of General Custer and his Seventh Cavalry regiment. The Hebrews, whether they were few or many, would have been marked for implacable pursuit - immediately, soon, or eventually, repeatedly, too, if the Empire of Egypt were not prostrated. For centuries the peoples of Sinai, Transjordan, and Canaan were left free of Egypt and Babylon to fight among themselves.

Perhaps the most aggressive of the peoples was the new nation, the heterogeneous federation of Israelites, forged by the steel-willed Moses in the name of the electric god of war, Yahweh.

In the miraculous turbulent atmosphere of the wilderness, Moses established the illumination and voice of Yahweh upon the Ark. Speaking then for Yahweh, he organized the people, taught it a new law and discipline, and injected it with an inextinguishable monotheism, proofed by fire against enemies within and without. Israel scourged the borderlands before finally descending upon Canaan. Moses, the archetype of the mad scientist and religious prophet, beat down successive rebellions that, if successful, would have dissolved the new identity of Israel into the larger surrounding culture. Then, the terribly oppressive and vindictive old man mysteriously died.

CHAPTER THREE

CATASTROPHE AND DIVINE FIRES

If the Israelites did not know that a great comet was visiting disaster upon the Earth, they would be the only people in the world from whom the knowledge was withheld. In fact, they did know. And they called it by god-names just as everybody else did in those days. But it is also true that a peculiar kind of suppression of cometary evidence is present in the Israelite record, for which there is an explanation.

In Chapter 1, I offered several pieces of evidence that the Israelites knew a comet was in the sky, and that the disasters on Earth were from heaven, and, furthermore, that the Lord bore them "on Eagle's wings" from Egypt. (See Figure 6) More evidence is due here. I must reason out the position as well. Was the whole world electrified beyond any later historical awareness? Is there an alternative to the comet: could there be another cause of all the disturbances? What was the fate of the comet?

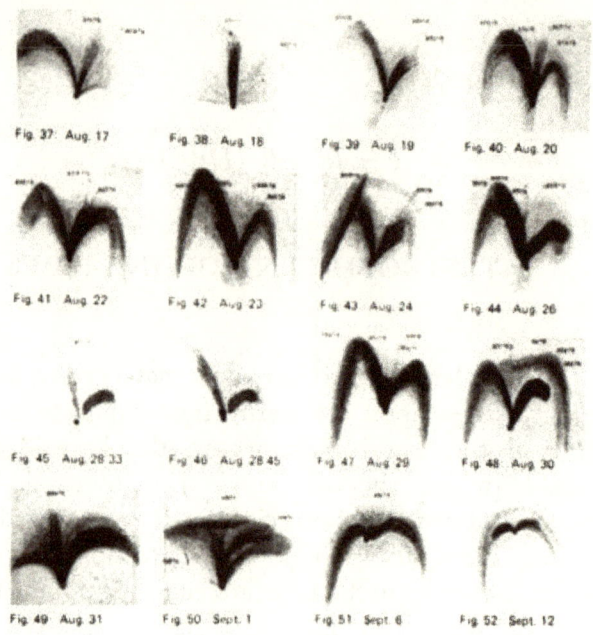

Figure 6. On Eagle's Wings "You have seen what I did to the Egyptians, how I bore you on eagle's wings and brought you to me." Ex. 19-4 *(The Torah: The Five Books of Moses,* trans from the Masoretic text. Philadelphia: Jewish Publications Society, 1962) Cf. Deut. 32: 10-3. The cometary images are of Comet Swift-Tuttle (1962) III, NASA, op cit., 29.

WHOSE ANGEL?

It is said that the Israelites were frightened in their Exodus by the sight of the Angel of Egypt darting through the air, "as he flew to the assistance of the people under his tutelage."[1] This tutelary angel was also called Uzza by the Jews [2], strangely, because the name is found among the ancient Arabian people in reference to the planet Venus [3]. It is to be identified with Seth, god of the Hyksos and the anti-god of the Egyptians, with Lucifer, and Phaeton-Typhon. Hence the "Egypt" referred to is already the conquered Egypt. Uzza is also Azazel, the devil to whom the Jews dispatched the scape-goat carrying their sins on the annual Day of Atonement. A very large body it would be.

Uzza, goes the legend, accosted the Lord, with a plea to return the Israelites to Egypt. A debate ensued between Uzza and the champion of the Jews, the Angel Michael. Archangel Michael is identified by Velikovsky as a Hebrew equivalent of the planet Venus. So that we had here the same figure debating itself, that is reasonable, for a myth as for a dream.

Uzza claimed that the bondage of the Hebrews had not been completed; only 86 years, not 400 had passed. No explanation is given of the 86 years; Auerbach and others believe that the Jews had been in Egypt for that time or less; perhaps only 60 years had passed since Joseph's death, since the pharaoh who "did not know Joseph, succeeding to one who did, laid heavy hands upon the Jews." The point may not be important [4]; the characters to the debate are. Uzza, of course, loses the debate. The Jews owned the comet, not the Egyptians (or the Hyksos).

Another of the explicit references to the comet is contained in a legendary speech of Moses to Yahweh, following upon the adoration by so many Jews of the Golden Calf. Imploring the angry Yahweh not to annihilate the chosen people, Moses says: "Fulfil not, I implore Thee, the prophecies of the Egyptian magicians, who predicted to their king that the star "Ra'ah" would move as a harbinger of blood and death before the Israelites."[5] "Ra'ah" in Egyptian must mean "the Great Sun," the comet luminous and larger than the sun.

The night before departure from Goshen, the terrible night of the killing of the first-born, was said by one legend to be a bright night, as bright as the brightest day of the year [6]. This legend contrasts with another, that the darkness persisted in the Egyptian capital. Might the comet tail be falling so densely in some places as to block the light, while the comet appeared larger than the sun in others, at least to accommodate these particular differences? Perhaps. The prophet Isaiah, recalling the Exodus long afterwards, preached: "The People that walked in darkness have seen a great light; they that dwell in the land of the shadow of death (which must mean Egypt), the light of Noga was upon them." Noga, insists Velikovsky, means planet Venus in Hebrew [7].

In the year 1666, a young man called Moses Suriel from Brussa, Turkey, claimed to be a prophet and supported Shabatai Zevi as savior of the Jews. He pointed to a comet that had appeared and explained that this, too, had appeared in the sky during the Exodus. (In 1665, G.A. Borelli probably used the same comet in calculating the parabolic forms of cometary paths.)[8] We infer that an insistent Jewish tradition

Catastrophe and Divine Fires

tied the cometary form to Exodus.

Velikovsky claims that the adventuring Israelites saw this and more. That they saw the full comet in the apparition of a serpent. When Moses, later on, made a serpent of brass and put it upon a pole[9], he was in fact modelling the image of the great comet as it snaked through the sky [10]. The same sculpture had, as we shall see, electrical utility, and could well have been a symbol that united the electrical events of heaven with those of the ground.

Legend has Yahweh at the Burning Bush foretelling to Moses: "I behold what cometh after, how the people will worship the steer, the figure of which they see upon My chariot..."[11] This has a four-fold significance: it conforms to cometary images in general; it connects the comet with the "golden calf to come;" it puts Yahweh into the driver's seat of the cometary chariot, and it parallels the Greek myth of Phaeton, searing the world from his solar chariot.

But the most powerful and exercised of cometary references is the towering column of smoke and fire that was first before and then behind the Israelites as they crossed into the desert. In ancient history and in folklore comets are often "hairy" and "'smoking" stars. I have already quoted this apparition of the lord that had led them from the beginning; it "did not depart from before the people."[12] The Lord here must be the comet. Ilse Fuhr, writing of comets in 1967, says [13]:

> "A comet which approached the Earth moving for a time - for the sake of argument - in synchronous orbit with the Earth between latitudes 33° north and south, would move back and forth in a flat figure eight with the two halves meeting at zero (this was demonstrated by the orbit of the synchronous satellite

Syncom II), in other words, during a period of 24 hours it would seem by an Earth-based observer as appearing once behind him and once in front of him in the sky (cf. *Exodus* 13:21)."

It is not announced when this apparition ceased, but it was the veritable incarnation of their god in their eyes. It was a monstrous verification that they were being watched over by the god whose protection and leadership Moses had prophesied.

We never escape this deity during Moses' life, for it assumed terrestrial form. It was Yahweh who led them on their wanderings, in a column of smoke by day and a pillar of fire by night, he who encamped with them and whose very same manifestations emerged from the sacred enclosure that Moses had built for him.

There is a naive myth, founded indeed upon the very words and acts of Moses, that the Israelites shunned the gods of the sky - the sun and moon, planets, and stars and would not fashion religious images. Although Yahweh is reconciled to the existence of other gods, he is zealous to be first and exclusive with his chosen people, on pain of their destruction. Yet the people knew there was more to the sky-scene than Yahweh.

Heaven to the people of Israel was a thickly populated region. Besides the gods of their enemies, there were hosts of angels, animals and ancestors, not represented alone in the stars but by all the meteorites that flew in the disturbed skies. The heavenly host rained down fiery darts, lightning balls and wheels of light, stones, and coals of fire. The Bible is purged of most of these visions, but the legends carried forward the visions of the people[14]. They are admitted to the Scriptures on occasion, as in the Revelation of John of the Apocalypse in the New Testament.

"In a somewhat indefinite way some Biblical scholars have recognized that Jacob's Bethel might have been a meteorite."[15] The Greek word for Bethel was Baetyli, meaning a Jovian thunderbolt. Baetyls are sacred thunderstones or meteorites carried by the holy litters or arks of various Bedouin tribes. Originally, directly or indirectly, the Ark of Moses carried the Ten Commandments on such tablets, as we shall understand later on. Very material things from the sky, then, were connected with Yahwism.

THE CENSORED DESIGNS OF HEAVEN

The Israelites were therefore eager to construct their habitat on earth in the image which they transported of heaven, and felt constrained to carry out as closely as possible the instructions that Moses received from Yahweh in this regard. These were numerous and the designs that he carried down from his first forty days and nights of isolation atop the sacred mountain of Sinai were particularly impressive. "And see that you make them after the pattern for them, which is being shown to you on the mountain."[16] Yahweh's 'commands were not so easy to execute: "Upon the occasion of the erection of the Tabernacle, God gave red, blue, black and white fire to see and imitate. To the question of how this might be possible, God answered: "I fabricate my glory; you make your own colors..."[17]

A legend conveys what must have been the feeling of the people, that the existence of the world depended upon the construction of the Tabernacle, sanctuary of Yahweh, "for when the sanctuary had been erected, the world stood firmly founded, whereas until then it had always been swaying hither and thither."[18]

If, as now seems probable, the Earth suffered a moderate tilt at the climax of the Exodus, a celestial unsteadiness would be perceived, both in the general turbulence and in the erratic movements of the stars and heavenly bodies. And one can be sure that in the retelling, if not in actuality, the earthly and heavenly climaxes would be brought together for maximum effect and symbolism. Perhaps the new awareness came in intervals of light in darkness or from reports received from the larger world. Nor can one be positive that the reference is not to continuous earthquakes. Then, too, "The land (world) turns round as does a potter's wheel," in Ipuwer's metaphor [19]. And the Psalm sings out: "God, when you set out at the head of your people, and marched across the desert, the earth rocked... The heavens deluged at God's coming..."[20]

It may be premature to claim definitive proof, but we can make the following statements with some confidence: no settlement anywhere in the world escaped heavy destruction in the finale of the Middle Bronze Age, at the time of the Exodus, that is, about 1450 B.C.; further, no temple that existed before 1450, and that was reconstructed or added to afterwards, was given the same astronomical orientation than it possessed before.

The implication of these statements will not escape the reader. With the accumulating evidence of worldwide destruction, it will no longer be permitted scholars to cast the Exodus in whatever form they please - as a stroll in the

Catastrophe and Divine Fires

desert, the flight of some slaves, a Jewish fairy tale. The Exodus occurred in a catastrophic setting.

Secondly, shifts in temple orientation form the strongest possible proof of an historical shift in the angle of the axis of the globe with respect to the ecliptical plane. And when an axial tilt occurs, great destruction is visited upon the Earth: tidal waves, adjustment of the equatorial (rotational) bulge by rising and sinking land, earthquakes and volcanism, vast and violent storms, and electrical discharges of all kinds. Further, the almost certain cause of an axial tilt is the near encounter of Earth with a great passing body.

Some of the objects of the Tabernacle stood for celestial bodies - stars, cherubim, the curtain of the sky [21]. "The separate parts of the Tabernacle had each a symbolical significance, for to all that is above there is something corresponding below."[22] The great encampment of the Israelites follows a celestial plan.

> The division of the tribes of Israel according to four standards, as well as their subdivision at each standard, is not arbitrary and accidental; it corresponds to the same plan and directions as that of which God made use in heaven. The celestial throne is surrounded by four angels: to the right Michael, in front Gabriel, to the left Uriel, and to the rear Raphael. To these four angels corresponded the four tribes of Reuben, Judah, Dan, and Ephraim, the standard bearers [23].

The sacred ball-courts of the Olmecs of the same age and of other Meso-Americans are authoritatively acknowledged to be tied to the cardinal points of the sky. The planet Venus is prominently represented in the games [24]. The players fought to the death. The Roman circus had on its axis altars of the planets [25]. There, too, blood flowed freely. "Ninevah proclaimed itself the seat of stable order and power by its seven-times crenellated circle of walls, colored by the seven planetary colors." [26] Chariots would run along the top of the walls.

"Thy will be done on Earth as it is in Heaven..." So goes the Lord's Prayer. The idea is worldwide. "Ancients believed that earthly temples and their cultic equipment were made according to the pattern or prototype of heavenly models."[27] The comment is too mild; it was imperative to imitate heaven, to placate, identify with, and control heaven. In most of this construction is to be seen a cultural heritage going back long before Moses and deriving from many gentile nations. Yahweh, himself an old god in many ways, puts old things together to make new ones.

But when it comes to mirroring himself, Yahweh is avant-garde. There is no throne in the Tabernacle. He is not carried about as a beautifully enthroned image, as Arabs carried their palladium and Europeans carry their saints and the Son of God. He has a "Mercy Seat" - strange contradictory words of the King James translation - the lid of the Ark-box a "vehicle" is the more literal translation - where he makes himself visible from time to time.

That invisibility had drawbacks is indicated by the Revolt of the Golden Calf when, before Moses' designs can be implemented, a great many Israelites melt their gold and fashion an animal form whom they immediately term their god. (See figure 7.) This is usually regarded as Baal, but "what Baal?" is the question, for Baal means "god" unless a special context or appellation is provided to further distinguish the Baal.

Here, say some scholars, it is Baal the Cow, or Baal the Bull, which could mean Baal Venus, inasmuch as the great comet, so often identified with the planet Venus, took on the appearance of a cow, its head elongated, its coma looking like horns and its tail pulling itself into the perspective of a great thick body dropping ambrosia or manna like milk, and like excrement, too.

The legend has it that the Golden Calf heresy "is in part explained by the circumstance that, while passing through the Red Sea, they beheld the Celestial Throne, and most distinctly of the four creatures about the Throne, they saw the ox. "[28]

On Earth, in those days of high electrical effects, the homology is proven by the discharge of fire between the horns of the animal. (A sculpture in the Athens Museum from Mycenean times, perhaps paralleling the Exodus period, carries a bull's head with a double-edged ax between the horns; the ax, as well as the ox horns, conveys electricity - mountain climbers write about the lights streaming from their axes.) The altar of the Tabernacle carried four gilded horns at its corners.

But why is this Baal of the Israelites a calf and not an adult animal [29]? It is called a "bull" on occasion in Jewish legend, however. "The word (translated 'calf' from Hebrew) is not a pejorative term for an ox, as many surmised. It denotes a young ox, an ox in the full vigour of its youth."[30] The only reason I can offer for this modification of the universal cow-bull theme is that the Israelites knew that the comet was a young body in the sky. It had not been known to them for long. The bison and bull, always with a divine celestial connection, had been worshipped and were sacred since time immemorial [31]. Zeus, the thunderbolter, assumed the image of the bull. Thoth (or Hermes or Mercury) took the image of a ram, afterwards.

Zeus, it will be recalled, had fathered and mothered Athene who was the Greek planet Venus. The new heavenly body, the Messiah, would take the form of a calf. The Venus connection is obvious, with Baal, then, being Venus. And for some hundreds of years the Baal Venus cult occupied a great many Jews. It was not generally admitted, but usually the god who competed with Yahweh and aroused the indignation of the Yahwists was the cometary Baal.

That the rebels of the Sinai incident had deep roots in the community was evidenced much later on, when the writers of Judah had to mention them again in order to demonstrate the terrible end that awaited their likes: when the Northern Kingdom of Israel, hundreds of years later, under Jeroboam, built two golden calves, one for each of its principal sanctuaries, in competition with and defiance of the Kingdom of Judah that possessed the Ark of the Covenant and the Temple at Jerusalem. But even before Moses' death, the Hyksos in Egypt had elevated the new young bull to divine status as Apis [32].

Enough sights, apparitions, effects, events, and experiences come with a large-body near-collision to supply readily all the personnel and myths of a full-fledged religion. Yet Moses was not alone in rejecting the absolute identification of a comet as a mainstay of his god. Generally so-called planetary, solar, or lunar religions are not exclusively such: there is a marked body giving substance to their god, and its behavior is carefully observed for indications of how to conduct themselves. In addition, there

Figure 7. Moses' Tablets and Golden Calf Heretics. (La Somme le Roy, ca. A.D. 1295 British museum Add. MS 54180, folio 5v)

occur innumerable god-named manifestations and designations in the sky, the biosphere, the air, and the falling stones. When the profound prejudices in favor of the Hebraic religions are waived, their resemblances to other religions, even to planetary religions, are great.

But Moses probably had something special in mind, and the subsequent Judaic priesthood in their mind, in laboring against cometary (or planetary) worship. Moses wanted to root his religion in earthly phenomena to the maximum extent possible so that he could control it. And the priesthood, too, had the same motive, plus a strong desire to make ritual all-important, so that they might control the worshippers as well as the god. The transition from the charismatic religion of Moses to the ritualistic anti-charismatic religion of the body of priests can be so understood.

Another reason occurs for banishing sky-body worship, and suppressing reference to any distinguishable body as being part of Exodus. If a named natural object were worshipped, even only as a manifestation or presence of the god, then all other peoples who saw the same body could pretend to the same god. They could match their experience, and counter their claims against those of the Jews. This would not do for Moses' exclusive people, exclusive god, exclusive religion.

Furthermore, the comet was terrible and damaging to the Jews. Undoubtedly the behavior of the god immanent in it was a large factor in permitting the extremely harsh rule that Moses imposed upon them. But the relation to Yahweh could be controlled; deep down there was an ambivalence, a hatred that could hardly be governed, working against a gratitude for an escape from "slavery," together with all that was provided for survival - water, manna and the poor subsistence coming from hard labor.

Moses himself could not help but feel this intense ambivalence, for of all people he could understand how the comet was wrecking the Earth. So he would not wish to make the phenomena of the skies of Exodus any conscious part, much less any identifiable part of the new religion and new god that he was building. Other religions with multiple gods, or gods and devils - and we should note that Moses would deny the existence of a devil - could handle ambivalence toward divinities much more easily than Yahwism could.

Now we are face-to-face with the phenomena of psychic repression. Yahwism sees no comet; it sees as little of the sky as possible; it allows only the fire of Yahweh to be seen. Z. Rix is "convinced that the prohibition to show an image of Yahweh is a repression, very injurious to the human mind."[33] What begins as traumatic terror is suppressed in memory; then, rather than gradually becoming adjusted to the memory, the mind is committed to the suppression by priests and ritual. And it never can adjust to the reality of recollection, and hence never can accommodate to the reality of the present. This mental condition is bound up with the invisible god and is a large factor in the psychological operations of mosaism and Yahwism.

If the mental process were to be divided into phases, in the first phase a perception occurred: the sight and force is then accorded life, that is, anthropomorphization. The reality of the comet passes and the memory remains, but not a memory of a comet as such; rather the memory of a divine intervention, of a god who can be controlled by sacrifices and subservience.

Memory always has a function and, to have this function, especially in terrible instances, must be distorted. The trauma of anthropomorphic natural force can be managed; a great natural force cannot, and hence must be denied. Thus, the Romans had gods with human qualities and permitted themselves psychologically to associate these gods with planets - as in the case of Mars - but in only one case, cited by Pliny, was an actual comet consciously named and admitted to the pantheon as a god, that of Augustus Caesar.

THE GENTILE EXODUS

The experience of Exodus was critical in the history of the Jews; further, a long chain of history has bound up over a billion people, indirectly the whole human race, in its consequences. Yet, at the time, the Israelite experience was special, affecting only a small fraction of the world's people. I say this not only to extend history but to contract it, and then I contract it in order to extend it differently. It has been a source both of pride and sorrow to the Jews in that they have unwittingly made the whole world suffer their Exodus. But every people of the world suffered its exodus at the same time. By taking on the record of the Hebrew Exodus it has been substituting the Jewish Exodus for one of its own, or blending them, or reviving its own. Whether this is for better or worse depends upon how each of hundreds of surviving cultures and many more dead cultures incorporated their own catastrophe.

Catastrophe and Divine Fires

In this age of one humanity and a sense of the good of all, I cannot but feel sympathy for the hapless nations and tribes that succumbed or survived in wretchedness. If only all had written books and these had been preserved, what a sense of common destiny, amounting practically to a common humanistic religion, we might share. Nevertheless, we have this one, with its terror, strife, and striving. And, here and there within it, we glimpse the distraught other peoples, the Egyptians of Ipuwer and El Arish accounts, but also especially of the Bible, written by their presumed enemies, the Israelites.

In the chant of Moses, already quoted, we hear of the people by their great highway into the Near East, the Philistines, Edomites, Moabites - all prostrated by disaster [34]. Velikovsky is like many people when he forgives the desperate Jews their transgressions upon others, while denouncing their equally desperate enemies such as the Hyksos-Amalekites for their transgressions. This is not only unfair; it obscures also the motives of peoples, their common fates, and the origins of their gods. It continues the destructive notion of the chosen people whether it be Israel or the mosaic-inspired Kaiserdom of "Deutschland Über Alles."

From the scene of the Exodus we can fan out in all directions, finding everywhere in the records and ruins of the time the same elemental fury. We look of course for the same things that we have found in the Biblical setting: the plagues, the years of darkness, floods, earthquakes, wanderings of people, continuous heavenly fire, electrical effects, new frenzied and obsessive forms of worship and gods on the ruins of shattered cities and among groups of survivors.

"Plagues of insects, drought, earthquake in the night, the most terrible devastation, clouds sweeping the ground, a tidal flood carrying away entire tribes - these disturbances and upheavals were experienced in Arabia and Egypt alike."[35] Amidst tumult and disorder, the Amalekites-Hyksos managed to reach and conquer Egypt.

During the Late Holocene period, which may actually have included the time of Exodus and later catastrophic episodes as well, the Sinai subplate was subjected to heavy uplifting, folding and submerging at its East and West margins. This is the scene of the Exodus drama; however, archaeological evidence is not yet available to tie a phase of this turbulence to the end of the Middle Bronze Age. (As matters stand, a connection can be made with an uplifting event and the disturbed astronomical years 776 to 687 B.C. that I refer to and describe in *Chaos and Creation,* in *The Disastrous Love Affair of Moon and Mars,* and, with Earl R. Milton, in *Solaria Binaria.*) [36]

In a paper published elsewhere[37], I surveyed the evidence for the catastrophes of the Near and Middle East, which I can summarize here. Claude Schaeffer, whose archaeological work in Syria brought him many honors, published as early as 1948 a great compendium of the destruction of settlements in the second millennium before Christ. The end of the Middle Bronze Age, corresponding to the end of the Egyptian Middle Kingdom that we have been studying, seems to have witnessed the complete destruction of every city that had been excavated. The effects of earthquakes were most common.

Since it is believed sometimes that the pyramids and other strong stone structures have escaped damage through

Catastrophe and Divine Fires

the ages, it is worthwhile mentioning that even the Great Pyramid exhibits severe damage by earthquake[38]. I do not make more of this case and others because there is presently no way of judging whether the damage was caused in the earthquakes of the Exodus.

The destruction of Minoan Crete around the same time was exposed by Evans. Evidence of a Chinese catastrophe with a hiatus between the Hia and the Chang dynasties was adduced by Schaeffer and Velikovsky. Previously, the Indus River civilization was shown to have collapsed in ruins then, too, and the extent of the fall has been steadily expanded north, east and south on the Indian subcontinent in the past half century of excavation[39]. The Euphrates River systems of channels moved west at this time and hundreds of settlements were abandoned in a long dark age[40]. It was then, too, that "the ancient cities of Southern Turkmenian civilization perished at about the same time as the proto-Indian, and the reasons are still unknown."[41] The antiquity of Meso-American civilization is only now being discovered. The Olmec civilization, which had the lodestone compass before the Chinese, suffered devastation by fire and flood at this time [42].

To the evidence of the spade may be added the evidence of legend from around the world. Greco-Roman civilization knew of the Exodus catastrophe, which Pliny gives passing mention to, in part by way of the stories of Typhon and Phaeton. Phaeton loses control of the chariot of the sun and sets fire to the world; Zeus has to strike him down with a cosmic thunderbolt to save the world from destruction. (See figure 8.)

Stecchini has recently publicized the work of the

Babylonian astronomical scholar, F.X. Kugler, that assigns to about 1550 B.C. the adventure of Phaeton. By Kugler's reconstruction, "a sunlike meteorite" passed by Earth from South to North creating various disasters until it, or some portion of it, fell in the Thracian region. This would be the region of the Celts, whose representatives, when asked one time by Alexander the Great what it was that they feared most, replied "that the sky might fall."

Typhon, too, was part or all of a monstrous sky body, which Zeus was supposed to have felled with his thunderbolts. Bimson shows that Typhon has another identity, that of the first Hyksos king of Egypt following the Exodus. Either the comet or the king was named for the other. The typhoons of the South Seas carry the name, too, and resemble, as do the American tornados, the pillar of smoke, water and fire.

The legends of the world are rich in material probably of this period. From Egypt we have a depiction of the "red (angry) eye of Horus in the mouth of Seth," who is the Typhonic monster. Sutherland has given us an account of how the unlucky dragon of China originated at this time and developed into the "lucky dragon" of later times, honored by being woven into the Emperors gown, even as magnificent as the ephod, robe and breastplate of Aaron. He depicts a large serpent-like creature with stubby feet and jets of flame flashing the length of its body as it pursues with jaws agape a round globe that may be taken to be the head of a comet [43]. Obviously the Jews were not alone in converting the harbinger of disaster into a benevolent and beneficent being.

Catastrophe and Divine Fires

Figure 8. Zeus Strikes Down Phaeton.
(Source: Sixteenth century embroidery of scenes from Ovid's *Metamorphoses*)

On what must be the last day of Passover week, but in every month, the Babylonians celebrated a 'Day of Wrath' of the goddess Ishtar with the stoppage of work and lamentations; Ishtar was Athene, Minerva, Venus, and Baalzevuv. Baal Zevuv or "god of the flies," whom Americans know by the popular devil's name of Beelzebub, was also Baal of the Ten Tribes of the Northern Kingdom of Israel and of the Canaanites; god Ares in the Iliad calls Athene: "dog-fly;" a reading of the voluminous cross-cultural evidence brought forward in Velikovsky's books should provide assurance that the four plagues of diverse insects or vermin before Exodus were inextricable from a celestial, catastrophic event.

THE HORROR OF RED

The horror of the color red in Egypt after 1450 B. C. is an understandable result of the Exodus catastrophe and most precisely the red plague. "Red is regarded as a purely calamitous color."[44] Yet the heavenly gods of Edfu (third dynasty of the Old Kingdom) were clad in festive red. The tracing of just this detail of a culture, the color red, illuminates how the cometary disaster produced long-lasting psychological and material changes,

The Egyptians could not even enjoy a red sunset or sunrise for a long time thereafter, deeming the sun to be ominous of danger and anger. It was "Horus raging with red eyes." The Red Sea was probably named for those days of the red plague. "It is remarkable that the designation of 'Red Sea' has no precedent in Old Egyptian; to the contrary, expressions regularly contained no mention of color."[45] The seas all around were feared and the Egyptians did not go to sea but left the waters to other peoples. The whole foreign world was called "the red " with the same loathing that a modern capitalist might talk of the "reds" of communism.
While the murex, the shell that makes a beautiful red dye, was the object of brisk trade elsewhere, the Egyptians would never deal in it. In the sarcophagi, a bull at one end of the tomb was painted red. The dead who were buried with broken red pots were said thus to ward off Seth and recognize Osiris.

The Egyptians were probably the source of imagining the devil to be red. Seth - god of the conquering Hyksos, but eternal foe of Horus - was sent into the underground after the expulsion of the Hyksos. The color of Seth was red. So was the color of Typhon, who came to be a monstrous identity of Seth. Human sacrifices - the highest compliment that humans can make to a deity - were offered to repeat and thus reassure the destruction of Typhon. According to Rix, Jews were often chosen for Typhonic sacrifices, especially red-headed Jews. Possibly thus the historical connection of the Jews with the red plague could be more sharply symbolized. "Therefore the *nuggoi* (red) people were persecuted, therefore only *nuggoi* animals were chosen for sacrifice, therefore also fiery colored people (Typhonians) according to Diodorus in ancient times were offered at the tomb of Osiris, and according to Plutarch, later, were burnt in Eileithyia and their ashes winnowed to the winds."[46] Yet, "the name (or nickname) 'the red one,' referring to skin color or hair color had at first no negative value."[47] When animals were substituted for humans, "the sacrifice of a red bull is represented at Denderah with the formal statement that the animal was Typhon."[48] Cows, bulls and asses were portrayed as red on ceremonial occasions. Seth was also the red ass and hippopotamus. However, the bull-god Apis, object of the Hyksos cult, is colored black [49].

The Pharaoh of Egypt wore a double crown to represent both Upper Egypt and Lower Egypt, which includes Memphis and the Nile River Delta whence occurred the Exodus: the crown of Upper Egypt was white, the crown of Lower Egypt red. This was to show the domination of Lower Egypt by Upper Egypt. But this domination meant probably the disaster, suppression, and finally liberation of Lower Egypt from the Hyksos, the people of Typhon. "Because red had an evil meaning, the red crown was referred to euphemistically as 'the green.'" A district governor from Siut declares his resolve "to bring order to the red."[50]

The god, Horus, was connected with the color white but when angry, his eyes became red. Isis, when siding with her brother Osiris, is black; when shown as the sister of Seth, she is red. Although red originally was used on a papyrus as "the color of high rank" it "becomes later the symbol of the unfavorable and dangerous." The Pharaoh's name is in red in the Book of the Dead. Calendars marked their unlucky and evil days in red ink [51]. The pervasiveness of the attitude toward red as evil is a measure of the trauma of cosmic catastrophe, followed by foreign oppression, that befell Egypt as the Israelites under Moses departed.

THE ELECTROSTATIC AGE

His lightnings lighten the world;
the Earth sees and trembles.
The mountains melt like wax before the Lord,
before the Lord of all the earth.

This Psalm 97 of the Bible seems to have been composed by a devout but advanced electrician. So also seems Deborah: "The mountains melted... even that Sinai." (*Judges* 5:4-5). Only lately, and by means of satellites, have scientists known of mega-lightning, 100 times more intense than the typical thunderstorms discharges, which shoots bolts of 1013 watts and 109 joules between the highest atmosphere and low clouds or earth [52]. Such discharges, of which there are many and which were probably once more common, can transmute heavy elements and create

Catastrophe and Divine Fires 95

radioactivity in abundance.

Since we have had no recent experience of lightning-like electrical discharges between a large body and Earth, we need to draw analogies from extra-terrestrial astronomy to imagine what can have happened during Exodus times. The closest analogy may be what is happening between planet Jupiter and its moon-sized satellite Io.

"Probably the most spectacular discovery of the Voyager mission has been the existence of active volcanoes on Io, erupting material to heights of several hundred kilometers above the surface."[53] According to T. Gold, these "volcanoes" are probably of electrical origin. Seeking out points of high potential and conductivity on Io, lightning from Jupiter shoots ten trillion watts of power repeatedly across the space gap between the two bodies. It digs volcano-like craters with high heat and explosive force, raising pillars of material to heights of up to 270 kilometers, whereupon most of it falls back around its caldera. The electric current or arc "can be expected to be an accurately repeating process."[54]

I would add here, and discuss later, the comment that the Earth-to-comet discharges would range from such enormous discharges (which would however be not so repetitive) to much less powerful, non-explosive electrical melts of mountain-tops. The tie-in of electrostatic discharges with a thermal flow through mountaintops is still a problem for a future science. Meteorologists and geologists have no sense of its history, possibility, and effects. Hence for thousands of years Psalmist 97 has been regarded merely as an exuberant poet.

The Age of Exodus was perforce electrical, judging

by the traits and behavior of the greatest gods of the age, such as Zeus, Jupiter, Thor, Marduk, Thoth, Amon and Yahweh, electric phenomena were pervasive and intense, and took many forms. As G.B. Vico wrote, every gentile nation had its Zeus. Every mountain had its fire sanctuary. The Etruscans, probably in the Near East in Moses' time and, later on, a powerful and advanced Italian nation, are a case in point. They exhibited the most frenetic obsession with lightning; every stroke made its target sacred and approachable only by one of the powerful priesthood; today every eminence in Tuscany seems to reveal to the aerial infra-red camera a ruined development beneath its soil. The Etruscans gave the Romans Jupiter, who was Jove or Ioweh or, who knows, Yahweh; they originated in the Near East and some of their linguistic roots are in Sumer, their blood types resemble an Anatolian group, and they possessed creation and flood legends strikingly like those of Genesis.

Throughout the world, altars were placed on eminences, where a "priesthood of the mountain" would collect and administer static electricity in the course of its rituals, orgies, and oracles. These would not necessarily be the highest peaks. Very tall mountains discharge readily and invisibly into the vapor clouds that hover over them and frequently envelop them. For electrical purposes, lesser eminences, with the proper types of conductive rock, the proper network of fractures, and the presence of groundwater steeply descending would facilitate the religious function. Everywhere priesthood developed an expertness in selecting and shaping sites for the exploitation of divine fire. The Druids of Britain distinguished between the lightning of priesthood *(drui-lanack)* and the lightning of god *(dis-lanack)*.

Catastrophe and Divine Fires

In Egypt, the age of pyramids preceding Exodus brought the mountain priesthoods to the flat Nile Valley.

Everything that was luminescent, that emitted a high density of photons, was termed "fire." Left with this general word, we of this age, when much less of fire is left in nature, are likely to regard all ancient references as combustion or lightning. The term may mean these two forms; or it may be a metaphor; but very often it refers to strikingly different manifestations.

The incessant attention given to many forms of fire is one reason why I believe that certain ancient periods were undergoing a universal change in electrical conditions. Already highly electrical before Exodus, the world was impelled by the comet of those years into a yet more widespread and intense electrical condition.

There is every reason to believe that "present conditions" - meaning by this the past 2500 years - have experienced in no way the conditions of the Jovean age which we are discussing, and the Bible misleads or is read wrongly when Moses is pictured as a traveling magician with a tent full of trinkets. Seneca, the great Roman stoic, recalls in a tragedy a Jupiter whose bolts would level mountains; this is the kind of god with whom we are dealing. Experts on lightning who have looked into paleontological lightning evidences - such as E. V. Komarek [55] - draw pictures of heavy past electrical activities; immense fields of lightning-caused fulgerites are to be found embedded around the world. No such processes have been reported in historical times.

Electrical fires may have been responsible for scorching of some sealed tombs of the period [56]. The pyramids or Egypt may seem to have evaded divine melting, but calcination is manifested in certain places, and the plated stone that covered the pyramids is missing. We do have a provocative instance of burning in Babylon, such that it has been considered by some as the original Tower of Babel, whose brick and bitumen construction was struck by divine fire [57]. It was of the stepped, ziggurat type.

> It appeared that the fire had struck the tower and split it down to the very foundation. In different parts of the ruins immense brown and black masses of brickwork had changed into a vitrified state. At a distance, the ruins looked like edifices torn apart at their foundations. Evidently the fiercest kind of fire created the havoc. The most curious of the fragments found were several misshapen masses of brickwork, black, subjected to some kind of heat, and completely molten.

> The whole ruin has the appearance of a burnt mountain. On one side of it, beneath the crowning masonry, lay huge fragments torn from the pile itself. The calcinated and vitreous surface of the brick had fused into rock-like masses. It is difficult to explain the cause of the vitrification of the upper building. Great boulders were vitrified, and brickwork had been fused by fire [58].

It is probable that thousands of burnt eminences exist around the world whose tops have seen the electrical fusion of rocks, perhaps even Troy IIg, the "Burnt City" so-called [59]. The famous site, whether or not it was the real Troy, is on an eminence. While not high, the city would have had many small reservoirs of water, whereas the ground outside might already have been dried out. In Troy IIg a sulphurous color suffuses all outdoor spaces and passageways

Catastrophe and Divine Fires

of the town. A deposit of lead and copper melted and flowed around the town. (It is possible that this melt had been scavenged after Schliemann reported it in the 1880s and the discoloration was all that was discoverable when the Blegen expedition re-excavated the site in the 1930s.) No human hand could have or would have set such a fire. The heat was fierce. The ash was far too abundant for a deliberate fire from local materials, and carried a red color. No one would have wanted to destroy precious metals (not to mention even more precious metal left in abundance in the scorched houses and the "treasure of Priam," found on a wall.)

Noteworthy is the almost complete absence of human and animal skeletal material in the ruins. Either they turned to dust from the heat, or the electrical buildup was sensed, as it is by animals before earthquakes for example, and they fled from the hill onto the plain where the sensations were absent. Troy IIg, however, should be dated around the time of the Tower of Babel, and exemplifies the unusual play of electrical forces in pre-Exodus times, rather than during the Exodus itself.

In this connection, it is suggested that a great many eminences without settlements or special conditions may, in the process of conducting a charge to or from deep below the surface, have liquified silicates and ferruginous substances together as a conductor, or fused them from the ancient rocks and from by-products, and brought these materials up to the top of the eminence where they are today found, resting on loose, hardly consolidated rocks, as a hard dense cap. This phenomenon is usually explained as a metamorphosis, of very old age, that somehow raised the temperature of water-laden deep limestones and granites and caused them to nearly melt and to rise.

Silification is abundant around igneous metamorphism. In a hot and fast reaction, siliceous fluid is introduced hydrothermally and replaces the host rock, such as limestone, into which it intrudes. It is possible, with or without water, for an electric discharge to assemble and flow quickly as a current up the core of a hill, heating as it moves. Resistant rock heats up like the resistant coils of an ordinary electric room-heater. The taller the mountain, the less time and chance for the siliceous fluid to reach and cap its peak before the current is dissipated in heat or finds enough discontinuities of strata and faults to disperse in different directions.

YAHWEH'S ELECTRICAL FIRE CONGLOMERATE

Yahweh is present in smoke and fire both in the Tabernacle and elsewhere, giving rise to the naive view that he was simply a typical volcano god, of which, presumably, there are as many as there are volcanoes [60]. Freud adopted this view as part of accepting the primitivist bedouin theory of much of Exodus. The volcano gods that inspire this belief are the small "retail" gods of today, not the wholesale volcano and fire gods of old - like Hephaistos. And Yahweh was more than a wholesale volcano god; he was a giant fire conglomerate god.

When Moses invited the elders to visit Yahweh with him, they came upon his presence on a vitrified surface, sapphire as of heaven. This was the Sinai that "burned like wax." On the occasion when Moses had spent days and

Catastrophe and Divine Fires 101

nights on the Holy Mountain, the electrical currents were so heavy that he had crouched in a cleft for fear of electrocution as Yahweh passed by. The Israelites had their own electrical mountain:

> There were thunders and lightnings, and a thick cloud upon the mountain, and a very loud trumpet blast... And Mount Sinai was wrapped in smoke, because the Lord descended it in fire [61].

The fire came down to the mountain. Only Moses could approach its heights safely. The people had to stand below, which is something nevertheless that they might not do if it were a violently erupting volcano. A column of smoke went up. The horns sounded ever louder. Fiery darts dropped everywhere. There were frightening electrical storms and earth movements. Stones were cast down from the sky. The people scarcely dared approach the foot of the mountain for fear that they would be destroyed by fire. They did finally run away.

Since Mount Sinai does not behave like a volcano, one is not surprised to learn that explorers have not found a volcano, whether extinct or alive, at any of the sites proposed for the location of Moses' Holy Mountain. The two major contenders for the position are Jebel Músa in the South Central Sinai Peninsula and a mountainous location at the northeastern head of the Gulf of Aquaba (see map of Figure 5) referred to as Mount Horeb. Following Winnett's tracing of the Wilderness itinerary, I am adopting the latter in my considerations, partly because this is in Midian and Horeb is placed in Midian by *Ex.* 3:1 and Moses has had so much to do with Midian otherwise [62]. Geological investigations are required before Mount Sinai-Jebel Musa is definitely pronounced a possibility for "electrico-vulcanism," and even less is known of the geology of the several locations heretofore proposed near modern Eilath, in ancient Midian or modern North Hêgaz.

On various occasions, Yahweh sent consuming fires upon the Israelites, once even at a place renamed Teberah, "the Burning Place."[63] The fire: "wrought havoc among...the murmuring and complaining multitude that had joined the Israelites upon their Exodus from Egypt."[64] It was a fire that destroyed fire. It spread on all sides. It was the same fire that "found its place on the altar of the Tabernacle," and that destroyed Aaron's sons and Korah's company. "Moses took bundles of wool and laid them upon the divine fire, which thereupon went out."[65] Wool is of course more effective than water in extinguishing electrical fires.

One cannot be sure what kind of fire it is that runs along the ground. It is not ordinary combustion; it may be fleets of ball-lightning such as have rarely been observed in recent times [66]. "Fire has mounted up on high" (Ipuwer) is significant. This is not lightning: the combination indicates a type of St. Elmo's conflagration - there are cases reported even recently like this with a climbing of whatever eminences are accessible. Pyramids, obelisks, buildings, perhaps even balls and jets of fire leaving the ground and moving through the dense atmosphere upwards, like a clutch of balloons, are probable.

The repeated Biblical references to Yahweh's sending darts of fire, jets of fire upon the enemies of Israel and even upon the Israelites when they displease him, inspires one to seek the corresponding natural phenomenon, even though it would be enormously amplified in a general catastrophic encounter. Juergens has suggested plasmoids, pieces of plasma, as being formed and bombarding earth on some ancient occasions. These electrical footballs are formed of a balance of positive ions and electrons. They retain their identity and appear as luminous objects of the size of missiles. They would cause explosions near the ground and/or dig craters [67].

It is the voltage difference that promotes electrical activity; opposite charges that attract are not necessary for a discharge. A high negative charge will discharge to a low negative charge; the electrons explode or spark to the less dense negative region, or follow a highly conductive medium. The difference in potential is the setting for an activity.

The Earth as a sphere carries an overall charge but no one knows what it is [68]. The concept of "charge" is effectively meaningless except in relation to other aggregates that carry an electric charge. The charge of the Earth as a whole then is significant when any part of the whole - its rocks, its waters, its atmosphere, its depths and heights - becomes electrically differentiated, which means that these are electrically potentiated for activity when their charges or distances or media of conduction change in relation to one another. Also the Globe is charged in relation to other aggregates of the solar system environment, be they plasma, gases, meteoroids, planet or sun, just as it may have a gravitational relationship to them. And just as that gravitational relationship varies exponentially with the distance of the aggregates, so does the electrical relationship vary.

The solar system as a whole, moving as it does in

relation to millions of bodies of the Milky Way Galaxy, operates in a changing electrical environment. This is constant so long as the solar system as a point in the Galaxy retains a stable position, though moving, in relation to all other significant charged points. And it does so too, so long as such body-points are not rapidly changing their electrical condition, as for example happens when a star explodes as a nova or supernova.

In good weather a point on the Earth's surface carries in the meter of atmosphere above it a negative charge of about 100 volts. (Ground zero is a relative concept; an immense voltage might conceivably be in the Earth.) The luminous halo-discharges from points, known as St. Elmo's fire, "are caused by a sharp increase in the voltage field to a value a thousand times greater than the average 120-150V/m."[69] At a height of 50 kilometers, the ionosphere carries a positive charge of about 400,000 volts, which would indicate an average vertical voltage gradient of about 8 volts per meter. This difference produces no visible or felt effects ordinarily. A sudden change, such as occurs just before an earthquake, will excite greatly the biosphere and produce weakness, giddiness, and tense feelings among people [70]. Eric Crew points out that there is a normal leakage in the atmospheric column; this current is tiny and totals 1800 amperes, which is balanced by the charging effect of lightning carrying negative charge to the ground [71]. Changing atmospheric conditions also play upon this voltage gradient causing electrical effects.

Any changed deployment of external aggregates also plays upon this voltage gradient and often it is by no means child's play. A volcanic eruption or a meteorite fall plays

Catastrophe and Divine Fires   105

havoc with its ambiance, electrically as well as otherwise. Sun spots, which are electrified explosive events, have meteorological and climatic effects on the Earth and may even disturb the Earth's motion.

If two large bodies - such as the earth and a great comet - approach each other, they will invariably be carrying unequal charges at various lines of potential contact. They will exchange charges between their plasma sheaths (magnetospheres), between their atmospheres, between their surface prominences, and between their surfaces, which are graded according to conductivity and resistances. Even if all of these changed states and all bodily motions were known and this data were fed into a computer, and even if all the laws of electricity now known were programmed to manipulate the data, the pattern of exchanges would be exceedingly complicated, fast, often violent, and in any event impossible to plot given the present state of knowledge and the many behaviors that are beyond history.

A long-term charge exchange of Earth with its atmosphere and interplanetary space is postulated, together with a large-body encounter, to explain the apparently heavy electrical effects of the mid-second millennium B.C. A third major producer of electricity would be the crustal stresses of the Earth in the aftermath of a large-body encounter, whether involving a slight or major deceleration or axial re-orientation of part or all of the Earth's crust, mantle and core. These would bring about a long period of earthquakes and piezoelectric effects.

The relation between earthquakes and lightning has been foolishly neglected for two centuries until now. The Chinese earthquake of July 28, 1976 lit up the sky in red and white colors for 200 miles around its epicenters for hours [72]. Observers, from antiquity to the present day, have spoken of the flames emerging from earthquake fissures; one student counted ten such reports in a survey of several hundred earthquakes.[73]

Piezoelectricity comes from stresses of pressure and heat upon quartz rock, which is widely dispersed over the Earth's crust, particularly in lavas. "The North Idu peninsula earthquake on November 26, 1930, the best documented instance of seismoelectricity (over fifteen hundred sightings), occurred in a region with widespread quartz rich lava flows."[74] In quartz whose axis has been lined up by tectonic strains, an earthquake can create "an average electric field of 500-5000 volts/cm. For distances in the order of half the seismic wavelength, the general voltage is 5×10^7 to 5×10^8 V, which is comparable with the voltage responsible for lightning in storms. The discharge will seek outlets through tooth-like (Sinai=Sinn=Tooth?), sword-like (Horeb=sword), and especially quartz-loaded eminences, or in fissures, or, if needs be, in fires "running along the ground" (plagues of Egypt). The piezoelectric effects, occurring from earth strains, would long outlast the cometary encounter, and provide continuous high voltage above ground.

E. A. Von Fange quotes 37 passages from the Old Testament referring to great destruction by fire, only one of them from *Exodus,* which we find has numerous references to fire. He also mentions "a total of 28 fields of burned and broken stones called *harras,* has been found in Western Arabia, covering up to 7000
square miles each. "[75]

A comprehensive list of all electrical phenomena that

are mentioned or hinted at in the Bible and Jewish legends would include: celestial eyes; angels and other apparitions on prominences; St. Elmo's fire; blasts; jagged lightning; jets or darts of fire; exploded gas pockets or petroleum fires; electrically induced or electrically accompanied dust and water typhoons and tornados; ionized winds; charged and ionized dust-falls; illuminated skies, including earthquake lights; the electrical flashes from volcanoes; point discharges on controlled machines or near to such apparatus; smoke clouds of luminous quality; night lights; phosphorescence; thunder, trumpets and singing; piezoelectric effects; and natural electrochemical compositions of manna and other substances. To these should be added the fall-outs of electro-jet transported stones and dust, and electrically accompanied radioactive fall-out or explosion. Nor should one neglect the many electrical changes overcoming the great comet in its movements through space, that gave it so many different identities - animal, human and divine.

We can be sure that a full range of electrical effects - visual, auditory and physiological - would be experienced by the whole population and that many changes would occur in the atmosphere, lithosphere, hydrosphere and biosphere. Furthermore, the effects would be enduring. Centuries would pass before the numerous causal chains would emerge into an apparent equilibrium. Then all spheres of nature would gradually have been adjusted to all others. Earth rock strata, discontinuities, faults, and contours would carry differing currents, generate piezoelectricity, and so-on, but at a level finally recognizable as of the present day. Like water seeks its own level, electricity gropes for a balance of charges.

THE CELESTIAL FIRST CAUSE

Given the Exodus symptoms which were exhibited in the Near East and elsewhere, which were not all confined to Lower Egypt, we can surmise that physical convulsions overcame the Earth. These were provoked either by internal causes or external ones. But what would provoke a quiescent Earth, as we know it today, to such energetic reactions as we observe during the Exodus? If the Earth's interior were as it is now, and as many believe it to have been for a billion years or more, and if its motions were then as they are now, as they are believed to have been for a billion years or more, neither Exodus nor any other such general catastrophe would have been experienced in history and prehistory.

We have a convenient test of this statement. The island of Thera-Santorini, north of Crete, and only some hundreds miles from the scene of the Exodus plagues and tides, has recently been accredited with that disaster [76]. Thera, an ancient center of Minoan civilization, suffered more than one explosion in the second half of the second millennium. The date of its climactic destruction may be about 1000 B.C. based on Isaacson's matching of cultural remains with Bronze Age remains of Egyptian origin also found there [77]. The incredible blast, 50 times that of Krakatoa offshore Java in 1883, is known to have filled the sky with a fall of ashes and excited great tidal waves.

I eliminate Thera as the source of the Exodus catastrophe, not only because of the late date of the most destructive outburst, but also because it alone could not have brought about the long period of ground and air turbulence of Exodus, the biosphere behavior, the sky scenes of moving

Catastrophe and Divine Fires

bodies, or the years of dust, chemicals, and dark clouds. Further, it is more likely that a general thermo-electric effect of the Earth's crustal torsion brought on the explosive series of Thera than the reverse. Mount Vesuvius exploded with a force equal to the climactic Thera explosion about 3500 years ago [78]. Many other eruptions would have occurred, both conical and fissure in type. The great explosion of Thera, when it did happen hundreds of years later, may have contributed to the rapid decline and fall of the Hyksos empire of Syria and Lower Egypt, a fall made final by an alliance of King Saul of Israel and Pharaoh Ahmose of Egypt [79].

Therefore, there must have been some extra-terrestrial cause of the Exodus catastrophe. There might have been a change in the sun, which we consider because of its great size to represent also any considerable change in the galactic environment. Or there might have been a wandering cloud of gases or meteoroids that invaded the Earth's "air-space." Or there might have been some large-body intrusion, coming close enough to the Earth to provoke the destructive effects experienced on Earth.

This large body would be by definition a comet, because any body on an irregular orbit or path near us cannot be called a planet, and further, there is no fundamental difference between a meteoroid and a comet (although it used to be thought that meteoroids were short-distance travelers in the solar system and comets long-distance travelers [80]. As for the coma, or "hair" (Latin) that characterizes the comet, any body moving through different types of space will react gaseously and electrically to the differences, and grow or lose its "hair" or "tail."

Since large meteoroids behave like comets, we may turn to smaller meteoroids. A meteoroid of, say, the diameter that caused the Berringer Crater of Arizona, or the Tunguska blast in Siberia, which exploded aboveground, falls on rare occasion. Today Earth experiences incursions by swarms of meteorites from time to time. A regular swarm hits the atmosphere and is to be seen on or about August 10 of each year. Their effects go generally unnoticed. Several reliable accounts of meteorite swarms of greater moment are available: the widespread terror is noticeable; the incitement of earth's tremors has been attributed to some meteors. Strange effects such as gas clouds, ball-lightning, and small gelatinous masses have been partially verified. No effects comparable to those of Exodus are demonstrated.

Especially in view of the astonishing irregularities that have been ascribed to the sun in the past several years [81], one might think of blaming the sun for the Exodus catastrophe. But here the problem is that those who experienced Exodus did not blame the sun. The Phaeton legend is practically alone in asserting that the son of Helios stole his chariot and lost control of it, careening about the sky to the great distress of the Earth and its inhabitants. I have already referred to the study of Kugler who severed any relationship between Phaeton and the sun, giving an independent existence, path and destruction to this large sun-like body. The Greek legend of Zeus striking down Typhon, and the Egyptian legend of Horus defeating Seth and sending him to hell represent much better the celestial events surrounding Exodus. It is probable, however, as I explain in another work *(Chaos and Creation)*, that changes in the sun and solar system precipitated the great body upon its

Catastrophe and Divine Fires

errant course.

Nevertheless, the body is independent, very large, and distinct in the eyes of the beholders. Velikovsky says it was the planet Venus; I term it elsewhere the protoplanet Venus or Cometary Venus. This is because of the abundant connections made in antiquity that associate the great body of the Exodus skies with the planet Venus. But this point has been heavily discussed in many places and we can be satisfied, for the purposes of this book, with the realization that an enormous body passed near the Earth and that only such a body could have produced the Exodus effects.

CHAPTER FOUR

THE ARK IN ACTION

Salem, Massachusetts, a century after it achieved fame in witchcraft, became an exciting center of the new science of "electric fire." Of an evening, for instance, according to an advertisement of March 7, 1765, one might attend lectures at David Mason's house, learning there:

> That the Electric Fire is a real Element,- That our Bodies at all times contain enough of it to set a House on Fire,- That this Fire will live in Water,- A Representation of the Seven Planets, showing a probable Cause of their keeping their due Distances from each other, and the Sun in the Center...[1]

Until the 17th century, "experiment (what little of it there was) belonged to 'natural magic,'..."[2] Then, three thousand years after Moses, the European-American world rediscovered electricity through experiment, that is, "natural magic." We see clearly now why the tradition that Moses was a great magician, no matter how often "rebutted" by his admirers and "advanced" theologians, persisted. He who was an experimenter was thought to be a magician. He who was a magician performed experiments.

It is not surprising that Moses regarded the electrical fire as divine. Nor that Jesuit priests were among the most active modern experimenters. A prolonged debate divided

The Ark in Action

early modern electricians into those who believed electricity to be a substance, and those who considered it to be an influence (both attractive and repulsive). It is of the essence of Yahweh that he be such an "incorporeal" substance on a cosmic and microscopic scale and be at the same time an invisible influence for good and evil.

Long before the early modern scientists found their *deus ex machina*, Moses displayed Yahweh from the Ark of the Covenant. The divine presence luminesces from the pillar of cloud [3] and from between the two cherubim "visible to the people... as the radiation of the divine substance, as the kabod... always visibly directed towards or pointing to the tent."[4]

The invention of the Leyden jar in 1745 aroused great scientific and public interest. The Jar, which has found its way into hundreds of classrooms in elementary physics since then, was independently contrived by two scholars. One was the German scientist E. G. von Kleist. The other, a Dutch scholar, Peter van Musschenbroek, was affiliated with the University of Leyden. Innumerable ingenious applications took place,

Working with materials and instruments that would have been available to Moses, the new scientists literally played with every device and scheme that, according to my study here, was employed by Moses. So secular were the new scientists and so futuristic their pride, that practically never did they think to search among the most ancient records for their origins. A few years after the invention of the Leyden jar, Georg Wilhelm Lichtenberg (1743-1799), one of the founders of electrical science, called attention to its resemblance to the Ark of the Covenant, to the "Powerful

One of Jacob."[5]

Another distinguished electro-physicist, Maurice Denis-Papin (b.1900) asserted that the ark as an electrical capacitor was capable of producing from 500 to 700 volts [6]. This is quite enough to electrocute humans and animals as well as to perform many other electrical operations such as apparitions, smoke, and fire-making. However, neither scholar had in mind the effects upon the ark of the electrical turbulence of the Exodus period, a condition that was deduced from many circumstances and the Bible itself by Jerry Ziegler (1977), in his book *YHWH*.

The Leyden jar collects electricity. In its simplest form it consists of a pointed metal aerial conducting rod that is insulated from the ground by being immersed in water inside a glass jar. An electrical charge accumulates on the rod and will discharge to any grounded conducting element that touches it or comes close enough for the charge to jump the gap with a spark. (see figure 9)

A similar device will add a conductor to load the opposite ground charge. A jar is coated with a metal foil on the outside, and another metal foil on the inside; the glass, which will not conduct a charge effectively, insulates the one charge from the other. Water is unnecessary. A metal rod affixed to the inner foil helps to gather the atmospheric charge. A potential difference of voltage will build up between the two conductors and if it is heavy enough, will discharge by a spark or by a conducting contact like a wire, between the two, or by a deliberate or accidental interposition of a hand or another resistant or short-circuiting medium.

The voltage between the stored charges is dependent

The Ark in Action 115

upon: the electrical condition of the earth and the atmosphere; the material of which the conductors are made; their shape and size; and the time elapsed for the accumulation of charge. Various means can be taken to enhance the electrical potential, and therefore the force of the discharge. Benjamin Franklin in 1752 charged a Leyden jar by attaching to it a silk thread that could conduct electricity from a kite that entered a thunderstorm. He was taking a great risk.

He drew up a list of ways in which the "electrical fluid" of the Leyden jar resembled lightning [7]. Concluding that the phenomena were identical, he thought to capture and store lightning, but luckily he did not pursue his dangerous designs; a Swedish scientist did so and was struck dead by the badly stored charge (see case of Dr. Richmann below). The abundant electrostatic phenomena, both natural and humanly induced, of the Exodus, have been generally attributed to "lightning" as we know it today; this is a convenient category that disguises all references to other types of "fire."

Nicola Tesla in 1881, produced spark discharges five inches long in his New York loft; the potential was estimated at 100,000 volts. He elicited "a variety of new forms of illumination."[8] By 1900 Tesla was imitating lightning. He claimed he could produce two-mile long sparks conveying ten million horsepower. He wanted to create electric power by using the whole earth as a kind of Leyden jar (condenser) and resonating coil combined [9].

Franklin and others experimented with "the power of points ... drawing off and throwing off the electrical fire." He exploded cork balls from a muzzle and said that at night the muzzle cast off lights. He observed that the shots caused halos of smoke [10]. Sulphurous smells were associated with them in other instances.

Franklin also set up an electrostatic device to ring a bell when the atmosphere was charging up. Aaron, High Priest of Israel, had to wear the blue ephod, a gorgeous pullover to whose skirt are attached golden bells, "and it shall be upon Aaron when he ministers, and its sound shall be heard when he goes into the holy place before the Lord, and when he comes out, lest he die."[11]

Petrie reproduces from an Egyptian priestly garment a border of "lotus-flowers and seed-vessels" that seem like "bells and pomegranates." Few doubt, however, that the Israelite bells would ring. Cassuto says that they would sound so that the priest would not enter the sanctuary unannounced and irreverently. And in departure the priest would prostrate himself and the bells' sound be a blessing [12]. But perhaps Moses grafted electronics upon the original design. Thus, at Dodona, seat of the oldest Greek oracle, dedicated to Zeus Naios, there was "an oak grove hung with vessels of brass, by which the god's voice was thought to be made audible."[13]

This Zeus Naios was related to Zeus Ammon of Libya and Amon of Egypt, who is not unrelated to Yahweh. Priestley describes eighteenth century electrical experiments with bells besides those of Benjamin Franklin [14]. The bells of Aaron's *ephod* might usefully have been agitated by an excess of electricity about him, warning him not to come into the Inner Sanctum or sometimes to get out while he could ("lest he die…")

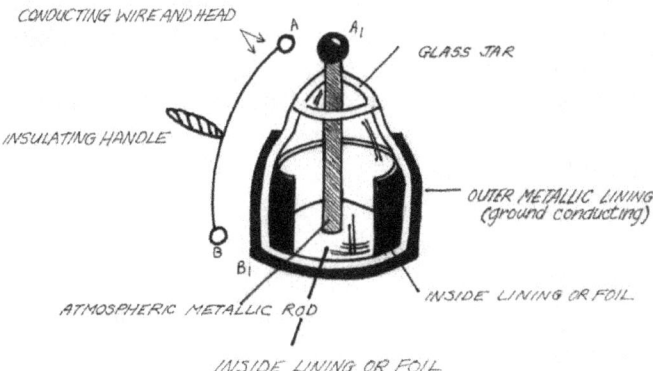

Figure 9. The Leyden Jar. If A is touched to A1, and B to B1, simultaneously, the jar will discharge at the points of contact and sparks will probably illuminate the two points of contact.

Franklin did not escape unscathed from his experiments. On one occasion he was knocked unconscious when he made an accidental connection while hooking up two Leyden jars to electrocute a turkey. Franklin was a humane man who liked turkeys - he once nominated the turkey for the American national bird in preference to the eagle totem - and was probably seeking a less painful way of butchering them. The device, it needs be said, does not display its charged condition to the eye; it is an invisible power of "an invisible god."

Musschenbrock, foreseeing such accidents, wrote: "The hand and the whole body is struck in such a terrible fashion that it is hard to describe. In a word, I thought the end had come." He advised a friend to "never repeat this new and terrible experiment."[15]

THE GOLDEN BOX

The Ark of the Covenant, so named because its hollow interior probably contained at first solely the stone tablets that Moses had brought down from Mt. Sinai with the words of Yahweh, measured probably between 45 x 27 x 27 and 63 x 38 x 38 inches. That would be close to the bulk size of a secretarial desk. Tradition maintains that the Ark itself was fashioned by Moses[16], and, of course, the design was his, dictated to him by Yahweh on the sacred mountain.

An ark "denotes here a kind of chest or box."[17] Its Hebrew word is 'aron.' It may have meant once something other than a box; that is, the structure embracing the function may have appropriated the name of the function in later ages. The root of 'aron,' says Strong's Concordance, signifies a gathering in; in this case, charges are collected and Aaron is the collector. The name of Aaron thus may be closer to the function, the priest of the ark or arc science.

Flinders Petrie, the greatest of Egyptologists, used the word 'ark' to describe one of a number of Egyptian depictions, such as is portrayed in Figure 10 here[18]. One is tempted to speculate that it is an engineering sketch of the Ark itself, lacking the box below. There would be little reason for the construction of these poles or this arch, aesthetic or otherwise, except to manage an electric arc or system of sparks. This ark in operation would flare at the junctions of the grounded poles and the top horizontal bar.

Why would the Egyptians set up an ark upon a boat? The implications are surprising. We think first of where a box to generate an electric arc would function more continuously and intensely. This would be a location on water, where charges gather more readily because of high conductivity of the medium. Especially in pre-cometary or post-cometary times, when the Earth was discharging less strongly, the ark as pictured in the illustration would create a more active arc discharge.

Secondly we revert to the puzzle of why the Jews named the Ark of Noah and the Ark of the Covenant similarly. The answer is probably that the electrical phenomena of Noah's Ark were stupendous, that the Egyptians generated their arcs on boats, and that Moses derived his land-based Ark from the aquatic models. These may have descended to the Egyptians from the Noah tradition via the Hebrews, or may have been indeed Moses' invention, whether in the aquatic forms, the land forms, or both. Regarding this last item, we may recall that Moses the

Figure 10. Egyptian Ark Procession
Source: Hugo Gressman, *Die Lade Jahves and das Allerheiligste des Solomonischen Temples*. Leipzig: Kohlhammer, 1920, from III Denkmaler 14. See also F. Petrie, Egypt and Isreal, p.62a

The Ark in Action

infant floated on the Nile in an "ark," the same rare word.

Priestley tells us that "as the electric fire may be made to take whatever circuit the operator shall please to direct, it may be thrown into a great variety of beautiful forms."[19] With various adjustments, all of which were recapitulated in the renaissance of electrical science in the eighteenth century, the poles or bars could be made to scintillate throughout their lengths, the wings of the cherubim would light up, and a glow would occupy the space beneath or shrouded by the wings, with the four ankhs (pictured at the corners of figure 10) sparking like brilliant, erratic candles. A god was present. The only meaning of 'Ark' in the dictionary of Egyptian hieroglyphics is the name of a god.

But when was this Egyptian ark constructed? Was it for a shrine made before 1450 B.C. or afterwards? The ankh answers the question. It is the paramount symbol of the planet Venus. Though it is also a symbol meaning 'life' and 'salvation' and the procreative *membrum virilis,* it reverts to Typhonic Venus in the end [20]. Therefore it is mostly of the period after 1450 B.C., by the chronology I am following. Thus were joined the Ark of Noah, the Egyptian ark, the ark and ankh of the gods, and the Ark of Moses.

Then five possibilities occur, assuming the gift of the design from Yahweh (see figure 12) to be a theological invention. The Ark of the Covenant may be an invention of Moses based directly upon Egyptian models known to him as a member of the Egyptian theocratic-scientific establishment. Or the Egyptian ark may be a copy of Moses' Ark. Or the ark might have been independently invented in both countries. Or Moses' Ark may be an outright theft of an Egyptian ark. Fifth, the Arks of Moses and of Egypt may be

Hyksos inventions that Moses acquired under Hyksos subjection.

The independent invention I would regard as impossible; the details are too close and are not found elsewhere in the world. Continuing, it cannot be a copy of Moses' Ark because Egypt was not free to copy until the Ark had lost its puissance. Therefore, the Ark must come from possibility 1, 4 or 5. Number 5 is possible, but the Hyksos were on a lower technical level, before and for long after their conquest of Egypt. Numbers 1 and 4 are compatible. They move towards each other. Moses knew and worked with Egyptian science and technology. He would certainly draw on them for the design of the Ark. Then the question of whether a specific ark or set of arks was operating in Egypt before the Exodus is not too important. The ark was in Egypt. The Ark was also Moses' (and possibly Aaron's) invention for Israel [21].

A capacitor or condenser of the size of the Ark might be rated in many thousands of volts if atmospheric electricity were more continuous and abundant then it is today and if the earth had suffered shocks and were emitting electricity in the aftermath. Large sources of leaking or gathering earth charges and a heavily electrified atmosphere would be required. The operators of the Ark system would, under such favorable conditions, be able to induce repeated sparks, of heavy or light intensity, slowly or rapidly.

Early modern science also discovered that electricity could be induced from the atmosphere and ground to produce differential charges and then sparking or shocking discharges. This discovery was combined with the knowledge that a charge could be built up by scraping the electrical

The Ark in Action

"fluid" off of certain materials and loading it onto other materials. So they went about rubbing and storing and discharging electricity with cloths and amber or glass or gem sticks. They devised machines to create ever larger charges. One experimenter was sure he could create a discharge attaining the power of a lightning bolt by enlarging the surface to hold the charge which a rubbing machine would create. Some inventors imagined they might fabricate a circular series of lugs that could turn a wheel whose bits would be alternately attracted and repelled until a perpetual motion machine was thought to be possible.

Did Moses and the Levites explore frictional electric manufacturing so thoroughly? They probably did; once begun, the logic and direction of experimentation is irresistible [22]. However, the difference between those days and nowadays is that the Exodus atmosphere had more than enough to offer to build any usable charges without further exertion. Like agriculture was unnecessary in the climate and ecology of Adam and Eve's Garden of Eden, electrical manufacture in Moses' time did not require hydraulic, fossil, animal, or human energy input.

I think that similar circumstances may have discouraged the development of wire for the transmission of electric charges or current. Early modern scientists used fibre and silk lines to transmit charges; these could have been employed by the Israelites as well. The moderns used hammered and stretched metallic wires; the technology was obviously within Israelite capabilities. Hundreds of copper necklaces have been recovered from Middle Kingdom sources.

In Petrie's catalogue of Egyptian artifacts, we read

that "the necklet of a single stout wire of metal belongs almost entirely to the Twelfth Dynasty [before Moses] and the Ptolemaic to Coptic period." Number 28 is "a silver wire with curled ends." Number 32 is of "two silver wires bent double and linked together..." Petrie describes the sophisticated technology of wiring and soldering in the Twelfth Dynasty. A single piece evidences soldering, wire stretching, die stamping, and a gold tube to carry a thread wire.

Whenever a spark jumps a gap, a conductor suggests itself to induce the discharge, be it a hand, a dagger, or a metal rod. We reexamine the Egyptian ark in Figure 11; it is bent at 90° in two places. Would it be wood or metal? Most likely metal. Why is it then, that museums do not exhibit lines and wires? Does it matter that Moses had an affinity with the Kenites? Their "name means 'smiths,' so we take it that some of the Midianites were coppersmiths."[23] Sometime afterwards, Kenites worked for the Egyptian government at the Sinai copper mines and were using the alphabet, "the earliest known."[24]

A curator would not be likely to postulate an electrical science if handed fragments of stretched organic or metal line. Nor likely would any be received by the museum in the first place; the materials are quite decomposable. In contemporary paintings they would appear as indistinct lines, on the rare occasion when they would be drawn. Wires would be short; insulation, new technology, and much metal alloy is needed for long wires. Telegraphy inspired wire technology in the nineteenth century. The ancients used fires and torches from eminences and may have employed "divine fire" in the electrified ages. There are hints of this in ancient

The Ark in Action

historical ages a millennium and more after Moses, when technology generally was not much advanced over his times.

Moreover, natural electricity is erratic and powerful. It can disintegrate a line or wire, whether or not insulated, quickly, by explosion or intense heat. A heavy conductor, as in the Egyptian ark, would be prohibitively expensive. It would be used only for in-house contraptions, entirely religious or experimental (that is, playful).

So we return again to a basic reason: the sufficiency of atmospheric or natural electrical electricity, and add that its oversufficiency may have contributed to blocking further development. As natural electrification diminished in the environment, the religious "atmosphere" added its weight to the causes forestalling development of electrical manufacture and wires. The divine fires were for priests and the priests were for tradition. The early modern electrical scientists, although evincing surprise at how electricity seemed alive, (just as Thales, the Greek philosopher, remarked at the spirit that animated the electrified amber), paid no further attention to gods or church. They went ahead individually, men women and children excitedly and delightfully playing the new game.

Catastrophe, too, inspires great tragic games. It frees its survivors. Wars are games of catastrophe and play out the catastrophic mentality. Moses was induced and permitted by catastrophe to change and manipulate people and things in many ways, to invent with a rare freedom.

The Ark box was gold outside and gold inside with an insulating layer of hard wood in between. The lid of the box, the *kapporeth,* also of wood overlain with gold, held at each end a cherub of gold. These cherubim faced each other with their wings spread out. In between them, over the lid, when he chose to be among his people, hovered Yahweh. This was his "mercy seat," in the anachronous English translation. Here he manifested himself to his people and, it is important to stress, to their enemies.

The limitations of space on the *kapporeth* or coverpiece of the Ark define in part the sculpture. Unlike the winged lions and bulls, griffins and other animals fashioned as cherubim in Assyria and elsewhere, the Ark's cherubim were probably two-footed with unisexual human features [25]. A later Assyrian assemblage (Figure 11) is similar. So are two figures from Egypt, showing two winged goddesses hovering protectively over idols of Osiris, in one case, and Thoth in the other [26]. The cherubim could not be seated or squatting, because they were facing Yahweh, but would stand with faces elevated, says the legend [27]. Figure 12 may convey some notion of their appearance, in accord with legend and with the Bible. It may be seen that their wings would be spread wide as a covering of the box so that, in effect, two platform levels would be created, one on the ample but separated pair of wings and again on the lid of the box.

The Bible affords images of Yahweh enthroned on the wings, speaking of "the ark of the covenant of the Lord of hosts, who is enthroned on the cherubim."[28] He at the same time is "the Lord, that dwelleth between the cherubim, whose name is called on it." And another verse speaks of "the ark of God, whereupon is called the Name, even the name of the Lord of hosts who sits enthroned on the cherubim."[29]

Then Yahweh is appealed to, with the words: "Thou

The Ark in Action

that dwelleth between the cherubim, shine forth." Moreover, Yahweh says, I will speak with you from above the Kapporeth, from between the two cherubim that are upon the ark of the testimony of all that I will give you in commandment for the children of Israel."[30]

If Yahweh sits upon the wings as a throne, then the lid below is his footstool. Thus, "Let us go to His dwelling; let us prostrate ourselves at His footstool."[31] Hence, Yahweh when present in name, voice, or image might be above the wings, between the wing separations, and between the wings and the footstool. The variant expressions imply what Priestley said earlier of the electrical effects he had achieved by similar devices, that they make different and beautiful figures as the charges move and sparkle. When conditions were propitious, a great leaflike sheet of fire might define itself over the sculptured golden group as a whole. It would be three-dimensional, like a hologram. (See Figure 12.)

Buber, apparently dissatisfied with biblical description, writes that "The Royal covenant is followed by the building of a throne," generally speaking. But "we have no reliable reports as to the original appearance of the Ark... We do not know why the description 'Throne' for the Ark was avoided. "[32] What bothers Buber is that it is not a throne, not a shrine, although it is like the litters carrying the throne of god that the Bedouin tribes possessed. It is yet a "genuine migrating sanctuary." It comes from the time of Moses, as various archaeological findings have proven.

Figure 11. Cherubim of Nimrud. In this piece of open work of ivory, a pair of winged female figures wearing the Egyptian double crown protect with their outstretched wings the aegis of Bastet on the flowering "Lily" tree between them. Since Nimrud (or Kalah) became the Assyrian capital city only after 880 BC the plaque must be post- Mosaic. The resemblance to the floral pattern to flames and even the Lion of Judah may indicate the invisible electrical flames. A very old principle of opposing and yet cooperative forces seems to be incorporated in the twin figures so often encountered around the world - from Castor and Pollux to Yin and Yang (Martin, pp 293ff: Ziegler, pp 113ff). It appears more likely than not that the two identical cherubim of the Ark are mosaic version of this universal twinship. (source: redrawn from Kenyon p58)

The Ark in Action

The learned Buber, a hero and good man in the terrible Nazi period, is at his wits' end when he approaches the obvious. He laboriously formulates the question: "Was there a moment in the life of Moses which drove him overpoweringly to unite and mould the elements familiar to him from extended observation and knowledge of tradition, and to make some new formation out of them?"[33]

"He said, to be sure, did that man, that God goes before them and that He makes His presence known by one or another sign; but the sole firm and unshakable fact was, in the last resort, that the God could not be seen; and all said and done you cannot actually follow something which you cannot see."[34]

Buber is now rationalizing why the Israelites should have preferred a Golden Calf to an empty litter. In the face of the most explicit references, *which he himself employs,* that the Ark was occupied, or would be, when Moses made it, he abandons his inquiry into its design.

Gressmann is also baffled by the apparent emptiness of the seat of Yahweh. He insists [35] that there must have been a little figure of Yahweh, or an animal, or at least a meteoritic stone that rested or could be placed beneath the wings of the cherubim. The perplexity is understandable but wrong-headed. What is to be found elsewhere, sometimes, and later, is not definitive of the Ark of Moses. And how, when the Bible says that Yahweh sits upon the cherubim, is a figure beneath the cherubim to be accounted for? The answer must be that Yaweh, the electrical god, was both present and invisible.

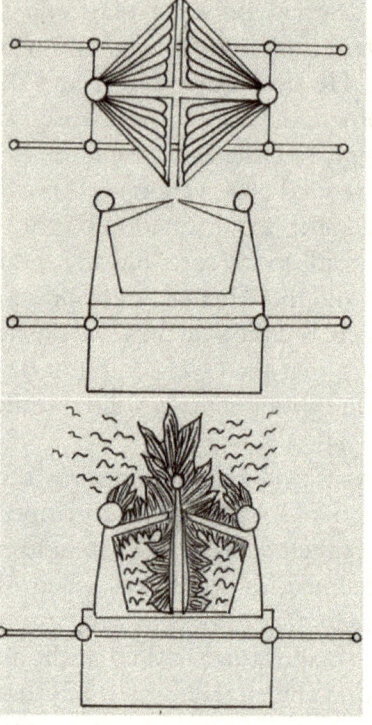

Figure 12. The Ark's Structure and Function.
Top: View from top Middle: View from side Bottom: "Thou that dwellest between the Cherubim shine forth." (Psalm 80:1) The Ark with Yahweh displayed. Legend claims the wing spread of the Cherubim was eleven spans(of the hand) plus a span for the head, and that the Cherubim were 10 spans tall from head to ground(III G 158-9)

The Ark in Action

Certainly the Bible does not go heavily into describing the functions of the Ark but it has many brief direct and explicit references to its electrical operations, and how and when its effects would come about. Nothing about the human mind is incredible, but it is almost incredible that for three thousand years the Ark has not been understood, whether by the friends or foes of Yahwism, or by theologians or scientists. Or, lacking absolute proof, why has this theory not been before the world as one of the most plausible explanations of Moses, of Yahweh, and of the Ark?

Perhaps the savants of ancient times preferred description to analysis, statics to dynamics, Aristotelianism (Maimonidism) to pragmatism. With all of their zeal for mummification, the Egyptians have left us no recipes for the technique. Perhaps the electrical powers were only vaguely known to those who may have inserted most of the description much later - that is, after it had ceased its active functions and become a "period-piece." Perhaps its externalia were more gaudy than its unknown, even sacred, interior dynamics - rather like, as they say, the automobile today that is sold on its appearance to people who never lift the hood of the motor.

Another answer, too facile, is that a few critical points of design were deliberately omitted from the Bible for the sake of secrecy. For instance, if the connections of the cherubim were machined to serve as opposing poles, and were minutely described, the secret would practically surely be revealed. Perhaps all of these reasons enter into the mystification, and to them we should add the strong, even unconsciously strong, wish to reject any mechanical explanation of the sacred. And it was precisely after the Ark ceased to be operative that the desire to explain its former workings would be suppressed.

The most perplexing problem of the Ark as an electrical worship, control, and weapons system does, in fact, involve the cherubim. Two descriptions of the Ark are provided [36]. In both, the cherubim are facing each other from the two ends of the Seat. But we note: "Of one piece with the [gold] mercy seat shall you make the cherubim on its two ends."[37] This would imply, if accurate, that the cherubim would be of the same charge and that the ark would not function electrically by a discharge between them. Against this seeming design defect are the dozen and more descriptions of the Ark in action.

Ziegler does not address this problem and says that one cherub would be grounded, the other affixed to the inner gold shell of the Ark. In short, only one cherubim was of a piece with the lid or seat. He thinks that the intricate mechanisms of the ark are kept secret. However he does assign a function to Aaron's rod which he believes would have been the aerial conductor.

This, it seems to me, is close to the solution. The Ark is a variable machine and the control of its power must be capable of modification. This is impossible with the fixed cherubim alone. They can only store charge, the same charge. But what can be varied is a rod, preferably and inevitably a sacred rod, Aaron's rod or Moses' rod. The rod would connect with the inner gold lining of the box while the cherubim connected with the outer, grounded lining. The rod would be adjustable in relation to the cherubim, in one or more of four directions, such that weak or powerful discharges, under unfavorable or favorable charging

The Ark in Action

conditions, could be made with the cherubim. Sockets and ratchets of simple design, and a telescoping rod, could manage all of the required motions.

Remarkable phenomena could be induced. Perhaps the most inspiring would be the luminous arcs of fire that would be emitted between the two cherubim and the pole, bringing into a high intensity image the presence of Yahweh at the center of the Mercy Seat.

The arc or spark will jump the gap as often and as rapidly as the voltage can build up. Writes Priestley: "If the knobs of two wires, one communicating with the inside, and the other with the outside of the phial, be brought within four or five inches of one another, the electrical spider... will dart from the one to the other in a very surprising manner, till the phial be discharged."[38] It can become almost a column of fire to the naked eye.

In the presence of prolonged discharges, an ionized cloud of dust will gather around, concealing the discharge in the daytime at least and making it less visible at night. There are ways of placing an arc apparatus more advantageously to produce electrical phenomena, ways of guarding it, of measuring its potency, of enlarging or diminishing its activity and noises, of enhancing the surrounding cloud, of using water and dirt and various stones for visual effects, and treating, blessing or magnetizing metals and metal alloys. One might also produce some mental phenomena by feeding and extracting ionized air to and from the device. We are dealing with a complicated technical apparatus and set of operations and effects.

Nor was any other religious device so activatable. The ark made the pyramid obsolete. In an age that saw no reason to distinguish between inanimate and animate natural forces, the liveliness of electricity would put it definitely in the sphere of the animate and, if not in a god, then in a voice of the immediate presence of a god. As Ziegler writes, the word electricity comes from the Greek electron, which may come from El, meaning "god" (as in Elohim) and ech meaning "to have," that is, "what gods have." And ark is surely related to the arc that it creates, and to the form of arch that an arc takes, and probably to early ages (archeons and archaic) and forms of rule (monarchy, oligarchy). The archaic electrical age may have sponsored these words [39].

DANGERS OF ELECTROCUTION

The Ark was a highly dangerous machine. Ordinary Bible reading and anthropological training about primitive customs condition one to pass over indifferently its taboos. The people, officers, dissenters, priests and in fact everyone except Moses are warned to avoid the Ark, or to approach it carefully on pain of death. The Holy of Holies is well away from strange hands when Israel is in camp. (See Figure 13.)

The invisibility of electric charges is, of course, a major concern. The danger is unseen. People must have faith and discipline to observe safety precautions respecting electricity. Not until the studies of S. Jellinek in Austria during the 1920's did it become quite clear "that death from electric shock could be instantaneous and without any visible signs of injury."[40]

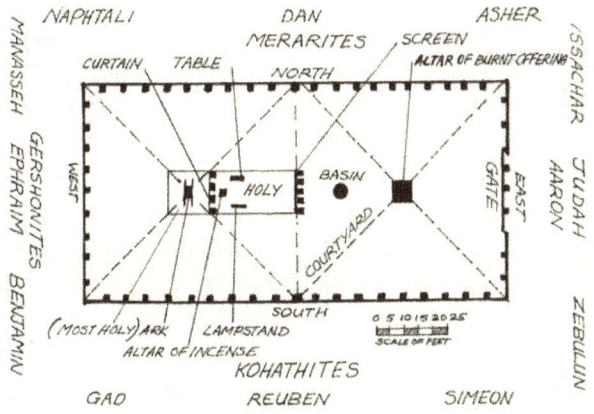

Figure 13. Ground plan and Design of the Tabernacle. (Source: redrawn from the *New World Translation* of the Bible, after a reconstruction by Conrad Schick)

Some body areas are more sensitive than others: the back of the hand, the neck, the shoulders, the temples. Some persons - perhaps Moses - are less sensitive to electric injury than others. Perspiration (and all water) heightens conductivity; the minute burns discoverable sometimes in different places on the body of a person who has suffered electrocution may signify resistances in such conductive spots. Washing therefore helps to avoid or pass a shock, as priests of various cultures still do, even if symbolically, when approaching an altar. Burns can be severe, but occur at voltages of 200 or more; meanwhile, lower voltages can cause death with little or no visible markings on the corpse. Voltages as low as 10 have been known to kill, according to the Russian expert, Manoilov. The heart or brain electrical systems need only be interrupted for life to quickly cease, often with the disruption of breathing control, hence asphyxiation.

Yet high voltages are used in penal death by the electric chair, 1200 to 2000 volts, and excruciating minutes of time can be required to kill. This may be owing to a strange fact, that a person who is anticipating an electrical current or sparks can, especially if not too fearful, absorb or pass a larger voltage without death or with less serious an injury than otherwise [41]. Four-legged animals are more sensitive to death by ground charges or lightning than two-legged people or birds.

The electrical potency of the Ark or a similar mechanism varies with the differences in charge between air and ground. If the air is losing charge rapidly, the ground will concentrate a charge rapidly and on a point contact discharge will cause a heavy explosion, a brilliant arc, and a deadly

The Ark in Action

experience for anyone or even a group who short-circuit the contact. If St. Elmo's fire is arising naturally from an elevated point, an arc machine nearby would carry a heavy static charge, capable of jumping more forcibly.

Amidst general rejoicing at the fine manner in which Yahweh was coming down upon their offerings at the new shrine, Nadab and Abihu, sons of Aaron, priests themselves, "each took his censer, and put fire in it, and laid incense on it, and offered unholy fire before the Lord, such as he had not commanded. And fire came forth from the presence of the Lord and devoured them, and they died before the Lord."[42]

According to a legend: "From the Holy of Holies issued two flames of fire, as thin as threads, then parted into four, and two each pierced the nostrils of Nadab and Abihu, whose souls were burnt, although no external injury was visible."[43] Modern medicine knows that the nostrils are peculiarly susceptible to electric shock. It is generally known that electroshock can kill and injure without signs of burning. The Bible implies that the two men were drunk and hence unholy before Yahweh, whence we may see in the accident the kind of negligence that does occasionally cause fatal accidents among skilled electricians.

Rabbi J.H. Hertz, in one of his enthusiastic interpretations, blames the sons of Aaron for their "intoxication, unholy ambition, arbitrary tampering with the service, and introducing 'strange fire' into the Sanctuary."[44] Hertz believes (p.445) that they were struck by lightning, since their garments were not destroyed. Further he defines "strange fire" as "unconsecrated fire, not from the Divinely kindled flames on the Altar." It is a more meaningful translation of the words "unholy fire," which can mean anything or nothing. "Strange" or "alien" means that it is not the fire that is appropriate to the fire of the Holy of Holies; it is fossil, not electric, fire [45].

Moses explained then to Aaron what the Lord was doing: "I will show myself holy among those who are near me, and before all the people I will be glorified," says the Bible, "and Aaron held his peace." As they were carrying off the corpses, Moses, in his genial manner, tells Aaron and the remaining sons: "Do not let the hair of your heads hang loose, and do not rend your clothes, lest you die..." He says that it is up to the general congregation to mourn for them. Further, he says, apparently not sure of their self-control: "And do not go out from the door of the tent of meeting, lest you die." For there was a crowd of spectators outside [46]. Poor Aaron had to take much scolding with his bereavement and hear many safety lessons:

> The Lord spoke to Moses, after the death of the two sons of Aaron, when they drew near before the Lord and died; and the Lord said to Moses: 'Tell Aaron your brother not to come at all times into the holy place, within the veil, before the mercy seat which is upon the ark, lest he die; for I will appear in the cloud upon the mercy seat [47].

One must also bow low before Yahweh, if only to avoid a shock. But this practice presumes that a divine fire is hovering above [48]. In a history of electrical science, we read the following:

> A.D. 1753, Prof. George William Richmann (1711-1753), native of Sweden and member of the Imperial Academy of St. Petersburg, who had already constructed an apparatus for

The Ark in Action

obtaining atmospherical electricity according to Franklin's plans, was attending a meeting of the Russian Academy of Science, on the 6th of August, 1753, when his ear caught the sound of a very heavy thunder clap. He hastened away in company with his engraver, M. Sokolow, and upon their arrival home they found the plummet of the electrometer elevated four degrees from the perpendicular. Richmann stooped toward the latter to ascertain the force of the electricity, and "as he stood in that posture, a great white and bluish fire appeared between the rod of the electrometer and his head. At the same time a sort of steam or vapour arose, which entirely benumbed the engraver and made him sink on the ground." Sokolow recovered, but Richmann had met with instant death [49].

The sad story of Uzzah who was electrocuted for trying to steady the ark which was on its way to Mount Zion in a cart will be told shortly. He was not a Levite. But the Levites had their problems too.

The most distinguished among the Levites were the sons of Kohath, whose charge during the march through the desert was the Holy of Holies, and among the vessels particularly the Holy Ark. This latter was a dangerous trust, for out of the staves attached to it would issue sparks that consumed Israel's enemies, but now and then this fire wrought havoc among the bearers of the Ark. It therefore became a customary thing, when the camp was about to be moved, for Kohath's sons to hasten into the sanctuary and seek to pack up the different portions of it, each one planning cautiously to shift the carrying of the Ark upon another. But this even more kindled God's anger against them, and He slew many of the Kohathites because they ministered to the Ark with an unwilling heart. To avert the danger that threatened them, God ordered Aaron and his sons to enter first into the sanctuary, and 'to appoint to the Kohathites, every one, his service and his burden, that they might not go in to see when the holy things are covered, lest they die.' This was done because previous to this command the sons of Kohath had been accustomed to feast their eyes on the sight of the Ark, which brought them instantaneous death. But, according to this order, Aaron and his sons first took apart the different portions of the sanctuary, covered the Ark, and not till then called the sons of Kohath to bear the burden [50].

This legend is technically and behaviorally so clear that little interpretation need be supplied by this author. As a modern example, one needs only picture the scene of deadly sputtering which occurs when some object like a pole falls against a gang of live wires and machines.

The Ark makes a noise, a hissing, crackling, moaning complex that can rise to near-deafening decibels. If the air-ground differential remains large, the arc and the noise can continue for minutes, hours or days. Various observers have written that electrostatic discharges on mountain-tops and elsewhere make a noise like vast swarms of bees. Yahweh tells the Israelites: "I will send hornets before you, which shall drive out Hivite, Canaanite, and Hittite before you."[51]

THE ARK AT WORK

An obvious first function of the Ark is to be the main vehicle of a procession. All too many students have ceased their inquiries after making this observation[52]. They are reinforced in their belief by witnessing religions where litters carrying sacred images are borne - whether on camels of bedouin tribes supposedly like the primitive Jews, or upon the shoulders of devout males in Catholic feasts of the

The Ark in Action

Virgin, or even in the form of the wagon of juggernaut of India. Yet practically the only reference to the Ark in procession is hidden in Psalm 24:7-10:

> Raise your head, O you gates,
> And raise yourselves up, O you long-lasting entrances,
> That the glorious King may come in!
> Who, then, is this glorious King?
> Jehovah strong and mighty, Jehovah mighty in battle.
> Raise your heads, O you gates;
> Yes, raise [them] up, O you long-lasting entrances,
> That the glorious King may come in!
> Who, then, is he, this glorious King?
> Jehovah of armies - he is the glorious King. Se'lah.

The staid editors of the *Oxford Bible,* Revised Standard Version, comment blandly that the Ark "served to guide Israel in wandering (*Num.* 10:33), to lead in war (*Num.* 10:35-6), and to be a medium for oracles (1 *Sam.* ch. 3.)."[53] From this, one might imagine the Ark to be a kind of brave flag carried at the head of a troop; the flag is also used when swearing to agreements and making promises for the future. The Jews, however, had plenty of banners inscribed with tribal legends and Israelite mottoes.

The Ark was no mere banner or image. The Ark would always give psychological consolation, of course. It would indicate by its activity and sounds the comforting presence of Yahweh. In what seemed to be interminable periods of despair and starvation, it lived for its people. Thus:

> And they departed from the mount of the Lord three days journey: and the Ark of the Covenant of the Lord went before them in the three days journey, to search out a resting place for

them [54].

I would stress here the separation of the Ark from its people; it went ahead with its special guard of Levites to spy out a camping ground. There is no reason for this tactic unless the Ark was required to perform a real special function.

> Although it was the clouds that gave the signal for taking down and pitching tents, still they always awaited the word of Moses. Before starting the pillar of cloud would contract and stand still before Moses, waiting for him to say: 'Rise up, Lord, and let Thine enemies be scattered; and let them that hate Thee flee before Thee,' whereupon the pillar of cloud would be set in motion. It was the same when they pitched camp [55].

Ziegler tells us: "The mysterious Ark seems endowed with intelligence. With this viewpoint we see that the ark was an instrument carried by men and was capable of measuring to some extent the electrical activity of the atmosphere. In a safe place, the ark or electrical capacitor would charge up little, if at all, and no electrical discharge would occur. If placed in a dangerous region, the ark would build up a charge quickly and give a strong discharge."[56]

The rule was to rest when the ark was active. A pillar of smoke by day (or smoke and fire by night) indicated that the Lord was present and the people must remain encamped. When the ark was less active and the smoke vanished, the hosts of Israel moved on, carrying the ark in their front ranks.

"And it came to pass, when the ark set forward, that Moses said, Rise up Lord and let thine enemies be scattered; and let them that hate thee flee before thee. And when it rested, he said, Return, o Lord, unto the many thousands of Israel."[57]

No Jew could or, later, was allowed to speak the real name of Yahweh. Yahweh means "I be," according to Moses. Clear enough: He is the basic principle of life and existence. He cannot be known in his full being. I doubt those Jews and gentiles who say the "word" Yahweh was the name of God and not to be spoken. More likely, Yahweh spoke his own name from the Ark, which could not and should not be mimicked.

THE ELECTRIC ORACLE

That the ark had oracular powers can be explained. The ark would charge even at low potentials. No electricity would be manifest here. But the ultimate discharge would give some measure of how rapidly a charge had been accumulating. "This same idea is used to measure the electric potentials of the atmosphere by modern scientists," comments Ziegler[58]. The fatal accident to Professor Richmann, recounted above, occurred when he stooped to examine an atmospheric electrometer. The Ark in the hands of Moses and the Levites was a fire-measuring instrument. Dangerous ground could be avoided, not only high places, such as all could soon learn of, but lower places where underground water could result in quick accumulation and discharge or where unseen rock formations fostered lightning exchanges with the atmosphere through the unhappy animate contacts moving in-between ground and air.

But, too, insofar as the voice of Yahweh was heard coming from the "mercy seat" or divine vehicle emplaced between the two sparking cherubim, and there are actual variations in the sounds of rapidity, rhythm, pitch and tone[59], oracular instructions could be systematized and related to reality with a degree of reason much superior, let us say, to the kinds of relationship among the stars that astrologers used then and now to prophesy and advise.

The Jews did not ignore the predictive science of astrology: far from it; a Roman author called them "star-obsessed." But their astrology was purged from the Bible over time for being close to a violation of the commandment against worshipping other gods before Yahweh. And besides, these earliest times were not adapted to astrology, since the skies of the Exodus period were largely obscured. During the Egyptian crisis, the crisis of the plagues, and during the many years in the wilderness thereafter, careful astrology would have been of little help, except for watching the cometary behavior of Venus-Baal.

Hence, we have another practical reason for the preoccupation with electricity. It was temporarily the only major method of discussing the will of God and the movements of the cosmos in a systematic way. So it was not only that electrical phenomena were abundant, but also that the basis for another oracular technology was inaccessible. Without the Ark, how could Yahweh communicate to His people? "There I will meet with thee and I will commune with thee above the mercy seat from between the two cherubim which are upon the ark of the testimony." Not only

The Ark in Action 145

was the ark voluble, speaking for Yahweh in tongues, but also visible: in Psalm 80:1 the direct statement is made: "Thou that dwellest between the Cherubim, shine forth."

Ancient Greek theurgy sought sometimes to induce the presence of a god in an inanimate receptacle, and sometimes in a human form. Luminous apparitions were favored, as in the Chaldean Oracles, which promised that by pronouncing certain spells the operator should see 'fire shaped like a boy,' or 'an unshaped... fire with a voice proceeding from it."[60] An oracle of Porphyry speaks of "the pure fire being compressed into sacred forms..." Elsewhere, "the 'strong immortal light' replaces the mortal light of the lamp... the watcher sees the light of the lamp become 'vault-shaped,' then finds it replaced by a 'very great light within a void,' and beholds the god."[61] Such practices, a thousand years after Moses, suffered from a paucity of god's fire; they seem to reach back in time for more auspicious electrical conditions.

THE BATTLE OF JERICHO

At the time of Aaron's death, legend has it, the skies cleared and the sun and moon came forth. This was not long before Moses' death and towards the end of the wanderings. The lower atmosphere would carry less charge and the Ark could not be so continuously loaded.

Recalling, however, the simple rule of potential difference, we would be able to judge the new conditions if we knew whether the earth was still releasing charge regionally as the lithosphere sought electrical equilibrium.

Indications of disequilibrium could be obtained if we knew whether volcanism was still raging in many places, if earthquakes were frequent, if St. Elmo's fire were common on higher places, and if the state of all such activities were changing not only in the Palestinian area but in the broader areas with which Palestine was connected, such as the great Syro-African-Mediterranean rifts, the Danubian region, the Upper Nile, the Anatolian mountains, and so on. Further, we would wish to know the conditions of the upper atmosphere, whether the dust on high had dissipated, whether large meteoroids were circling and occasionally falling, whether the great comet were returning on an earth-approaching orbit from time to time.

If Velikovsky is correct in ascribing the 52-year jubilee cycle of the Jews and the 52-year ceremony of atonement of the Mexicans to the regular return of the great comet, we would expect a renewal of electrical activity regularly, and a heavy residual effect during the interval between visitations. The jubilee was a time for the cancellation of obligations such as land tenure and slavery [62], and for repentance among the Mayans and the Aztecs; there human sacrifices were made, fearful convocations were held, and then great bonfires celebrated the passage of the 52nd anniversary without a new catastrophe [63]. I am accepting the attack upon Jericho as an event close to the 52-year cycle and as probably affected in its outcome by the cosmic event.

Strong traditions attest to forty years of wandering in the wilderness; perhaps another dozen years found the Israelites before Jericho and then before Gibeon; the conquest of Canaan is said to have occupied 14 years and

The Ark in Action

Joshua's leadership in all 28 years, so the time schedule seems appropriate. I am sceptical of the old ages attained by both Moses and Joshua, and think that they may have been measured on a shorter-year sacred calendar from a prior epoch. Studies of earlier and later human remains indicate a younger average adult age of death than in modern times.

The Ark was used many times in battle. Going to war without it was foolhardy. One time Moses said to a gang who wanted to raid the enemy: "Go not up, for Yahweh is not among you."[64] They disregarded his words and were thrashed by a combined Amalekite and Canaanite force. Moses was not an infallible oracle, but he had more foresight than others, partly because Yahweh's vehicle was providing him with intelligence on fighting conditions.

And Yahweh, too, was worth a regiment. When the Ark behaved in an excited fashion, it foretold heavier discharges. The enemy, observing the Jews, could see their renowned Yahweh. When the same phenomena began to manifest themselves inside their fortress, they would imagine that "Israel - the Fighting God" - was in their very midst. (People unacquainted with the immediate circumstances of battles are inclined to judge their outcomes in terms of gross figures of men and equipment committed. The spearhead of the vast armada of Americans that descended on "D-Day" upon Normandy in 1944 was blunted for many hours by a single German artillery piece, well-emplaced and manned by a stubborn, well-trained crew.)

"In any terrain Israel had the advantage with the Ark of the Covenant," argues Ziegler. "They were warned earlier of the electricity by it and could seek out a better shelter."[65] Cities that were built up for protection found themselves vulnerable to Israel. In some cases, with advance knowledge of a cosmic electrical storm, the Jews could surround the town and capture the population as it came fleeing down the hill.

The conquest of Canaan by Moses' successor, Joshua, was swift and decisive. Many small kingdoms were destroyed, many towns burned, many people slaughtered, many idols smashed.

The ark worked well. Its use in the battle of Jericho is exemplary. When, some 52 years after Exodus, Joshua's army approached Jericho, his spies reported the city already in a state of fright. They were huddled behind the massive stone revetment of their hilltop town [66].

Very likely the heavens were disturbed, and a return of the great comet was expected by the Jews (and most likely, the Canaanites as well). Joshua could have timed his invasion in anticipation of it. The Jews were already, as Moses and the Levites would have them, a "People of the Book," obsessed in their tactics and memory. When the earth shook and the river's northern sources were blocked [67], the Jordan River was regarded and treated as another Sea of Reeds. The whole people marched across the river-bed saluting the Ark there upheld to view.

The tactics for Ark employment called sometimes for electrical disengagement. Thus the people were kept at 2000 cubits from it during the approach to Jericho but then ordered to pass close by it on the stopped-up river bed of the Jordan. Disengagement would be accomplished by removing the center pole affixed to the Lord's seat between the cherubim and elevating the cherubim. A crossing of the dry river bed of the Jordan might be accomplished at a speed of

The Ark in Action

three miles an hour. We can allow therefore that a two-mile column of people could walk across in an hour. Perhaps there were 40,000 in all that day. The whole Jewish nation with its impedimenta and herds could cross readily in four hours, if they didn't stop to stare at the Ark. Even in historical times, the Jordan has been blocked by seismic landslides for that long and longer.

Figure 14 gives us the story in the collapsed time perspective of a medieval mosaic. Yahweh commanded a daily march around the beleaguered citadel for six days, and seven rounds of the city on the seventh day. Armed men went first, then seven priests blowing rams' horns, then the Ark whose behavior by now must have been transfixing the garrison, and finally a rear guard. On the seventh day's seventh round of the hill, the trumpeters blew their horns, and the expectant people of Israel, hitherto silent by command (probably to let the voice of Yahweh give the city "the screaming meamies") huzzahed as they had been told to do. The walls collapsed in a great blast. The slaughter began. The terrified survivors of the blast tried to flee and the Jewish shock troops poured through the breaches. Their comrades stationed below walked up the hill, cutting down the people attempting to escape. Only the whore, Rahab, and her family were permitted to survive, for she had earlier helped the Jewish spies to hide [68].

Jericho is on a western rise of the Jordan Valley, seat of the catastrophe of the Cities of the Plain, which forms part of the northern line of the great African Rift. Its earthquakes have been frequent, and electrical phenomena are associated with seismism. Joshua was maneuvering in accord with the ionization and charge-up of the ground and air. He expected electrical display and fires, and a nervous enemy. He could hardly have expected the huge walls to be overturned, although the connection among electricity, fire, and seismism must already have been known to him.

Archaeologists have discovered that the great Middle Bronze Age walls of Jericho were in fact overturned by a great earth shock. John J. Bimson presents archaeological confirmation of the events [69].

> MBA [Middle Bronze Age] Jericho was destroyed by Joshua, around 1400 BC. Then followed a long gap in occupation [Joshua cursed whoever would try to rebuild the city]. In the time of David a settlement of some kind was established on the site, though this was very small and no traces of it have been found on the mound, pottery and scarab from Tomb 5 being the only indications of its existence. A proper town... was rebuilt in the Amarna period, ninth century BC...

The blast must have included cosmic electricity as well as seismism, because one excavator, John Garstang, found plenty of evidence of intense fires; storerooms were burned; stone houses were reduced to calcinated debris and white ash was overlain with thick layers of charcoal and burnt debris[70]. (I am reminded here of the Trojan case, recited in the preceding chapter.) Granted that the Jews had made the eradication of Jericho a holy war; there is still a limit to the amount of ash that can accumulate from hand-burned stone houses with a few wooden utensils and some wooden beams. An atmospheric discharge probably occurred, accompanied by numerous thermoelectric pyres,

Figure 14. The destruction of Jericho.(Source: Mosaic in Church of Santa Maria Maggiore, Rome, about 432-440) MBA [Middle Bronze Age] Jericho was destroyed by Joshua, around 1400 B.C. Then followed a long gap in occupation [Joshua cursed whoever should try to rebuild the city.] In the time of David a settlement of some kind was established on the site, though this was very small and no traces of it have been found on the mound, pottery and scarab from Tomb 5 being the only indication of its existence. A proper town ... was rebuilt in the Amarna period, ninth century B.C...

concurrent with the earthquake.

That is not all: Jericho, like the typical Middle Bronze Age ruin, presents several mysteries. Kenyon reports a plague in Jericho then[71]. Bimson links this plague with the death of 24,000 in Israelite territory shortly before the crossing of the Jordan[72]. The Bible says this was a plague in punishment for the Beth Peor popular heresy[73]. The Beth Peor plague or scourge may have been a massacre or civil war; we discuss it at the end of Chapter 5. The Jericho plague or scourge, evidenced by tombs crowded with bodies, may not have been a disease either.

Zeuner found an extraordinary preservation of organic material in the tombs of the multiple burials[74]. He ascribes the phenomenon to natural gas, a combination of methane and carbon dioxide, which may have entered the tombs shortly after burial. The gas, he believes, may have originated from fissuring of the ground during an earthquake.

The Bible reports that the last fall of manna occurred just before the Jews entered the Holy Land, that is, at this moment of time. Formaldehyde vapor, also a preservative, falls with manna and is poisonous, apart from whatever chemicals may be falling with it. The cause of death, then, and the cause of the plague, may have been external and atmospheric; the bodies were preserved before burial. A cometary origin of the gases, and even of viral material, cannot be ruled out.

THE ARK'S END

Apparently the Ark was used less and less as a mobile

The Ark in Action

weapon. Electrical conditions were changing so that it became more difficult to operate along the full range of its original functions. "The clouds of glory" vanished for the first time with the death of Aaron. People born in the desert saw the sun and moon. They had to be warned against worshipping the heavenly host [75].

Also the skills of the personnel assigned to it after Joshua may not have been adequate; perhaps they knew the procedures well enough but could not adapt them to new conditions or invent new procedures. I would suppose, too, that as the division of labor proceeded after Moses, the priests might be content with managing a tractable ornamental ark, and the military men would like to get rid of "civilian" participation in matters of the sword [76]. The very sacred nature of the Ark and the taboos surrounding it would also obstruct any bright young scientist from tampering with its structure.

We hear on one occasion that the ark was duplicated by a young man named Micah in his home, a surprising occurrence, reminiscent of claims that the nuclear bomb can be home-made. The lad's mother was quite proud of him; she had consecrated her silver for the purpose.[77] He made a graven image, a molten image, an ephod, a teraphim and hired a priest. Nothing untoward occurred save that the tribe of Dan descended upon the household and carried away the ark and the priest.

Later we learn that the true Ark was kept at Shiloh, whence it was occasionally employed. Once the Philistines captured the Ark in battle, killing its attendants. They sent it from one city to another, but it acted so disastrously at each place in turn - perhaps as they sought to make it work - that the Philistines finally made a substantial offering of gold objects and a sacrifice of beasts to it and conveyed it back to the Israelites. The propitiatory golden mice of the offering are connected with Apollo Smintheus of Crete and Palestine, sminthos meaning "mouse."[78]

In several passages, Ziegler reaches for connections between the mouse and electricity [79]. "Sminthos" was "mouse" in Greek and "mus" in Latin. "Mys" is another word for "mouse" in Greek, and "Mystery" (as in Eleusian Mysteries) is a cognate term and appears variously in connection with electrified rites. Apollo is also called "Mysagetes," which relates him to mouse and to his role as protector of the Muses.

Much later, and the historian Herodotus relates the story told him, the army of Sennacherib, besieging Jerusalem, was set upon by an army of mice in the night; they gnawed the bowstrings of the archers and caused the army's total discomfiture. The Bible has it, and the date must be around 687 B.C., that a blast from heaven destroyed the Assyrian army. I discuss elsewhere this incident and ascribe the blast to an electro-gas explosion. Whether or not the cloud descended in the form of a mouse, a horde of mice would be drawn from the ground by the electricity. At all events, the Egyptians memorialized them by erecting a statue of a mouse (for they, too, opposed the Assyrians), at a city called, significantly, Letopolis, meaning "City of the Thunderbolt." At least two Greek towns were named Leptopolis ("Mouseville").

Josephus said that "Moses" should be written "Mouses."[80] This seems ridiculous; but let us ponder the matter. The usual Hebrew for Moses is "Mosche." The

The Ark in Action

French version is "Moïse" but was once "Moyse." Depending upon the vowels that go between the consonants "M" and "s" we can be dealing with Moses, a mouse, a god, a ritual, a statue, or a musical muse, all of these somehow in an electrical context. The root flourishes, too, in several cultures, and attaches to events stretching at least from 1450 B.C. to the present era.

The mouse involved is sacred, as at Letopolis and other mouse-named places, and has some association with a god, and in the present case sacrally with the Philistines and the Jews. In Chapter VI we shall trace and assign the name "Moses" to the Egyptian word for "child." Could it also be the Egyptian word for "a little being"? For a "mouse"? Probably not; we are fairly certain of our etymology.

However, this is not to say that a mouse in the age after Moses might not have acquired from Moses the root of his name, especially since electricity seems to have been connected over some centuries with both Moses and Mice. Words often derive from the names of famous practitioners of what they refer to. An electric figure rather like a mouse could clump at the top of a rod like that of Moses or Mercury (brother of Apollo); it can surmount a turret, crouch upon a church steeple, or move restlessly about the top of a promontory. Numerous modern reports have ball-lightning "'scurrying like a mouse" around a house. A connection between Moses and the mice of the Philistines may, therefore, not be entirely fanciful.

The Philistines also placed in the Ark as a propitiatory offering several modelled gold hemorrhoids. This would appear to be a singularly unaesthetic gift; it has quite baffled and embarrassed biblical students. Finally, now, we have clues. Thoth, we know, was the god of healing and is associated with Hebrew-Egyptian mosaic religions, even in the Bronze Serpent Rod (or caduceus) of Moses. Serious electrical shocks can cause nose-bleeding and anal bleeding. So can radiation. The membranes of both organs are electrically hyper-sensitive. Electrical and magnetic shifts promote plagues and changed incidences of heart disease and other troubles[81]. Not to be dismissed is the possibility that, during the Philistine affair, electrical conditions were disturbed. A disturbed electrical situation and probably radioactive fall-out, or some heavily ionized fallout would provoke simultaneously epidemics of several illnesses, hemorrhoidal and general bleeding, enhanced and uncontrolled Ark activity, and thence the religious, unitary "solution" of the biblical scenario.

But, still, a model of hemorrhoids or piles seems unlikely and inexplicable. Then a solution appears, from deep in the etymology of the word "hemorrhoids." We find "haemorrhoid" also "haemorrhe," from the Greek meaning "blood-discharging." It is "a serpent whose bite was fabled to cause unstaunchable bleeding."[82] The Bible refers to these "serpents" and the plague of bleeding that they caused. These serpents (could they be leeches?) are the same as caused the plague which led to the fabrication of Moses' homeopathic Serpent Rod of Brass, sparks and jets of hissing fire breaking out in connection with radiation and electrical storms. The specific disease of hemorrhoids was probably a conspicuous part of the general bleeding epidemic and was attached to the word after general bleeding epidemics were long forgotten.

The totem and taboo of the Ark would deter other enemies (or allies) who might have been tempted to acquire or imitate the Ark. It is noteworthy that the Bethshemites, in whose territory the Ark was abandoned by the Philistines, and who were connected with the Israelite, suffered the plague, too, and pleaded with the Israelites to come down from the hills and take the Ark away. It had the tabooed reputation of being the Jews' god. Those would properly be accepting Yahweh who accepted the Ark. Other peoples lacked, too, the history - the mixture of catastrophe and science in the Egyptian context - that the Ark grew out of.

Then again it was difficult to construct and operate. Moses was a genius at synthesizing elements and a terrible bully at seeing that the machine was handled properly. Also, the others were probably too sky-oriented, astrological, and the idea of Baal, say, marching along with them humming his own name, would appear weird. Then there was the ever-present problem of technological change: what would their feather-bedding priests do without their sacred time-honored tasks to perform? (only the machine-gun finally broke the centuries-old habit of European armies to attack in fine straight rows.) In all of this, I am not arguing that the ark machine was solely Israel's. The same may have been invented elsewhere, even in Egypt, but would not be adaptable to the central complex of functions - military, theological, political, and managerial - which it performed among the Israelites.

When David was King he wished to bring the Ark to Zion where he ruled. So "David went up and all Israel... to bring up thence the ark of God, the Lord, that dwelleth between the cherubim, whose name is called on it."[83] Yahweh was still there saying "Yahweh."

A great festive party accompanied the ark as it moved

on its way drawn by oxen. But at the threshing floor of Nacon, a man named Uzzah "took hold of it, for the oxen stumbled... and God smote him there because he put forth his hand to the ark; and he died there besides the ark of God."[84] The electrocution frightened David so that he waited three months before his second attempt to move it, and this time installed it beside him. (One wonders why the Levites were not tending to the Ark; they are not mentioned.) In a queer incident, David is so happy at having the Ark that he dances naked around it, incurring the reproaches of his wife for making a public display of himself. She is suitably punished for her prudery by becoming barren for the rest of her life.

    Now the Ark was ensconced on high ground. It no longer went to war. Yet it is not known whether the Ark was regularly employed for its remaining functions. With David we are in the tenth century, five hundred years after Moses. We wonder whether electrical conditions can any longer support the Ark and whether Yahweh's presence will ever again grace the mercy seat between the cherubim.

    In a plaintive passage, Yahweh tells the Prophet Nathan to tell King David that he has not had a decent house but has had to live in tents since leaving Egypt. And we are informed that "the people were sacrificing in high places... because no home had yet been built for the name of the Lord."[85] He asks therefore for a temple, but warns David against rushing into the job. David thereupon designs the Temple and leaves it for his son, Solomon, to build.

    Meanwhile it is clear that the Ark needs artificially supporting conditions to work at all. This bodes ill for the Ark as a mobile weapon, and as "inspector-general" of the

The Ark in Action

tribal centers. It is discovered that the Ark works best standing upon a source of natural heat. The proper thermal conditions may be found usually on threshing floors, where in some ancient time the threshing of grain and the heat have become associated [86]. Matthew refers metaphorically to "unquenchable fire" that "will burn up the chaff."[87] David goes looking for a threshing floor on which to place the Ark [88]. Beneath the floor may be a source of ionization, a conduction of charge through rock - many floors being of smooth bare rock.

Gressmann wonders at the Ark being regularly placed upon stones [89]. The Ark has no legs; very well, one might think; therefore it must be placed upon a stand of stones. Rather, the Ark had no legs so that it might be placed on stone. For it is on stone and rock, whether from the Jordan River or an old threshing floor or whatever, and especially on meteoritic stones, that the Ark can charge up negative electricity.

The next artificial support of the Ark comes from being elevated. On high, it can profit from the accumulation of ground charge for point discharge into the atmosphere. Mt. Zion is a hill of Jerusalem. The Ark is there more active. Yet it should now be confessed that the original principle of the Ark is being lost - that it was a weapon of the plains and desert capable of being moved and of assaulting the mountain fortresses where St. Elmo's fire was active, and sometimes too active, as in the case of Jericho.

A third artificial stimulant was water. Water conducts electricity and wetted conductors function better [90]. If the Ark were on deep smooth rock whose surface was wetted, the chances of the Ark becoming operational would be much greater.

Any sacrificial object to be burnt by Yahweh had also to be wetted. So we find King David pouring water around the altar to assist in his sacrifices [91]. He may have also supplied water to the grounding and casing of the Ark to promote its conduction of charge. The altar was on a bare rock threshing floor and Yahweh sent a fire down upon his burnt offering.

All facilitating conditions are brought together in the climactic Temple of Solomon high in Jerusalem - Ark, rock, height, top water, bottom water, and finally a temple that is itself designed as an Ark with devices in its Holy of Holy Rooms, the Inner Sanctum to connect the Ark to the building itself. Seven years were required to build it.

The roof was of gold-plated wood. Indeed there was a separate house of wood inside the outer walls, which were of stone. Inside, "no stone was seen."[92] No metal connections were used on the outer wall; no hammering or metal work resounded during the construction. Stone, then wood, the insulator; then gold, the conductor. In the Temple court, a "molten sea" holding 12,000 gallons of water rested upon twelve couchant bulls facing in the four cardinal directions; it was for the priests to wash themselves [93].

A multitude of sharp gold points covered the roof of the Temple. The Temple was never struck by lightning during its long existence [94]. Michaelis and others have identified the points as lightning rods and he says that they connected "with the caverns in the hill upon which the temple was situated, by means of pipes in connection with the guilding which covered all the exterior of the building..."[95] Ancient Hindu fountains were also protected

The Ark in Action

from lightning by rods that grounded charges, and the Temple of Juno in Rome was protected by a roof of many pointed sword-blades [96].

One may surmise that the Ark was connected with the deep natural rock and water, and that the smaller cherubim of the Ark were in contact with the giant cherubim, that in turn connected with the roof where exterior rods or spires induced the atmospheric charging.

Scrutinizing the appropriate Biblical passages, we can reconstruct the ultimate setting of the Ark of the Covenant. The Ark was set in a windowless room that was a perfect cube of 20 cubits (about 30 feet). It was placed below two giant cherubim of wood, covered with gold, the tips of whose wings touched each other and the golden walls of the rooms; that is, each cherub had a wingspread of 10 cubits. Gold covered the whole inside of the Temple including the inside ceiling of the roof.

Three possibilities appear: that the whole was a purely symbolic creation not intended to work; that the design was intended to function under the new and weak atmospheric conditions, but could not work without blowing up the Inner Sanctum; that the system was designed to work but could not function, or its functioning was believed to be too dangerous and the connections were deliberately broken. King Solomon, in his dedication speech, is supposed to have said to the assembled throng: "But will God indeed dwell on the earth? Behold, heaven and the highest heaven cannot contain thee; how much less this house which I have built."[97] The speech does not ring out with confidence.

In the very next verse, Solomon prays that "thy eyes may be open night and day toward this house, the place of which thou hast said, "My Name shall be there."' Electric eyes and electric name! "When the priests came out of the holy place," on this first occasion, "a cloud filled the house of the Lord, so that the priests could not stand to minister because of the cloud; for the glory of the Lord filled the house of the Lord."[98] Either the system worked, or the priests lit a phosphorous smoke and bungled it in the closed quarters. I doubt that it worked. The conditions were not propitious; if the gigantic apparatus had loaded and sparked, the lightning bolt would have blasted the room of wood and gold to pieces.

Thus stands the Ark. Ultimate perfection. But the "Holy Ghost," so to speak, is gone. Yahweh says little: the mobile weapon of the plains has surrendered to the pyramidal weapon of the mountains. The assimilation is completed. Still the gods of the mountain scarcely speak, nor does Yahweh, now also a god of the heights.

It may be appropriate to use the fact that out of Egypt, in the fifth year of King Rehoboam, son of Solomon, came Shishak, Pharaoh of Egypt. Jerusalem was surrendered without siege. Shishak "took away the treasures of the house of the Lord and the treasure of the King's house; he took away everything,"[99] It is ironic that Shishak should be identified as Thut-Moses III [100] - "Child of Thut" echo of Moses, "the Child. "

It is doubly ironic that Thut (Thoth) should mean the god "Thoth," "Mercury" in Latin, "Hermes" in Greek, who was an electrical god - distinct from the "greater god" Horus or Yahweh or Zeus-Jupiter; his famous caduceus, composed of a winged rod with a serpent entwined upon it is nothing other than Moses' rod of the brazen serpent, the original of

The Ark in Action

which probably ended up in the trophy rooms of Shishak-Thutmoses [101]. It is trebly ironic that Thut-Moses III might have had, as aunt and Queen Mother, Hatshepsut, who has been identified by Velikovsky as the Queen of Sheba who visited Solomon and admired so his treasures [102].

An inscription of hers has recently been publicized, in which she boasts that "when I became king, my uraeus threw fire against my enemies."[103] The uraeus denotes a symbol of royal power, but here may refer to an Ark display, employed hundreds of years after Moses and at the time of King Solomon.

Finally, it is ironic that the Ark ended where its idea had begun with Moses - in Egypt, impotent [104]. Nor perhaps were the pyramids employed under Shishak of the New Kingdom as they had been under Thoum and his predecessors of the Middle Kingdom. The "Ark School" of Moses was moribund. So was the "Pyramid School" of electricity. The age of pyramids was over.

The Romans relied upon heated oil, levered projectiles, assault towers, well-worked battering rams. Somewhere in the Near East was invented "Greek fire," a sticky, nearly inextinguishable mixture, that was hurled upon the enemy. Everyone relied upon banners, trumpets, drums and images to inspire themselves and terrorize the enemy. Not until the deployment of explosive power in bursting units or by blunderbuss were the effects of the Ark achieved. But then, of course, the natural conditions for the progressive development of an electrical weapon had disappeared. And there was no Moses around and about to develop electrostatics into other electrical forms - unless it was Nicola Tesla (1856-1943), who sought to make of the whole world globe and its atmosphere an electrostatic machine. But Tesla, a lonely genius akin to Moses, lacked Aaron and Joshua, and led no revolutionary people. He encountered the effective neglect of the "Motor and Wire School" which he himself had helped create. Nor had he the Great Comet or Yahweh.

GOD'S FIRE GONE

What was left of the electrical function was carried out on altars in high places, which would serve on occasion to induce St. Elmo's fire upon sacrifices to produce burnt offerings.
Psalm 78 chants:

> For they provoked him to anger with their high places;
> They moved him to jealousy with their graven images.
> When God heard, he was full of wrath,
> and he utterly rejected Israel.
> He forsook his dwelling at Shiloh,
> the tent where he dwelt among men,
> and delivered his power to captivity,
> his glory to the hand of the foe.

It is registered that as the Jews were being carried into captivity in Babylonia, Jeremiah the Prophet hid the fire of the Altar in a secret waterless pit [105]. Upon the return from captivity, the priestly posterity repaired to the place and found only "thick water." They took this and placed it upon the Altar, whereupon, the sun striking it, a great flame was

The Ark in Action

kindled. The pit was made a sacred enclosure, sometimes called the chamber of Nephtar (Naphta, oil). The thick water was probably petroleum. The incident is connected with the celebration of the Festival of Lights (Hanukkah). The possible use of petroleum then, at such other times, would supplement the true "Lord's fire" when this became unavailable, or, as may have happened here, too[106], when a chemical fire was needed to excite an electrical discharge.

The age of the prophets had been an age of renewed electrical phenomena. We ought not here discuss this subject, which is extensive in itself, because the Ark was not in action. Then, as Ziegler writes, "The age of the Prophets came to an end with the death of Haggai, Zachariah and Malachi. A Rabbinic book says at this time: "The Holy Spirit ceased out of Israel."[107]

Electricity might still be induced in sacrifices on high places. The Jewish historian, Josephus, writing in the first century of this era, said that the light which "shined out when God was present at their sacrifices" ceased for the Jews two hundred years before his time, "'God having been displeased at the transgression of his laws. "[108]

Under special conditions and with the most elaborate arrangement, high sites such as that of the famous Delphic oracle would still produce electric shocks. These would inspire the Pythoness to utter sounds, which would be interpreted by the priests. A young Scythian visitor, who paid his charges and watched the scene, exclaimed in disgust in a letter afterwards at the great many personal decisions and determinations of public policy which had been arrived at by these means. Plutarch, 1500 years after the Exodus, wondered "Why oracles cease to give answers." He had been himself a priest at Delphi [109]. During his tenure, as described by him, a Pythoness was killed in a way that suggests electrocution, after the oracle's weakness of response had induced unsafe practices – in fact, an over-watering of the ground in the oracle chamber.

Three centuries later, an anti-Christian emperor, Julian the Apostate, decided to help the Jews rebuild the Temple of Jerusalem, probably to spite the Christians. The project "was dropped when it was reported (as it was on both an earlier and a later occasion) that 'balls of fire' had issued from the old foundations and scared away the workmen."[110]

The name of Yahweh lapsed among the Jews upon their return from the Babylonian exile in the sixth century. One scholar [111] suggests that this happened because Elohim was a more universal god and the Jews began to proselytize in the Greco-Roman world. Or else, says he, the divine name may have been too sacred to utter, and the ritual of the synagogue replaced it by "My Lord Adonai." Both may be true reasons and connected with the third, more basic reason, that is, that Yahweh was no longer manifesting himself because he could not. Or he had retired, *deus otiosus,* and would not create the electrical conditions of the earlier world. The name is hidden, not because it was too sacred to utter, but because it was not to be heard.

CHAPTER FIVE

LEGENDS AND MIRACLES

Settled temporarily by the Holy Mountain, Israel awaits miracles. Moses and no one else must provide them. The Mountain is very active - smoke and fire abound. The scene is obscured by the continued high dusty and turbulent sky. Moses ascends the Mountain and gets initial instructions regarding preparation of a covenant. Moses returns and receives the assurances of the people: "All that Yahweh has spoken we will do."[1] Yahweh, hearing this, commands Israel to be present at the foot of the mountain on the third day of their consecration.

The third day broke with horrendous thunder, lightning, clouds, and trumpet blasts upon the mountain. The people assembled as instructed. Yahweh called up Moses and Aaron and delivered the Ten Commandments to the multitude. Apparently the people could not make out his words with all the thunderings, lightnings, the sound of the trumpets and the mountain smoking, so they said to Moses: "You speak to us and we will hear; but let not God speak to us, lest we die."[2] So Moses drew near again to the "thick darkness" where Yahweh was and he received many ordinances.

Moses is told to invite the leaders of the people up to see Yahweh; do not let the people come up. Before doing so,

Moses sacrificed oxen and sprinkled their blood over the people as they gave their pledge to the Covenant.

He brings the seventy elders and three priests - Aaron and his sons (later to be accidentally electrocuted) - up to a marvelous plateau, a table or pavement of sapphire stone, evidencing prolonged electrical discharging, raising a heat that glazed the rock, perhaps metamorphosing it [3]. There "they saw the God of Israel;" it is repeated: "They beheld God."[4] Not so, the exegetes say, Yahweh is invisible; ergo they could not have seen him; never mind the explicit language.

Nonetheless Moses is inspired and hears Yahweh calling to him. He tells the elders to await him and, during his absence, to refer any problems to his adjutants, Aaron and Hur. Joshua, who is called his servant, goes part of the way up, and halts. Moses waits because of a dangerous cloud that hovers over the summit. On the seventh day, Yahweh calls, and Moses enters the cloud. All Israel, meanwhile, can see from below "the glory of Yahweh… like a devouring fire on top of the mountain."[5]

After forty days and nights, Moses descends from the mountain with the laws, written by Yahweh on two stone tablets. Awaiting Moses is a full scale revolution - the Golden Calf. He destroys the tablets in shame and anger. He suppresses the revolt ruthlessly. He begs Yahweh for another chance. Again he goes up the Holy Mountain. This time, Yahweh admonishes him to hide himself from His person, so Moses enters a crevasse, a cleft, a kind of cave, and there crouches as far in as possible ("bows low") when Yahweh's brilliance passes by him. Not even a pinprick of light penetrated his cave, says a legend, or else he would have

Legends and Miracles

been consumed when Yahweh and his retinue passed by; still the intensity of illumination was such that "he caught the reflection of it so that from its radiance his face began to shine."[6]

When he descends, the people recoil from him in fright and awe. His countenance is radiant. He has a halo - the first halo, and the only one on earth - Neher states enthusiastically. Others give Moses horns on this occasion. Michelangelo's great conception of Moses depicts him with horns. Why didn't the Jews and Catholics complain of this? Daiches presents an unconvincing etymological argument [7]. All the medieval and Renaissance scholars and churchmen, led astray by St. Jerome, read a word wrong: Karen (H) is a verb meaning "shone" or "gave forth rays of light"; the noun keren means "horn" or ray of light" (Ex. 34:35). He objects to deriving the latter from the former word. But the words are obviously related; Hebrew vowels are notably unreliable in sounding words (as when a preference is sought between "Jehovah" and "Yahweh"); the earliest etymologies are often indefinite and partial. Perhaps something with connotations of both "horn" and "ray of light" may be intended, inasmuch as the phenomenon was capable of giving both impressions, and people were quite sensitive to "horns" in this aftermath of the revolt of the Golden Calf.

Ruth Mellinkoffs enchanting study of *The Horned Moses* concludes that St. Jerome's translation of *Exodus* 34:29 as 'horned' appears "in keeping with the context and meaning of 'horned' in the ancient world as well as the metaphorical meaning of 'horn' and 'horned' in the Bible. It meant strength, honor, victory, power, divinity, kingship, and salvation..." The scholar-theologians of the Church saw them as "horns of light, or light emanating in the manner of a horn" - an interpretation first suggested by Rashi, the famous eleventh-century Jewish commentator.[8]

Moses has unusual ways of conducting, storing, and discharging electricity. Or was there so much of a voltage gradient as he descended that he discharged static electricity in coming down? As mountaineers have testified, St. Elmo's fire under certain propitious conditions, even now, will stream like horns from the ears of a subject and from any tool he is carrying. The horns of animals stream fire, too, in such circumstances. And always in mind is the comet with its horns reaching far out from its head. Close the horns and there arises a halo, given to Moses and to saints. The later saints got their radiant 'halos' by traditional inference; for them it is a medal, like millions of Christians wear the crucifix without experiencing crucifixion. Earth and heaven are united in a single symbol once more.

Moses "did not know that the skin of his face shone because he had been talking to Yahweh." He ordered all to draw close so that he could give them the laws. The people's faces shone, too, briefly [9]. Perhaps they felt a sympathetic contagion. Afterwards Moses put a veil over his face whenever he was in public. He removed it when he spoke to Yahweh in the tent and then replaced it when he came out. St. Paul spoke of "Moses, who put a veil over his face so that the Israelites might not see the end of his fading splendor." His skin was probably desquamating. When it was cured, an explanation for removing the veil would not be difficult: to avoid claiming a permanent gift, or as punishment by Yahweh for some peccadillo. One rare picture of ca. 1000 A.D. gives Moses all three: horns, veil, and mask [10]. (See

Legends and Miracles   171

Figure 15.)
    We may go farther into the mysteries of Moses' halo. Hugo Gressmann [11], one of the greatest of Old Testament authorities, asserts that Moses always wore a mask, that Moses wanted to play god and, after he had come down radiant from the Holy Mountain, he assumed a sacred mask. Gressmann had no idea of the atmospheric turbulence nor of its affecting Moses' skin; he claimed that priestly masks were to be found elsewhere, whether among the Egyptians or Semitic tribes. By intensive linguistic analysis, Gressmann demonstrates elisions in the Bible where the word "mask" would occur, and says that the word "veil" is a weak and vague substitution of a thousand years later [12].
    On the contrary, I find a powerful connection between Moses' perilous sojourn on the mountain, the radiation disease symptoms, his donning the veil or mask, and his incorporating the mask into the required equipment of the priests when working amidst the divine smoke and fire of the Inner Sanctum. Gressmann lets us believe that Moses' mask was his permanent public face; if so, it can only mean that Moses was disfigured for life and therefore wore a mask, naturally proclaimed sacred; or more likely that Moses' facial disfiguration was itself considered a permanent mask of Yahweh, and that Aaron's and other masks were artificial, in imitation of Yahweh's mask and for protection against dangerous radiation and shocks around the Holy of Holies. I find additional support for this view in the advice of Hyam Maccoby, who asserts that the word in dispute is in fact Karan, the only occurrence in all of the Bible in this form. The phrase would then read that Moses' skin became of horn-like texture.

Figure 15: Moses with Horns, Veil and Mask.
(Source: Bible of Lübeck, 1494)

RADIATION DISEASES

The cause of Moses' halo may have been phosphorous burns, compounded by a dose of radiation. Both elements would be present in abundance in the clouds of the mountain and the artificial clouds of the Tent of the Tabernacle. Whoever entered the Tabernacle unless under order was to be stricken with leprosy [13]. Many sins are punishable by leprosy [14]. And there are various types of leprosy; despite all the detail on the diagnosis and treatment of leprosy in the *Book of Leviticus* (13:1-59; 14), no clear single

Legends and Miracles   173

disease emerges. A "leprosy" that is not excluded is radiation sickness, which of course during all the centuries when the Bible was seriously studied by scholars was an unknown disease. Skin lesions, blisters, and ultimately death among experimenters with radium and X-ray are a twentieth century phenomena. When the first atomic bomb was exploded over Hiroshima, and features of radiation disease began to emerge, it was thought at first that an infectious plague had followed in the wake of the disaster.

In the Revolt of the Golden Calf, Aaron, whom Moses had appointed high priest, lost hope for Moses and deserted briefly to the opposition. Later Aaron and their "sister," Miriam, who had become a kind of priestess for women and children, entered the Lord's tent and accused Moses of such irrelevances as taking for his wife a non-Jew. The woman in question may have been the daughter of Hobab, the Kenite, although referred to only as the Cushite (Ethiopian?) in the Bible. Thus suggests Winnett, who adds that this bigamous liaison was probably contracted for political reasons inasmuch as the Jews were now leaving Midianite territory and moving northwards into Kadesh, land of the related Kenites [15].

Moses promptly squelched his relatives. He said, in effect, that if it was Yahweh they would complain to, all three of them should have a talk with Himself. They did, and Miriam, I think, emerged from the tent with a mild case of radiation sickness and phosphorous poisoning that blanched her skin, and greatly frightened her and Aaron. She was to be permanently expelled from the camp for leprosy; but Moses put in a good word for her with Yahweh who limited the expulsion to seven days, after which she returned, healthy, perhaps having fed meanwhile upon the honey-like manna which, like honey, would have been an antidote for radiation sickness and blood-poisoning [16].

According to legend, when Moses wanted to cure Miriam, he drew a circle around himself and, in praying to God, concluded with: "If Thou do not heal her, I myself shall do so, for Thou has already revealed to me, how leprosy arises and how it disappears." Perhaps he was referring to his own "halo" case.

Miriam may have lost a lot of blood cells but she did not become bald. Many in those days were not so lucky. Isaiah probably had their history in mind when later he prophesies: "The Lord will give the women of Zion bald heads, the Lord will strip the hair from their foreheads."[17] Since he raises the same point twice elsewhere, Isaiah must have had an experience in mind in which he firmly believed. But then, far back, in the time of Exodus, the Egyptian Ipuwer had been lamenting: "Indeed, hair (has fallen out) for everybody, and the man of rank can no longer be distinguished from him who is nobody." The upper classes had worn their hair long.

A Swedish commentator, Ragnar Forshufvud, writes that "a dose of 300-400 rem will give temporary epilation while 700 rem will give permanent epilation." (1 rem = the radiation dose of 1 Roentgen of X or Y radiation.) If the whole body is subject to a single dosage of 450 rem, there is only a 50% chance of survival, which may be another reason why Ipuwer had written of Exodus in Egypt, "Indeed men are few, and he who places his brother in the ground is everywhere."[18]

Thomas Foster, "a physician of some note in the

scientific world and member of several learned societies in England and the Continent, in a work published in 1829, devotes forty-one pages to a catalogue of plagues and epidemics, in nearly every instance accompanied by a comet."[19] Sometimes beasts (the "murrain") are afflicted as well as or instead of humans.

The relation between chemical and radiation plagues and "real plagues" of viruses and germs is close in the history of Exodus and its aftermath. Realization that their sources may be cosmic disturbances will no doubt help in their investigation. In a recent BBC interview (1977) regarding his research on "Diseases from Outer Space," Professor Chandra Wickramasinghe maintained that "invasions of this type could be responsible for all the major plagues and epidemics which have punctuated our history from antiquity to modem times." He was seconded by his colleague, Fred Hoyle [20].

THE ELECTRO-CHEMICAL FACTORY

Of clouds in Exodus, there are the high clouds of obscuring the sky and causing the long-enduring darkness; next the cloud or pillar of smoke that leads the Jews out of Egypt; the cloud and pillar upon the mountain; the cloud arising from the Tabernacle sanctuary; the cloud that moves with the ark; the cloud above Moses' tent outside the camp; and occasional clouds that are dangerous to the camp. Yahweh's fire, which we find synonymous with electrostatic fire, is present in all the clouds. The fire can come before, with, and after the cloud's appearance.

The experience of clouds is frequent. These clouds

do not carry rain. They carry vapors which have serious consequences for evil and good. The clouds in all cases are associated with Yahweh; they are dangerous; Moses is uniquely competent to deal with them, and even he is overexposed on the mountain and perhaps on other occasions.

The great pillar of cloud and the high obscuring blanket of cloud are probably connected, the first being an earlier state of vision and contact with the comet's tail and the second being a later state of the elements of the tail that diffused throughout the earth's atmosphere. Comet tails can be millions of miles long and thousands of miles in diameter. Since we have had no late experience with large comets, their components are subject to debate. It has lately become permissible in scientific circles to attribute many kinds of materials to them - elemental and molecular gases, particles, ice and rocks. Should a large comet-tail pass through the atmosphere, it would deposit its own materials, and combine its materials with those of the earth, not only with normal atmospheric components but also with the discharges peculiar to volcanoes and typhoons or tornadoes.

In the major catastrophic columns or typhoons of a comet-earth encounter, therefore, would be discovered a variety of chemicals under turbulent conditions of pressure, heat, and electricity. Picture a vast gaseous and heavy meteoritic fall-out mingling with the eruptions of volcanoes and electrical discharges by the many thousands, and one has the beginnings of a conception of the event. In such a maelstrom, miracles would be multitudinous. We are dealing with a vast electro-chemical factory. The first response of a catastrophized human group is to relate itself to the turbulent

Legends and Miracles 177

skies. Moses was exceedingly busy - up and down the mountain - trying to reproduce on earth what he saw in heaven. Hence what we expect is that certain "miracles" happen naturally and others, much simpler and crude, but nevertheless amazing, happen as the artifices of man. Reciting the Biblical references, we can derive radiation and radiance of various types: a complex chemically-loaded dew; red phosphorus; hydrocarbons; unidentified poisons; sulfur; mercury; ammonia; cinnabar; formaldehyde; manna; and perfumes. The sky and earth are producing enough heat and electricity to manufacture many products.

The element phosphorus might have been prominent in the Exodus chemical environment. It may have had poisonous effects, especially if accompanied by radioactive materials, in the Nile and the wells of Egypt. It was probably present in the clouds of the mountain. It was a major ingredient in Moses' arsenal, possibly for helping to send up smoke when smoke did not originate in satisfactory abundance from the ark, possibly for communicating with Yahweh in his tent, possibly as smoke bombs. When Moses set up his tent far outside the camp for living and counseling, Yahweh would visit him there: witness the cloud or pillar of smoke that descended whenever Moses entered the tent door [21].

Phosphorus is "not found free in nature except in a few meteorites..." because "it takes fire spontaneously upon exposure to air and forms dense white fumes of the oxide."[22] It is a colorless, transparent, soft wax that glows in the dark. It converts to red phosphorus with sunlight or heat, after which it neither glows nor spontaneously combusts in air. White phosphorus is used to make smoke shells for military use.)

White phosphorus is easily made. Calcium phosphate, a stone, is ground into powder and combined with silversand (silicon dioxide) and charcoal. Carbon monoxide is a by-product. When exposed to air, the phosphorus burns with a bright hot flame, a voluminous dense white smoke, and gives off a poisonous gas. Moses would have known from Egypt the properties of these common materials, what they smelled like when burned, what the clouds on the mountain appeared to be. His main problem would have been to encapsulate the white phosphorus in order to deprive it of air until the moment of use. Small gourds, ceramic jars, or bladders would contain the material under seal. A poisonous grenade would be available to toss into the tents of opponents of Yahweh, such as Dathan and Abiram. They had refused Moses' summons and denied his authority. Moses supervised their execution by Yahweh. The ground was said to split open and swallow their households. The crowd fled the scene, which might have resembled the hell-fires bursting out and enveloping them. Small amounts of phosphorus would suffice to emit a smoke cloud about the Tabernacle and tent of Moses,

Phosphorescence, which may characterize many objects, is "the emission of light from a substance exposed to radiation and persisting as an afterglow after the radiation has been removed."[23] A phosphorescence may last for an instant, days, or years and will react whenever agitated by heat or optical waves. This refers to the cases of Moses and Miriam and a kind of leprosy, but also to the "footstool of Yahweh" that the elders witnessed; various apatite phosphate minerals are of a green glassy appearance and "are often fluorescent in ultra-violet light...; phosphorescent; sometimes

Legends and Miracles

strongly thermo-luminescent."[24] Although we cannot be sure of the processes of the clouds of Exodus, the existence of a special electro-chemical environment and an applied science thereof are fairly demonstrable.

The dew that fell in great abundance in the wilderness was no ordinary vapor. It was often red, often poisonous, often conductive and facilitative of electrical discharges. The wearing of Moses-designed heavy and full priestly garments, the washing that went on before and after rituals, the placement of veils and curtains within the Tabernacle, the holes in the tent tops, the arrangements of vessels and paraphernalia: - "Aaron and his sons are to do this lest they die" - these were safety practices and procedures for handling dangerous products. Only later could they be called psychological obsessions, when their functions had disappeared with the fading of the electrical age and the great electrochemical factories of nature.

One scholar, Von Fange, writes that "In the Middle East in Ancient times there was an amazing number of literary references to a garment of flame, the goatskin dyed red, or a ramskin dyed red, or a red-dyed goat. The meaning is completely obscure."[25] An editor's footnote reads: "Obviously references to ramskins dyed red as in *Exodus* 25:5 [describe] directions from God for construction of the sacred Tabernacle, and would have no connection with pagan use of goat skins dyed red." Both are connected probably to the red dust and dew that covered everything dead and alive in the Egyptian plagues and from time to time in the wilderness. The startling, ominous, and effective events are typically perpetuated in design and rites. Earlier, we had occasion to discuss the taboos of redness.

MANNA

"When the dew fell upon the camp in the night, the manna fell with it."[26]

Obviously, despite the darkness of the days, a solar heating and nocturnal cooling were occurring in the wilderness. The manna may cure the very radiation sickness often caused by the radiation-loaded dew. Both are part of the Exodus experience of Egypt and Israel. Few scholars doubt that something natural and edible was being made available to the starving Israelites. Almost always, they have sought some desert plant that by its excrescences or pollen fall-out would give nourishment. Buber writes as if the matter were settled [27]:

"The tale is told of manna (a secretion of cockineal insect, tasting like crystallized honey, which covers the tamarisk bushes at the time of the apricot harvest, drips to earth by day and becomes hard at night)."

This is a whit short of absurdity. The large volume of manna, its long duration, its fall from heaven, the technique of its baking, and other details of the story are shunted aside. More persuasive incidents are available, with lichen as the possible agent, thus: "In 1829, during the war between Persia and Russia, there was a great famine in Orumiah, south-west of the Caspian. One day, during a violent wind, the surface of the country was covered with a lichen which 'fell down from heaven.' The sheep immediately attacked and devoured it, which suggested to the inhabitants the idea of reducing it to flour and making bread of it, which was found to be good and nourishing."[28] Electrical winds have been blamed for

Legends and Miracles 181

such drops, which is a step in the right direction.

Manna is described in two places, in somewhat different terms [29]. "Almost any reasonably experienced confectioner will recognize the substance concerned as a common constituent of sugar confectionary, usually called invert sugar."[30] It fell nightly as seeds, for a long time then occasionally. The last fall was reported just before the Battle of Jericho, "and the people of Israel had manna no more."[31] It could be baked into sugar-carbohydrate loaves. Although at first delighted and grateful, the people ultimately became heartily sick of it.

The basis for its natural production was the huge volume of formaldehyde gas, formed by the incomplete combustion of many organic substances. "At least one worker has actually produced sugars directly from very freshly formed gaseous formaldehyde at a temperature of 150°-180°C (H. Vogel at the University of Geneva in 1928)."[32]

A British expert on the chemistry of confections, M.G. Reade, has followed the various processes whereby, from the formaldehyde of incomplete combustion in the atmosphere, edible manna could have been naturally fashioned. The problem is like that of artificially accomplishing photosynthesis. He concludes that "synthesis in a burning fiery cloud is feasible, even probable when other environment conditions are favourable."[33] He thinks that Moses designed the Tabernacle to produce manna, but only because of the tent's construction[34] and not because there is any evidence of manna being actually produced. (Reade does speculate ingeniously that the reason why the often grumpy people followed the leader and Tabernacle was in order to get the manna that Moses was producing artificially.) His comments on the tabernacle are revealing: "Perhaps the single most basic association is that between the 'Tabernacle of the Lord' and the physical characteristics of the cloud. In laying down guidelines for the construction of a tabernacle, or church, it was clearly stated that the whole was to be the same as had been seen by Moses in the cloud... A burning fiery cloud has to have a fresh air intake... This air intake would probably be at its base, and it would be tent-shaped." Here one can be best protected from "poisonous or asphyxiating fumes."

One might locate such air intakes on mountain tops or man-made tents. Observing, as a trained scientist, from the "eye of the cyclone," that is, for many days and nights, Moses produced the design and specifications for the ark, tent, and tabernacle. Here, as elsewhere, the imitation of nature is used as the basis for an applied science; a priest or layman or political boss or "just a guy hearing voices" could not produce the works of Moses.

THE BURNT OFFERING

Servius, a commentator on Virgil, writes that "the first inhabitants of the earth never carried fire to their altars, but by their prayers they brought down the heavenly fire."[35] Even in the first century after Christ, Josephus, the Jewish historian could describe a successful sacrifice to Yahweh: "There came a fire running out of the air, and rushed with violence upon the altar, in the sight of all, and caught hold of and consumed the sacrifice." But such fires of

Legends and Miracles 183

Yahweh had long been rare, Josephus himself having testified that the Holy Spirit disappeared two centuries before his time. I think that the great electrical flood was mostly dammed by the time of Joshua and then was reduced incrementally from century to century, with perhaps a century or two of revival of flow during the time of the prophets and the end of the Late Bronze Age.

I have paid little attention to the altars of Moses and those that followed. I do not mean the Israelite altar of unhewn, heaped-up stones that was called for by Yahweh at first[36], or the Altar of Incense, but the elaborate one for sacrifices designed by Moses during his mountain retreat. The design of altars generally was fairly straightforward. It is clear what the priests were seeking; it is evident what they found and what failures they experienced. What is most obvious is that altars were uniformly constructed to carry out a simple electrical function, throughout the Near and Middle East. The Cretans, for instance, had horned altars, as did others. Perhaps the very origin of altars goes back to the beginning of the electrical ages, about six thousand years ago, when Zeus in all his forms became a great god and Saturn withdrew.

The concept of archaeo-electrostatics permits us to imagine that altars were designed for burnt offerings when it was observed that the gods whom one wished to propitiate were in the habit of dispatching sparks upon metallized prominences such as horns, spears and elevated plates. This was direct contact of a most exciting kind between god and humans. One could scarcely doubt that the gods were receiving and acknowledging the offerings. When Yahweh's fire is not called for, the worshippers use ordinary combustion. When the oil lamps of the Tabernacle were readied upon their seven-pronged lampstand, Moses "then fit up the lamps."[37] Fire did not descend from the atmosphere to do the job.

The great horned altar of Israel in the wilderness was another of Yahweh's Mount Sinai designs that Moses applied at the foot of the mountain [38]. It was a hollow, ninety-inch square cabinet of bronze-plated wood, standing fifty-four inches high, with carrying poles. It was hollow to permit its being filled with stones and dirt according to Yahweh's first instructions out of Egypt. The horns of the four corners were one piece with the rest. According to tradition, this magnificent altar did not work at first; but finally "there came a fire out from before the Lord and consumed upon the altar the burnt offering and fat." The fire stayed there for 116 years without melting the brass or burning the wood, the legend concludes, leaving us to wonder: "why '116'"? [39]

A legend has Yahweh reproaching Moses, who wondered whether the divine fire would consume the thin altar brass and wood: "Thou judgest by the laws that apply to men, but will these also apply to Me?" Then, referring to the fires and ice of heaven, he goes on: "Doth the water quench their fire, or doth their fire consume the water? For, 'I am the Lord who maketh peace between these elements in My high places.' No more shall the brass overlay of the altar be injured by fire; even though it be no thicker than a denarium [a coin]."[40] Obviously, he had in mind an electric fire, not one of coals.

Cassuto [41] insists, against exegetes and legends, that the altar had an earthen and stone top. The legendary metal and wood top would be quickly destroyed by a heavy wood

Legends and Miracles 185

or coal fire, as other sceptics, too, have pointed out. I am inclined to disagree with the distinguished Cassuto; electrical conditions were such at this time and so well controlled by Moses that he could be confident of exciting an electrical fire whenever it was required. The sceptics have not considered an electrical fire.

As with the Ark, once the significance of electricity is perceived in regard to the altar, we may deduce certain behaviors and understand others. We appreciate, once again, the immensity of electrification in those days, the universality of electro-static applications in worship, and the possibility of following electrical sensitivities wherever they may lead over the lithosphere and especially up into the mountains, the "high places" to which the Jews repaired more and more as the Earth-charge in relation to near space diminished and the atmosphere cleared.

By "burnt offerings" the Bible means an offering destined for sacrifice on an altar, as well as the same sacrifice after it has been burnt. On one occasion, Moses and Aaron entered the Holy Tabernacle and came out again; then the glory of Yahweh appeared to all the people. And fire came forth from before the Lord and consumed the burnt offering [42].

So far as one may tell, a burnt offering is successfully burnt when it is struck by a spark discharged from above, a divine fire... It need not be cooked; it should be marked or signed. Occasionally the enthusiasm of the language lets one imagine that Yahweh in fact did sometimes voraciously "consume" the burnt offering.

To get Yahweh to accept an animal sacrifice, it may have been prudent to drain the animal of its blood, whence would perhaps come the Judaic taboo of animal blood. Blood conveys electric current. A spark might be dissipated if it short-circuited through a bloody offering.

On the other hand, the blood was useful in the sacrifice for inducing a charge to collect on the metal of the altar base. Moses taught the Israelites to pour the drained blood upon the sacrificial offering, on the altar, and on the ground around the altar. Levites, clean-shaven all over to minimize risks of shock, performed such tasks. Ordinary fires by friction and combustion were also built to burn offerings and to encourage, as with blood, the descent of divine fire. Water, we indicated in the last chapter, will also expedite an electrical discharge. Altars worked better if means were available to wet the same surfaces that Moses used to pour on blood - not inside the offering but over it, on the altar, around the altar, taking care not to move too close or in any way short-circuit an impending spark.

Elijah, the prophet, was mostly incredible as a worker of miracles. There was enough of the scientific in his behavior in his famous contest with the four hundred and fifty prophets of Baal to judge it correct as to structure even if exaggerated [43]. In a time of great drought for the Northern Kingdom of Israel, when the king and most others were whoring after false gods, Elijah, hiding out from sure death, suddenly catches the message that finally a great thunderstorm is coming to end the drought. He impatiently importunes a friend to ask the king for an interview. The friend says in effect : "Why are you in such a hurry to get killed and to get myself killed?" Elijah insists, and the king sees him. Elijah asks for a chance to confute all the false prophets and the king agrees. A contest is set up on Elijah's

Legends and Miracles 187

terms - the opposition is to choose a bull, sacrifice it, and ask for a sign of the Lord's acceptance. He, Elijah, will do likewise. Whoever receives the sign wins.

The opposition builds its fire, places its offering, dances about, and gets no response. Elijah builds an altar of stone, places his offering, and then pours twelve barrels of water upon the offering. He dowses the offering thrice. He digs a trench around the altar and fills it with water. The time is approaching evening. The water soaks down and makes contact with the water table. The approaching thunderstorm is preceded by a heavy, moist, ionized, and charged lowering atmosphere. The fire of Yahweh descends upon the offering of Elijah. His triumphant followers escort the prophets of Baal to a nearby place and kill them.

THE BRAZEN SERPENT AND OTHER RODS

A final "miracle-product" permitted by the electrical age to the ingenious scientist was a variety of rods. The most famous was the caduceus of the Greek god Hermes (in Egypt, Thoth), nowadays the symbol of the medical profession because Hermes was also the greatest healer. The next most famous rod was the Brazen Serpent of Moses, then Aaron's Rod, and then, of course, we hear of other wonderful staffs. Every shepherd needs a staff, every walker a cane, every boy a stick.

So we should expect great disbelief to be visited upon rods. Yet rods have a mysterious quality: they are "guns" in slang; they are phalluses among many prehistoric peoples; they are water-finders in the sensitive hands of dowsers; they are electric attractors and lightning-rods; they are Upper Paleolithic batons; they are lances, tilting weapons, flag-poles, may-poles, dolmens, bethels, etc.; no man is complete without one.

Yahweh, in a legend, advertises that "dead things come before Me and leave Me imbued with life," referring to the rod of Aaron which had lain in the inner sanctum of the Tabernacle one night and then "brought forth buds, and bloomed blossoms, and even yielded almonds."[44] This is a flagrant challenge to legend-analysis: what can be made of it?

The Bible tells that Moses, in need of proving why Aaron should be High Priest of Israel, decreed that a beam of wood should be cut into twelve staves, that the Levi's should have one marked for them, and all other tribes one each as well, the Levi staff being that of Aaron. The rods would be left with Yahweh overnight to see which tribe shall have its rod singled out by him as the rod of the High Priest. Aaron's, and Aaron's alone, was transformed in the night, and his priesthood was divinely authorized by test once more.

If there is a kernel of truth in this sacred competition, it must rest with the manipulation of Aaron's stick in the middle of the night. It may be conjectured that it was subjected to severe shock on the mercy seat of Yahweh until it evidenced changes sufficiently symbolic to suggest the buds, blossoms, and almonds described in the Bible and legends. The ark when operative is somewhat like a tornado: it discharges sparks that set up a column of gases and dust and modifies whatever conductor it may embrace.

A tremendous tornado occurred in Chatenay, France, in 1836, and an expert report was made upon it for insurance

Legends and Miracles 189

purposes:

> All those (trees) which came within the influence of the tornado, presented the same aspect; their sap was vaporized, and their igneous fibres had become as dry as if kept for forty-eight hours in a furnace heated to ninety degrees above the boiling point. Evidently there was a great mass of vapor instantaneously formed, which could only make its escape by bursting the tree in every direction; and as wood has less cohesion in a longitudinal than in a transverse direction, these trees were all, throughout one portion of their trunk, cloven into laths. Many trees attest, by their condition, that they served as conductors to continual discharges of electricity, and that the high temperature produced by this passage of the electric fluid, instantly vaporized all the moisture which they contained, and that this instantaneous vaporization burst all the trees open in the direction of their length, until the wood, dried up and split, had become unable to resist the force of the wind which accompanied the tornado [45].

Aaron's rod, by discontinuous and repeated sparks, could achieve something of the remarkable representations that the observers saw in it the next day. The other rods had been laid aside, of course. Moses had had several rods, the rod that impressed the Hebrew welcoming committee in Goshen, the rod that he carried into his negotiations with Pharaoh Thoum, the rod that he held high in the first battle with the Amalekites, the rod that he used to find water, and the rod that was the Brazen Serpent. I have mentioned some possible special quality of each in another chapter. Of these, only the battle-staff appears to have been luminously activated; "the Midrashim narrate that the Israelites encountered the Amalekites in a thick veil of clouds,"[46] hence it must have sparked a light to have such effect on friend and foe alike.

The early rods that behaved like snakes may have been metal or metalized for high conductivity, insulated at the grasping points, and with pointed head to encourage a discharge upwards. If they discharged they would rustle and hiss like snakes. Possibly, too, by a certain disjointing, sparks might be induced to leap the hinging points and cause a wriggling effect by attraction and repulsion. (Priestley, quoted earlier, was calling such a spark "spider.") As with other magical tricks, the competition of professional magicians would accord to someone the fame of being the best of magicians. If a god or demon is associated with the basic phenomenon, that god, that magician, and that device are altogether connected and acknowledged superior.

The Brazen Serpent (see Figure 16) was the outcome of popular grumblings and protests which provoked Yahweh into sending fiery serpents among the people to bite and kill many of them. Moses, begged to intercede, was told by Yahweh: "Make a fiery serpent, and set it on a pole; everyone who is bitten, when he sees it, shall live."[47] There was no doubt always cause to blame the people for their disagreeable temper. The snakes that caused anguish were probably innumerable animals driven above ground by thermoelectrical phenomena [48] accompanied by fiery electric charges snaking though the ground, else why so many? Why so homeopathic a solution as another fiery snake that is under control? And why the cure from seeing the model excepting that thus would Yahweh and Moses lend their authority to psychosomatic therapy? But the bronze serpent, as an independent spark-generator, might have occupied a private tent of healing. Dr. Mesmer, famous for

Legends and Miracles 191

"mesmerizing" people, was one of "a long line of electrotherapists, that even today practices with some success. Healing might originate in certain cases by electroshock with the priesthood as therapists administering sparks to patients. Other cases of healing might occur by the bactericidal effect of ozone in the rooms where the electro-static machines were operated" as with Mesmer [49].

The bronze serpent, representing unconsciously the comet by its shape and electrification, was carried with the Ark; as Ziegler has suggested elsewhere, it might have been used as an independent capacitor with its rod and snake separated by an insulator so as to permit the tongue to discharge against the head of the rod. It might, too, be employed just behind the mercy seat as the target for discharges from both of the grounded cherubim; and it might be operated as an independent electrical demonstrator affixed to the Ark. Numerous instrumental assemblies and adjustments could be managed for different purposes, with more or less sparking, smoking, noise-making, and explosions.

Since Pliny described the great comet of Typhon as spiral-shaped,[50] there is some reason to connect the serpent with the celestial apparitions of Exodus.

King Hezekiah broke into pieces the Serpent of Moses or a reproduction thereof six centuries later on grounds that it had become the object of idolatry. Or perhaps it could cause panic if it were electrified and, as Ziegler guesses, there would be nowhere to go from a city undergoing siege, or about to do so. The electrical signaling had to be astutely controlled to prevent its causing self-demoralization.

Twenty-five hundred years later, in the first modern

Figure 16: The Brazen Serpent is Formed
(Source: Bible of Lubeck, 1494.)

outburst of enthusiasm for the rediscovery of electrical fire, there comes once again the idea that electricity cures. The spark-spitting is not from snakes but from jars. Some religious evangelists, admirers of the new science, unconsciously emulate their Old Testmanet hero, Moses. So we find in a bibliography the following item, which speaks for itself: [51]

Legends and Miracles 193

A.D. 1759. - Wesley (John), the founder of Methodism (1703-1791) and the most eminent member of a very distinguished English family, publishes "The Desideratum; or Electricity made Plain and Useful, by a Lover of Mankind and of Common Sense." In this he relates at great length the cures of numerous physical and moral ailments, attributed to the employment of the electric fluid, under such curious headings as "Electricity, the Soul of the Universe," "Electricity, the Greatest of all Remedies," etc.

THE POUCH OF JUDGEMENT

Moses, who hates sorcery and divination, provides a special place for a pair of objects, the Urim and Thummim [52]. He orders to be made a pouch of cloth that is closed at top and bottom but open at its two sides, with gold chains attached to hang it from the High Priest's shoulders and to tie it around his waist. It is the size of a man's hand. To the front of the pouch is attached a gold plate into which are fitted twelve different precious stones, each containing the name of one of the Twelve Tribes. "And into the pouch of judgement you shall put the Urim and Thummim."'

No one has found an origin for these two words. They are thought to be a very ancient device. Their shape is "impossible to ascertain."[53] Only top officials, perhaps only heads of state or tribes, could ask the priest to employ them. "They served as a means of inquiring of God, that is to say, of obtaining from the deity, with the help of the priest, an answer concerning matters beyond human ken."[54] Since they were used to choose which of two goats would be sent into the desert to Azazel on the Day of Atonement, it is thought they were a kind of lot. Other incidents of their employment are known. They gave short answers, usually "yes" or "no," to carefully framed question about a highly uncertain decision. Only one question could be handled at a time.

Moses never used them, probably because he could speak directly to Yahweh. But Joshua did, and Saul, and David. After David, the two objects disappear from the Bible. Legend does not go farther than to implicate the Urim and Thummim in the processes of inquiry. The open-sided pouch indicates that the pieces were not carried in it, but employed in it, for at least a hand might enter it.

Legend says that the two words mean "Light and Truth." "Only a high priest who was permeated with the Holy Spirit, and over whom rested the Shekinah, might obtain an answer, for in other cases the stones withheld their answer. But if the high priest was worthy, he received an answer to every inquiry, for on these stones were engraved all the letters of the alphabet, so that all conceivable words could be constructed of them."[55]

For lack of any better explanation, we are impelled to think once more of electrical mysteries. The Holy Spirit and Shekinah, like angels, may be metaphors for a manifestation of electricity. The "Light" does not always appear. The priest must be worthy. King Saul could not get an answer one time, and searched then who had done wrong, for Yahweh "did not answer him that day."[56]

A successful attempt is described by the legend: after the King or head of the Sanhedrin looks into the face of the priest and makes inquiry,

Legends and Miracles   195

> The high priest, looking down on his breastplate, then looked to see which of the letters engraved on the stones shone out most brightly, and then constructed the answer out of these letters. Thus, for example, when David inquired of the Urim and Thummim if Saul would pursue him, the high priest Abiathar beheld gleaming forth the letter Yod in Judah's name, Resh in Reuben's name, and Dalet in Dan's name, hence the answer read as follows: Yered , 'He will pursue.'[57]

More electricity is revealed here: certain stones shine brighter than others, "gleaming forth." The priest ponders the letters and composes the reply as best he can.

We cannot truly solve this mystery with all of its mechanisms - or electronics. Relevant is the fact that the famous early modern scientist, Gilbert (1600), performed and described hundreds of small experiments to determine the electromagnetic properties of precious and semi-precious stones. For most of 200 years following him, scientists pursued the same type of experimentation. Efforts were made to classify all stones by their electrical properties. Jewish legend claims to know what the twelve stones of the Pouch of judgement were. A discussion of the truth of the legend and of these stones and other stones also proposed is not possible here. It suffices to speculate that the original stones fell into a similar order of electrical behavior; particularly, each engraved tribal gem would collect, hold, and emit the same charge under like conditions, as would befit a confederation of equals.

The Urim might be an electrifying brush, a "rubber" the modern scientists called it. The priest would rub the gems until they held a charge, or rub them one by one. This he could do more easily by steadying the pouch with one hand from inside it. The Thummin might be a stubby rod of metal. The priest would whirl it in the air a fixed number of times and then present it to a tribal stone. He would repeat the procedure with all other stones in succession. If a spark gleamed forth, the letter would be used, otherwise not. Then the full word would be combined from the letters that lit up. The procedure was not dangerous; nevertheless it was most holy. King Saul would have killed his son, Jonathan, that day, because, in successive inquiries of the pouch, Jonathan was blamed for the absence of Yahweh. But the people rebelled "and redeemed Jonathan and he did not die."[58]

CHAPTER SIX

THE CHARISMA OF MOSES

"To deny a people the man whom it praises as the greatest of its sons is not a deed to be undertaken lightheartedly - especially by one belonging to that people." So goes the first sentence of Sigmund Freud's book on *Moses and Monotheism,* that views Moses as an Egyptian disciple of Pharaoh Akhnaton, and he continues: "No consideration, however, will move me to set aside truth in favour of supposed national interests."[1]

If Freud had published his first line in 1980 rather than in 1937, he might perhaps have taken advantage of the reconciliation achieved by the leaders of Egypt and Israel to advertise his works as an historical gift to the reconciliation. For the first time in 3400 years, some people were speaking well of the Egyptians. (It matters little in the rhetoric of religion or ethnicism that neither the Egyptians nor the Israeli of today are much like their namesakes of Exodus.)

THE LOVE CHILD

What strikes me about Freud's determination that Moses was an Egyptian was that he should not ask whether Moses might have been both Egyptian and Hebrew. This I attribute to Freud's own problem of identification.

On the one hand, Freud believed himself consciously to be a latter-day Moses, a point that will be explained in Chapter VI here below. On the other hand, Freud disbelieved strongly in ethnicism and wished time and time again that psychoanalysis become universal, rather than an isolated Jewish school of thought, to the point where he conceived of himself unconsciously as an assimilated gentile, a Christ-figure, whose teachings would become universalized. Freud's first act, when he arrived in Rome on a long-delayed trip, was to go view the heroic statue of Moses done by Michelangelo.

It was, I say, psychologically easier for Freud to claim that Moses was all-Egyptian than to think sociologically and psychologically of the obvious possibility that Moses was half-Egyptian and half-Jewish. "How much" easier can be measured by the frail, yet psychologically significant, rationalization that Freud gave of the two sides of Moses - the universal Egyptian and the tribal Yahwist - that there were two Moses, separated by a century or so, and brought together later to rationalize Hebrew history.

Who is rationalizing what? Freud was irrationally led to postulate two Moses, rather than descry a half-gentile, half-Hebrew Moses. In doing so, he was perhaps unconsciously admitting the two elements of Moses, asserting, also surprisingly covertly, that Moses was schizophrenic, and revealing that he, Freud, was ambivalent about the relations of gentiles and Jews. Needless to say, Freud brought down upon his head the wrath of all mosaists. With such controversy over Moses' origins, perhaps the fairest resolution would be to divide Moses in half Hebrew, half Egyptian. Let both mothers claim him, à la Solomon's judgement. Philo Judaeus says that when the princess saw the beautiful weaned child of three months, "she adopted him as her son, having first put in practice all sorts of contrivances to increase the apparent bulk of her belly, so that he might be looked upon as her own genuine child, and not as a suppositious one."[2] One might believe this - and take the ethnic position - or half believe it, seeing in it a denial that confesses: that is, the princess was pregnant with Moses. Then several problems are solved, quite apart from ending the argument.

Moses would be the son of a Hebrew official and an Egyptian princess (or, as the Moslems claim, the wife of the Pharaoh). Probably only such a love-child would have received the adoption and attention that Moses got. Hebrew women would understandably be his wet-nurse (his "mother") and baby-sitter (Miriam, daughter of the wet-nurse); Aaron, older brother of Miriam, would be a devoted admirer of the young gentleman from childhood. Thus we solve the relationship with Aaron and Miriam - no brother and sister, but possibly half-brother and half-sister through their father, or cousins by an uncle, with his step-mother or aunt his wet-nurse.

The Jewish legends, unlike the Bible, make a number of references to the Egyptianizing of the Hebrews, their abandonment of their old religion, their working against their own people and for the Egyptians, and, of course, the non-tribal "mixed-multitude" that joined in Moses' expedition into another world. In a curious legend, Yahweh blames Moses for the Revolt of the Golden Calf [3], saying that it was Moses who wanted to bring along the mixed multitude that wanted to join them... It is now these people, 'thy people', that have seduced Israel to idolatry. And Moses replies that, yes, "that it was chiefly my people, the mixed multitude, that was to blame for this sin..."

Exogamous marriage and concubinage, as well as incest, were common among Egyptian royalty. If recent American statistics are any indication, among the upper-middle classes the Hebrews might have achieved a rate of miscegenation of 15% or more. In more than one legend, the loss of Hebrew race through intermarriage is denounced, it might even be that "Levites" was a generic term for mixed Hebrew-Egyptians (see our index to the book), a thesis defensible both in theory and on the evidence. Jacob-Israel, in his last words, blesses the descendents of Simeon and Levi (perhaps similar in composition)[4] by calling them ruthless, violent people, saying: "I will divide them in Jacob and scatter them in Israel."[5] This puzzling passage might mean: they will live individually spread among the Egyptians in Egypt, and (as occurred) they will be disposed in gangs among all the tribes as an arm of the central Israelite nation. Moses would perforce acquire his combination of arrogant and schizoid traits, his large erudition, his familiarity with the ways of the Egyptian court, his immense ambition and quarrelsomeness, his ready promotion in the Egyptian hierarchy and introduction into both cosmopolitan and esoteric scientific circles. He would be cut off from the line of inheritance to the throne, which would rankle him and bring him enemies too, even those who feared that he would in any event become a threat. He would have an access to the Pharaohs that would otherwise be incredible.

But, beneath the veneer of his life and character, he would actively identify with the Hebrews. He would know them and understand them in a special detached way, particularly the assimilated leading Hebraic-Egyptian types among them. If and when the time came to switch roles, the ground would be prepared. His birth would be nicely managed by a myth typical of the birth of heroes. His infant attendants, or relatives, would become his "true" family - mother, Aaron, Miriam. His Egyptianized friends and supporters would become the Levites. His tongue-tied speech would have an additional psychosomatic source in his fear of his loss of identity (nor would I discard completely Freud's suggestion that be might not have spoken Hebrew perfectly, at least not idiomatically). The land of Midian where he was exiled and married was an ally of Egypt; it is mentioned that when the Exodus army came upon them, the Midianites had to make apologies for their faith in Egypt. Much later on, the Midianites fell victim to an Israelite attack. One can only wonder, in the end, why Moses has not been considered the offspring of a Hebrew and Egyptian love-affair. Certainly because the word of the Bible is sacred to many people. Also, the legend of a chosen people demands a full-blooded leader for their birth as a nation (despite history's frequent waiving of this rule). Moreover, the Judaic rule that descent as a Jew occurs through the mother, regardless of the father, contributes to ignoring the possibility. Judaic traditionalists are prone to frown upon miscegenation. (Apropos of this feeling, Senator Barry Goldwater once quipped at the peak of Egyptian-Israeli hostilities that he would be shot at from both sides of the Nile.) But Joseph married an Egyptian beauty, Asenath, daughter of the priest of On, by whom he had Ephraim and Manasseh, who were blessed by Jacob (Israel) and destined to be founders of tribes. And David's grandmother was Ruth, the Moabite...

According to the Bible, Moses was born of humble but good Hebrew parents at a moment when the king, advised by a prophecy that a newly born child would live to kill him, had issued a blanket order to kill all Hebrew babies. Indefinitely, says the Bible; for nine months only, says the legend [6], and all babies of Egypt. When the edict was publicized, legend reports, Moses' Hebrew father divorced his Hebrew mother to avoid having a child [7]. This, too, gives pause. Is there some implication of illegitimacy here? Perhaps.

Put in a rough basket and set afloat amidst the marshy sidewaters of the Nile, says the Bible, the infant Moses was found there by none other than a princess, daughter of the very same king. He was raised in secret by her, even was nursed by his real mother, hired unknowingly by the princess for the purpose. He grew up a prince, but somehow realized that he was a Hebrew. Not much can be made of this story at first, which Otto Rank, Joseph Campbell, and other scholars would agree is a typical birth of a hero in myth and legend. We gather from it that Moses was probably born in Egypt during an anti-Hebrew period, that he was related to Hebrews, and that he was related to a highly placed Egyptian woman who raised him in a princely fashion. Everything else seems questionable and in need of analysis and reassembly according to a new theory.

It is possible, too, that a general heavy pressure of population was occurring, and infanticide would be a policy, not unknown in many lands, to reduce the numbers of people, with expectable suspicions or actual overtones of

The Charisma of Moses

genocide among minorities. The Pharaoh mentions overpopulation as a reason for his edict. Whether it was decided to let the minorities pay the price, we cannot say; the Jewish legend says that it was a temporary moratorium on births for all people. Even birth control policies in America have been declared forms of infanticide and genocide by religious and racial minority leaders and writers. Egypt was a heavily regulated, bureaucratic state.

There is something to be made of Moses' name. It is clearly Egyptian, meaning "child" or "son" [8] and lacks the surname or prefix as, for example, in the pharaoh's name, Thoth-Moses, or "Child of the God, Thoth" (Mercury, Hermes). A variant theory says Moses means the "born one" in Egyptian, which is only a clumsy version of "child."

Buber says: "That Moses bears an Egyptian name, no matter whether it means 'born, child (of somebody)' or something like 'seed of the pond, of the water,' is part of the historical character of the situation; he seems to derive from a largely Egyptianized section of the people."[9] Some say the Hebrew etymology is "he who is drawn from" the Nile River, which is the popular Sunday School meaning, but Buber reverses this to mean "he who draws forth" the Hebrew people.

Otto Rank, citing Winckler, gives Moses as "the Water-Drawer." Psychoanalytic theory permits a reversal of meaning, so it becomes "he who is drawn from the water." Whatever route is taken one comes back to the profound simple meaning of "the water-born one." All children are born in the water of the womb. And legendary heroes are sometimes placed amidst water imagery at birth, as King Sargon of Assyria, who, like Moses, was a real person. The box or ark *(tebah)* of the infant Moses represents the womb of the mother.

Eduard Meyer, upon whom both Freud and Rank draw, says that "Presumably Moses was originally the son of the tyrant's daughter (who is now his foster mother) and probably of divine origin."[10]

A DISLIKING FOR HEBREWS

Moses would have known Goshen by passing through it on the way here or there but would have little familiarity with the Hebrew people. Legend has him meeting his first connections when grown up; then it was that he observed the complaints and hardship of the Hebrews; he used his court connections to help lighten their burdens, says the legend [11]. It is likely that his relatives there would bring him problems from time to time. When he returned from exile to lead the Hebrews, he was a delegate of Yahweh, not a Hebrew who had met with Yahweh for new instructions. Yahweh, not Moses, chose the Hebrews.

Moses was launched upon a splendid career. The best teachers were brought in to educate him [12]. He is said to have exercised military command, to have traveled outside Egypt, and to have been well-versed in the science of the times. It is said, too, in a legend, that he had originally an evil disposition, that he was "covetous, haughty, sensual"[13] (reminding me of Mahatma Gandhi as a young man before his great alteration of character) [14]. He cured himself of his vices by a strong will to change.

He seems to have submerged his original traits in a

kind of inhibition and reserve. He is not "a man of the people," a kindly father-figure, and seems to reject, for himself, the paternal role in regard to the "Children of Israel", giving this all over to Yahweh. Any love that he might have for the people of Israel, and indeed for everyone, including Aaron but with the possible exception of his devoted aide-de-camp Joshua [15], is suppressed; he scarcely permits himself to use Yahweh to express love for the people. In the Pentateuch, forms of the word "love" occur only 41 times, disproportionately in *Genesis* with 15. (see Table II) Yahweh's "love" for the people is mentioned seven times, Moses' love for the people not at all. The duty to love Yahweh receives 13 mentions, love among individuals 13, social love 5, and the love of pleasure and things 3 [16]. For every word of affection there are a dozen words of reproach, censure, adverse criticism, and dogmatic command. One would be naive to search in the Torah for any but the most feeble sources of the often-experienced warmth and graciousness of the Jews. Two notable exceptions - the happiness over the Golden Calf and the union with the people of Beth-Peor - end in horrifying slaughters.

Almost never does Moses indicate that the Israelites are his people, and usually, in speaking to Yahweh, he refers to "your people." When Moses heard all the families weeping about the lack of meat, and saw Yahweh getting angry, he exclaimed to him: "Why have you caused evil to your servant... in placing the load of all this people upon me? Have I myself conceived all this people? Is it I who have given them birth...?" In fact, Moses urges Yahweh out of motives of self-esteem not to exterminate Israel: what would other people think if, after all his public boasting and Moses'

advertising, Yahweh were to destroy his chosen people?
This would be Moses himself speaking; Moses would look the fool (to his imaginary and now mostly deceased Egyptian reference group) if this great adventure were to fail and the people killed or scattered. The projected conscience is often more juvenile than its possessor; so we need not think it odd that Moses, through Yahweh, should be so unsophisticated. At best, then, Moses and Yahweh are ambivalent about the Jews, both hating and loving them. A peculiar, stunted affection for them exists, growing feebly amidst the abuse. It takes sometime the form of a feeling of responsibility for them, having brought them out of Egypt.

They were characteristically suspicious of the people's loyalty and affections. Time after time they allege that these are only pretenses, shams. And they allow no excuses, insisting that the people willed their own defects and aberrations. This refusal to accept and receive affection is the paranoiac expression of ambivalence.

Part of this suspicion was warranted. A considerable proportion of the people did hate Moses and Yahweh. Moses knew this and said so. Yahweh directly accuses them of knowingly defying him and breaking their promises. Of course the people had good reason to hate Yahweh since the god was the cause of their worst disasters as well as their savior. Moses would be strongly interested in their hating other gods, that is, in displacing the people's hostilities upon Baal and other heavenly gods, and in trying to suppress the destructive side of the great comet. Baal later became the devil figure, Lucifer, who was the "Light-bearer" in Latin (or "Phosphorus," and the word for the planet Venus in Greek). The process of displacement did not work perfectly.

Unconsciously many people hated Yahweh as well as or instead of Baal and certainly hated Moses, while Moses and Yahweh did not even try to divide and transform their ambivalence toward the people.

The love that is behind Jesus' feeling of atonement for the sins of humanity is not present in Moses and therefore the doctrine itself is largely absent. But Daiches goes too far when he writes that "the concept of vicarious atonement was quite foreign to Mosaic thought."[17] He adds, rightly, that Moses was a "mediator and intercessor" and that sins were forgiven even of all Israel for the sake of their great ancestors. (This latter atonement in reverse being also a way of getting them to focus favorably upon a line of national history.)

However, Moses based the authority of the Levites upon vicarious atonement. By taking on onerous sacred tasks, they relieved all Jews of the duty to sacrifice their first-born children and beasts to Yahweh [18]. Further there was the custom of the scapegoat. Annually the goat conveyed the load of Jewish sins away into the desert to the demon Azazel [19].

Following upon the worship of the Golden Calf, Moses himself is on the brink of atoning for Israel's crime, but lets Yahweh pull him back into his typical egotism. For he declares to the people: "you have sinned a great sin. And now I will go up to the Lord; perhaps I can make atonement for your sin."[20] Then to Yahweh he says: "If thou wilt, forgive their sin - and if not, blot me, I pray thee, out of thy book..." Yahweh refuses and lets Israel live as a personal favor to Moses [21].

THE MEEK KILLER

Machiavelli commented once: "Whoever reads the Bible sensibly will see that Moses, in order to push through his laws and orders, was compelled to kill an infinity of men who were guilty of nothing but opposing his designs."[22] Time after time, Moses imposes rules and hardship upon others in the name of Yahweh. His famous meekness, which the Bible stresses and his biographers claim to find is in psychological terms the "meekness" of an inhibited rage type, who cannot trust his deep passions to public display. He insists, in effect, that he cannot help himself, that he is executing the will of Yahweh, like the foreman who explains to his workers: "I'll see what I can do, but you know how things are up there. I can't do much about it." Such is his "meekness."

André Neher recalls that "one searches vainly in the Books of Moses for the exposition of a doctrine or theology." Moses "had no need of dreams, trances, quackery, ecstasies, but spoke with God man-to-man."[23] His was a down-to-earth religion. He was a cold, careful, bold manager of schemes and driver of men.

There is pressure by Miriam and others to begin a line of hereditary seers [24]. He rejects them. He is hardly ever called a prophet; the word is far too limited for him. Moses is called by Yahweh only three times: from the Burning Bush, from the Holy Mountain and then at the Tabernacle where Yahweh instructs him how sacrifices shall be done [25]. He is moderate, too, in hallucinating; he does so almost always in private and restricted circumstances. He does not prophesy hysterically.

The Charisma of Moses

His only outburst occurs when, returning triumphant from the Holy Mountain, he comes upon the Golden Calf worshippers, whereupon he dashes the sacred tablets of Yahweh upon the ground. The frequent violence that bears his imprimatur is phrased in divine rhetoric and impersonally ordered and executed. His murder of an Egyptian work-boss has a surprising explanation.

After this killing, Moses goes into exile. He has been betrayed to the government by two Hebrews (brothers, says a legend) who were fighting. These workmen know of the secret murder of the Egyptian, who had been beating a Hebrew, and when Moses, now perhaps 30 years old, intercedes between them and admonishes the assailant, this person replies in words typical of lower class insolence to an upper-class member of their minority group: "Who made you a prince and a judge over us? Do you mean to kill me as you killed the Egyptian?"

Moses was startled because he had "looked this way and that, and seeing no one he killed the Egyptian and hid him in the sand."[26] One wonders how they learned the secret, by the next day, too, unless they were working for or near Moses; and then how did Moses kill the foreman? Legend says be killed him not by violence, but by uttering the secret name of god [27]. We know that this word is the treasure of the Ark of the Covenant. It is the equivalent of the word YHWH.

Was the Hebrew who was being abused by the supervisor a Levite or helper of Moses? And did Moses electrocute the supervisor on one of his dangerous experimental contraptions? Ordinarily, in a highly stratified society, a highly placed person will not demean himself by physically fighting a member of a lower stratum, but will have the job done for him by the man's equals. Were the Hebrew accusers other workmen in the same establishment, who had perhaps helped Moses bury the body? A body is heavy and not easy to dispose of, nor would a prince dirty his hands with a body.

If my guess were correct, it would explain why a princely official could expect to be haled before the highest authority, and why he would in person or in absentia be condemned to exile. The enemies of Moses in the pyramid priest-science establishment would be awaiting such an occasion to demand the punishment of this rash and controversial man.

Philo Judaeus is close to arguing in this vein. Pharaoh punished Moses, not for killing the foreman but for siding with those perceived to be enemies of the Pharaoh. "When the Egyptian authorities had once got an opportunity of attacking the young man, having already reason for looking upon him with suspicion..., they even implanted in his (Pharaoh's] mind an apprehension that Moses was plotting to deprive him of his kingdom." They told Pharaoh, "He will strip you of your crown. He has no humble designs or notions."[28]

THE COURTLY SHEPHERD

Next we come upon Moses in exile among the Midianites. "In his general appearance and clothing he looks like an Egyptian."[29] Buber, too, comments on his "court dress" when he first appears at the water well in Midian.

The Charisma of Moses 211

At the well, the daughters of a priest-shepherd named Jethro, who came early to water their flock, are being pushed away (molested and sexually attacked, says the prurient legend)[30] by several rough shepherds. He must have been impressive, this stranger, to browbeat the local roughnecks. Upper-class Egyptian dress was known, most likely, and Egyptian authority was not far out of mind. Moses must have been generally well-equipped to appear so well turned out several days' journey from Memphis.

He rescues the damsels, and is presented to their father and referred to by him as "the Egyptian" who helped them so. "Egyptian?" goes the legend; that is why the Lord kept Moses from entering the Promised Land: Moses should have insisted immediately that he was Hebrew, not Egyptian [31].

Moses bought a flock, or tended the livestock of Jethro. He was a careful and methodical shepherd, the legend goes. And he fathered two boys by Zipporah, daughter of Jethro. His mind was on natural events and the court of Egypt; his ambitions raged within him. He explored the area, for the site where he came upon the Burning Bush was removed from his pastures.

Besides his trained and self-developed scientific acumen about things electric, he may have been one of those unusual persons who are hypersensitive to static electricity [32]. He would become the world's most famous dowser, finding water miraculously in the desert [33]. No student, to my knowledge, has yet graded a sample of people by test as to their electromagnetic fields which can be measured by vacuum-tube voltmeters and vary in intensity from 15 to 20 millivolts, depending upon emotional states and certainly upon hereditary or bred differences [34].

The famous "Burning Bush" was a "thornbush," its spikes pointed to heaven. (See Figure 17) It was speaking with the sounds of electricity and releasing fire without being consumed. Moses knew better than any man what this meant. His imagination began to work rapidly. He took off his shoes to help ground any electrical contact and examined the bush closely. He touched his staff to the active area and it jumped like a snake. A phosphorus dew whitened his hand and he wiped it off.

A surge of excitement might have overwhelmed him. He is said to have had a revelation that a great god was addressing him from out of the bush. The bush suddenly symbolized all that he wanted to be and would be. The portents of heaven were in the sound and flames. They culminated in the Burning Bush experience: Moses who had been watching carefully for changes in the sky, would tell of this experience when asked:

"When did your visions come together in you for the first time?"

He explained his prophetic revelation to Jethro: the new presence of the great god in the world, the fitting of this god to the aspirations and religion of a discontented Hebrew people. He sent a message to the priest Aaron (Yahweh had assured him that Aaron would come to meet him) and when the reply was received and was favorable, he was ready to return to Egypt. He departed with his family [35].

The Charisma of Moses 213

Figure 17. The Burning Bush.

CIRCUMCISION AND SPEECH PROBLEMS

An episode occurs on the way to Egypt that surprises and puzzles many students. Yahweh tries to kill his own representative on Earth. Some say by lightning, others by Satan, in serpent form, swallowing him. Moses simply cannot keep away from electricity in one form or another.

> At a lodging place on the way, the Lord met him and sought to kill him. Then Zipporah [his wife] took a flint and cut off her son's foreskin, and touched Moses' feet with it and said, "Surely you are a bridegroom to me." So he let him alone. Then it was

that she said, "You are a bridegroom of blood, because of the circumcision."

No more is written [36].

There is a question of pronouns here. Some say that Moses must have been already circumcised and all the pronouns refer to his son, making even "Moses' feet" "his" (the son's). Others say that Yahweh was trying to kill Moses because he had still not attended to his own circumcision. That is, lacking a proper scientific hypothesis, they make of Yahweh's action something arbitrary.

The Editors of the *Oxford Bible* become avant-garde and write in a footnote: "Feet, a euphemism for the sexual organs (Is. 7:20)." Isaiah does support this interpretation, speaking there of a razor shaving the head and "the hair of the feet." I would agree with this view.

It is surprising that Freud, who certainly knew of this psychoanalytic principle, if indeed he were not its discoverer, makes no mention of it in his *Moses and Monotheism*. Can it be that this great objective mind was too fixated upon his idea that Moses imposed circumcision upon the Jews to notice who was circumcising whom? Freud further ignores the son and has Moses being circumcised explicitly; but he says the story is false and that Moses must have been circumcised since he was Egyptian, a kind of *petitio principiis* that is not otherwise absent from Freud's book. Buber has Zipporah both circumcising the boy and touching the boy's legs. Daiches suggests that Yahweh was aiming his bolt at Zipporah and the boy.

Were the Hebrews circumcised at this time or not? Freud says no: the Sumerians, Semites, and Babylonians were

The Charisma of Moses

not; but the Egyptians generally were [37]. Hence another proof that Moses was an Egyptian and wanted his Israelites to do the same. But then why, if he were an Egyptian, would he not have long before been circumcised?

The situation seems totally confused, and I could make the situation worse by asking how Zipporah, a Midianite, happened to be expert with the flint and incantation? Or why did not Moses do the job himself? If Moses were a Hebrew or an Egyptian he would have been circumcised at one time or another. How could he expect to lead a circumcised people if he were not circumcised himself, and even demand their circumcision before admittance to full membership in the new nation?

I go into the matter because it may bear upon Moses' character. If Moses is part Hebrew and part Egyptian, and assimilated almost completely to Egyptian thought and ways, and his Levitic friends are almost all circumcised in the Egyptian mode, then he is under cross-pressures. But perhaps he has always been too proud to let himself be circumcised as a concession to Egyptianization. And by "proud" I mean "regards it as a threat to himself" and perhaps in this was defended by his freethinking Egyptian mother: "No part of my precious boy will be taken away." And there is no patriarchal father to put the boy in his place by circumcision.

At the same time, Moses has become in character extremely authoritarian and patriarchal. Thinking of himself as his own remote father plus the father who has rejected him, the Pharaoh, Moses projects all of his patriarchalism onto his god Yahweh, who becomes a most arbitrary and autocratic father, carrying all of Moses' subjective passion into the role, and letting Moses loose upon the world in his name.

Now Moses, the uncircumcised, becomes Moses, the all-powerful father, in favor of the circumcision of others. Here he may be supported by Levitical-Egyptian scientific opinion. It is the modern argument on behalf of the practice. The Levites and Moses were of a character to believe in health practices; it is only because of the modern tendency (certainly not of many younger scholars, though) to think of ancient thought forms as primitive and incapable of pragmatic behavior, that the idea of a "health practice" as opposed to a ritual is usually ignored. I would surmise that Moses believed the Egyptian practice sane and civilized so that "rational" as well as "unconscious" motives spurred him in his campaign for circumcision.

Again cross-pressures, if Moses were not circumcised himself. But profound and sincere hypocrisy is of the essence of the charismatic leader: Do as I say, not as I do; furthermore, I am symbolically circumcised before Yahweh himself, simply one more of the miracles that set me off from ordinary men. Joshua (5:1-9), beyond the Jordan, calls for the total population to be circumcised. Evidently, the practice had fallen into desuetude, implying either that all or some of those born in the desert had not been circumcised. Whether this had grown out of Moses' inability to exercise control over the many new adherents to Israel gathered up along the way, or whether a second mass circumcision of confirmation of unity and dedication to Yahweh was here performed is debated; probably both are true.

Moses has a speech defect. He is slow of speech and tongue [38]. The words do not come out. The legendary story of how Moses became thick of tongue is an excellent example of how myth speaks truth even when highly improbable. Moses was only three years old at the time and was sitting with his mother the Princess Bitriah, daughter of Pharaoh, at a dinner party. Moses took the crown from off the king's head and placed it upon his own head. The group was astounded and Balaam, son of Beor, reminded the Pharaoh how troublesome and clever the Hebrews could be and suggested killing him. Pharaoh called for advice, however, from wise men and so came Angel Gabriel in disguise. Let the boy choose between a coal of fire and an onyx stone. If he chooses the gem, slay him, but if he chooses the coal, he shall be judged a simple little child. Moses was forced by Gabriel to seize the live coal, and because he thrust his burnt hand into his mouth and burnt his lips and tongue, he became slow of speech and tongue.

Legend here expresses Moses' mind, I think. Possessed of great ambitions, Moses "burned his lips and tongue" psychologically so as not to confess them. One is reminded of a kind of common saying: "She bit her lip to keep from exclaiming in protest..." An alternate common expression, at least in Germanic culture, can occur when a person blurts out words that she instantly regrets: "Oh, I've burned my tongue." It is pertinent here as well to point out how frequently schizophrenics develop speech patterns of an odd, disjointed, fragmented, and irrational kind.

When he explains his lame speech to Yahweh at the Burning Bush to avoid going on his mission to liberate Israel, he is told that Yahweh will tell him what to say and Moses can put the words into the mouth of the eloquent Aaron who is coming to meet him.

In two further incidents, he is depressed and tells Yahweh that he cannot persuade the reluctant Hebrews nor the Pharaoh of what Yahweh wishes, because he is "a man of uncircumcised lips." And, again: "I am of uncircumcised lips." Yahweh dismisses him the first time and on the second occasion again says he needs only Aaron to speak for him. Yahweh then adds, significantly: "See, I make you as God to Pharaoh; and Aaron your brother shall be your prophet."[39] This metaphorical expression is not used again, for it does make Moses his two fathers - Yahweh and Pharaoh. It reveals for an instant the otherwise suppressed wish of Moses. In any event, the first metaphor is a transference from the genital region to the oral one, and vice versa.

Moses cannot get his words out for reasons also bearing upon sexuality. Jewish legend has it that at the same encounter by the Burning Bush, Yahweh instructs Moses to forego hereafter the pleasures of the marriage bed; two children are enough; he is now to be wedded to the female holy ghost, uniting with "the Shekinah, that she might descend to earth for his sake."[40]

But this is post-climactic in Moses' life. He has long been mumbling in an attempt to control his fierce resentments against the father who was not and the father who exiled him. (The pharaoh who exiled him was, besides the great father figure of political authority, his mother's father and, given the incestuous customs of the Egyptian royalty, perhaps his mother's spouse or lover and therefore his "father.")

I would therefore ascribe Moses' incoherent speech to his inhibited rage, a rage reaching the magnificent heights which only the most ambitious achieve [41]. "He repressed

The Charisma of Moses 219

all the principal impulses and most violent affections of the Soul..."[42] And the connection of his speech with his genital integrity - verbally as well as in fact - is psychologically and physiologically strong. From this powerful foundation in the unconscious, it is therefore possible to conclude, first, that Moses was never circumcised, that he seized upon a symbolic circumcision before Yahweh himself as adequate for his own conscience and to appease others, that his wife and son were apt tools for the purpose, that he could insist that all Israelites, as Yahweh's children, must do their duty by their father and be circumcised.

Moses neglected his wife sexually and was reproached by Miriam, one legend states [43]. Philo Judaeus wrote: "He never provided his stomach with any luxuries beyond those necessary tributes which nature has appointed to be paid to it, and as to the pleasures of the organs below the stomach he paid no attention to them at all except as far as the object of having legitimate children was concerned."[44] He scarcely neglected legislating on the subject. If the fulsome detailing of sexual taboos in the Pentateuch is more the product of unoccupied priestly successors and purist prophets than of Moses himself, he designed its framework. It is nothing new: the striving for absolute power and authority go along often with sexual impotency, or uninterest. Moses in de-imaging Yahweh did a more conscientious job in the sexual realm than in all other parts of the anatomy. The de-sexing of Yahweh may have been part of the motive for de-imaging him, in fact, rather than the reverse.

Every movement, whether political or religious, that has since been tinged with mosaism has stressed sexual repression. Aside from outright prohibitions in most life circumstances, there has occurred an infinity of regulations on the management of the sexual organs, making of Yahweh a gynecologist as well as an expert butcher.

Z. Rix and Peter Tompkins have traced some cometary sources for this painstaking religious interest in sex [45], and argue cogently that, when the comet lost its tail, whether it was cut off, struck off, or bit off, a fine precedent for all manner of sex neuroticism presented itself to human view. Hardly a glimpse of this enters the Bible of course; largely the effects occur without treating of the underlying causes, whether in Moses or in the great comet.

The lightning bolt, or serpent Satan, or nightmare inspired Moses to think, and to think meant for him to act upon some major problem. Since those who speak of a close escape from death infer a divine presence, Moses had to put his mind upon Yahweh. Here was his immense new revelation of a father "not trusting Moses," say the commentators. No; conversely, Moses was not trusting the father. Not yet. But in the decision to circumcise himself symbolically and to lead a group united by circumcision, be could gain one more measure of control of the father. He could accept and please his close followers, the Levites. He could preserve his own bodily integrity and possess the female Holy Ghost. Thus, three items of the Old Testament carry a profound illumination of Moses - the Burning Bush, the assault by Yahweh, and the case of the tongue-tied prophet.

More is to be made of Moses' speech problem; it has to do with the character of Yahweh, which is treated later on. The reader will probably guess correctly that a man with a

The Charisma of Moses

speech defect will prefer an ideal without one. Even better than this, a man with a speech defect will invent a model whose speech defect will be, not a source of humiliation, but a divine gibberish to which all must bow down, on pain of death, and who speaks to him alone so that he, who cannot be well understood, is the only one in the whole world capable of understanding all that is spoken by this other unintelligible being. Thus he punishes those who would not understand him, by the act of interpreting another voice for them.

SCIENTIST AND INVENTOR

Most of the scientific and inventive genius of Moses is shrouded in a general misunderstanding of the biblical language of fire, spirit, and the Ark. Much is short-circuited by the interjection of Yahweh in all affairs. Still, enough emerged even in early times to create a legend of Moses as a scientist.

Philo Judaeus wrote of his intellectual precocity [46]. A composite portrait can be drawn from the Pagan writers of Greece and Rome [47]. Moses was an Egyptian who invented sun dials for solar worship in place of obelisks. He was learned, a great magician. He was the best of alchemists, a copious writer, and was called Thoth-Moses by the Egyptians. The legend of Pythagoras influenced the writing of the life of Moses during the late Alexandrian times, writes Buber [48]. Another source relates that in the same general period, in a fashion then typical, Jewish legends grew up asserting "that Moses, blithely identified both with the semi-mythical poet Musaeus and with the Egyptian Thoth, had been the teacher of Orphaeus.. and the inventor of navigation, architecture, and the hieroglyphic script."[49] As the French say: "One lends only to the rich..."

We have already presented enough evidence (and there will be more) to show that Moses was a master of electrical science. Until it should be proven that the Egyptians possessed the Ark, that great technology must be credited to Moses in Israel. His altar does not stand out technically from the other altars of the priests of the high places [50]. The age of the Delphic altar technology is uncertain. It may well go back to Mosaic times. Here again, we await archaeological and mythological studies that are illuminated by appropriate hypotheses. We will question later how the god Thoth (Hermes) and Moses were connected.

There is an old tradition both flattering and uncomplimentary, that pictures Moses as a magician, a sorcerer, a medicine man, and a seer. From the presumptuous modern perspective, these words are insults and invitations to disputation. I see no reason for defining and distinguishing them, and fitting them well or illy to Moses.

Buber barely skirts the "our boy is no magician" attitude, yet we can quote him here as showing that Moses was a better magician, ergo a better scientist, than others, and I have argued earlier that Moses was tolerated up to the last plague precisely because the Egyptian court knew and respected his science, going back many years. Discussing the plague of frogs, Buber is moved to say: "That he has... foretold the incident, and unlike the usual magicians, has done so without any magical conjurations... and that he further knows how to interpret the signs of the incident; these facts have a somewhat weird atmosphere not inviting any too close contact. The unwieldy words, with which a strange God jerkily moves his throat, only serve to enhance the weirdness."[51] If correct prediction is the test of a scientist, then, never mind the sorcery, augury, conjuration or magic; Moses is a distinguished scientist.

Moses himself is at the same time interpreted as one who banishes magic, augury, and divination. But, even when we discover that science underlays the Ark, we must grant that the Ark is intended for augury and divination. No one except Moses can go to the Holy of Holies for oracles, but he does so himself. Judgement is rendered upon Korah and his band of rebels by seeking signs from Yahweh, and so on. One man's science is another man's magic. Our position here is that Moses exceeded by far the then normal ratio of science to non-science in a large realm of practices having to do with discovery, instrumentation, application, and foresight.

Moses' alleged detestation of the non-sciences is part fact (granted he was more of a scientist) and quite expected. His suppression of non-science is part of his desire to suppress science as well, for he did not want more than one Ark, nor more than one "research center," for reasons of political control. Nor did he want people to engage in practices, which, quite apart from their scientific validity, would make of them independent leaders in prophecy, ceremony, or combat. Yahwism was to be a central rule interpreted by priests after Moses and enforced by the security police. Free science was believed to be inimical to religion and good government.

We have already dealt with Moses' competence in the field of radiation diseases, phosphorus, and manna. According to legend [52], Moses claimed to know "how leprosy arises and how it disappears." He certainly knew in Miriam's case and could be sure that seven days outside the camp was enough to heal her "leprosy" or phosphorus burns. We should also remind ourselves of Moses' Brazen Serpent, probably his final perfected instrument of the type of the rod. Used in conjunction with the Ark, it found a place therein, and was exhibited for a long period as a healing caduceus on its own account until it was destroyed. The contraption could by itself act as an electrical sparker, and it is conceivable that it was used both for charismatic (psychosomatic) therapy and for electroshock therapy.

Moses was not an astrologer (except in the sense that any astronomer whose ideas are mistaken or outmoded is an astrologer). On the contrary, his preoccupation was earthly, and he hated astrological science. This probably stems from his controversies with the Egyptian "pyramid scientists" and his perceived "persecution" by them.

In *Deuteronomy* [53] he warns the Jews against worshipping the heavenly bodies, condemning to death by stoning any man or woman who is proven to have "gone and served other gods and worshipped them, or the sun, or the moon or any of the host of heaven..." But there is no question of his meteorological interests and competence; he is a master of atmospheric and electrical arts.

Why did he not expand Yahwism to take in the heavenly movements? The answer is fairly plain: there is too much fatalism, too little drive, permitted in the fascination with celestial bodies; further, other religions were performing

The Charisma of Moses

astrological services as effectively as the Jews with their scant resources might, and hence people would hear the fatal call of Egypt and Babylon. Again the problem of control. Precisely during Moses' tenure, also, the skies were usually clouded and dusted over; it was a poor period for astronomical observation. Finally, a sedentary observatory would be needed for star studies; this a wandering nation could not provide.

In Jewish tradition we hear that a new calendar was divinely ordained to begin in the month of Nisan, with the Passover to be celebrated on the 15th of Nisan, "but the computations for the calendar were so involved that Moses could not understand them until God showed him the movements of the moon plainly."[54] God ordered a court to be set up to attest to each new moon. Apparently there was some change in lunar, solar, and Earth apparent motions, together with an intervening cloudiness. New calendars were required.

One of Velikovsky's surprising hypotheses was that the 365 day year did not exist before Exodus, and that before Exodus the year was of only 360 days. He denied that available evidence supported such beliefs. He cites hints that the new Hyksos rulers introduced the 360-day year in Egypt and that while the Jews were in Egypt, 210 modern years passed, although 400 revolutions of the sun occurred [55]. Here I confine myself to the indication of mosaic calendar change, and to a second suggestion namely, that the year's length before Exodus may have been 260 days. This was the sacred year of the Mayans tenaciously adhered to by these great ancient American calendrists for long after they designed and employed a new calendar [56].

Evidence of Mayan-Egyptian interconnections is not absent, but the problem is too complex and controversial to treat briefly. Suffice it to suggest that the 260-day year would give Moses an age at death of 85, instead of 120, 360-day years, and other time counts of the several centuries before Moses would also make more sense. I fear however that the temporal confusion is so great that no easy formula will ever deal with all instances.

Perhaps the most enduring of Moses' scientific contributions has to do with the beginnings of popular records and historiography. Hardly had the Israelites left Egypt when Yahweh said to Moses: "Write this as a memorial in a book and recite it in the ears of Joshua..."[57] it being a curse upon the Amalekites. In another surprising sentence of *Exodus,* Yahweh declares: "Whoever has sinned against me, him will I blot out of My book."[58] History and anti-history: god as a writer and bookkeeper! Had this ever happened before? What faith in the record! Yahweh was supposed actually to have written the first set of tablets of the Decalogue. They were written with "the finger of Yahweh." When Moses broke them, he had to repair back to the Holy Mountain, like a dutiful schoolboy, with a new set of writing materials.

Moses made the Jews "the People of the Book." From then on, they were literate and regardful of the written word. That Moses was quite literate surprises no one, yet it should. Probably only scribes then wrote, and the priest scientists of Egypt. Neither common man nor noble would be able to write, one more indication that Moses had been more than a prince in Egypt.

Some scholars and an old tradition credit Moses with

The Charisma of Moses

inventing the alphabet [59]. The alphabet that matches sounds with signs, as contrasted with communicating written meaning by pictures and constructions, is accredited to a North Semitic person and group of the same mid-second millennium of which we are speaking in this book. We know, too, that the Israelites were a people forged - in a strict sense of integration of diverse elements - in anticipation of, and amidst catastrophe. They established their continuity precisely in the period between the Middle and Late Bronze Ages when other peoples that we know about were experiencing a rending asunder of their cultural continuity. Therefore, more rapidly than others, the Israelites might have captured the peak development of the Middle Bronze Age and applied it under the new conditions of the Late Bronze Age.

At the time of Exodus, Israelites knew probably three kinds of script, the Egyptian hieroglyphic, the Babylonian cuneiform, and a popular script. Ernst Sellin called it "a popular alphabetic writing." He says: "The only piece of evidence that goes to suggest that Israel may have been acquainted with it as early as the Mosaic period is that the Mosaic oracular symbols, the Urim and the Thummim, appear to be not unconnected with the first and last letters of this alphabet... but it would be perfectly possible that Moses might have taken it over from the Kenites. Cf. I *Chron.* 2:55. This alphabet made it possible to express everything with exactitude in the national idiom, which was not possible with the cuneiform.."[60] Sixty years after Sellin's remarks, Barry Page, employing the revised chronology used here for Egyptian history, can conclude:

> The initiation of a 'developed' linear alphabetic script in Canaan occurs after the conquest and occupation of Israel by Joshua, and one is strongly tempted to suggest that Israelite scribes brought a developed linear alphabetic system with them from Egypt to Canaan [61].

Moses is of the right time, the right place, and the right race(s). He has, too, a thorough education and literacy; he knows how to work with symbols. He has the explosive ingenuity as a person, and what is crucial, he exercises the necessary social control over his people; for an alphabet is a communication technology; it must be imparted with coercive sanctions or high voluntary motivation. With the adjustment of dates so that the Hyksos invasion of Egypt coincides with the Hebrew emigration from Egypt, the thought that the Hyksos may have carried an alphabet into Egypt is lamed by the fact that they did not impose the alphabet upon the Egyptians. There were many movements of tribes and peoples now, but was there any people whose particular situation was equally congenial to the invention? Several theories of Ugaritic and other origins must go by the way, because, by the chronology we are using, their alphabetic usage must be moved to a later period and the Israelite presence placed ahead of it.

Nor have we finished with the circumstantial evidence pointing toward Moses. The tongue-tied genius was inherently interested in sounds. He is, we know, also interested in communicating - both because he is a distant type of character and because he is embarrassed at his speech - through agents (Aaron, yes) as well as written messages. Further, he was the originator of the idea that Yahweh speaks his own name; Yahweh can be pronounced like a

The Charisma of Moses

string of phonetics proceeding from an electrical discharge of the Ark. If one imitates the various hums of live wires and St. Elmo's fires, one can imagine the name of Yahweh continuously repeated. If this name is written down as in the First Commandment of the Decalogue, it is a phonetic name, perhaps the very first.

But Moses is still adding to his points as inventor of the alphabet. He carries the Decalogue down from Mount Sinai on two tablets. Could he do so if they were written in hieroglyphs?

A scholar complains that the Decalogue could not be compressed into two tablets. But it could if it were Moses writing in the abbreviated and new script. Of course, one cannot prove that Moses was the principal effective inventor of the alphabet, but, on the evidence, he may be acknowledged as the leading contender for the honor with regard to the Near East.

With all this, I have hardly begun with the inventions of Moses. Bearing in mind that no invention comes without a build-up of antecedents and precedents and that Moses, as hero, even autobiographer, of the Pentateuch, will be credited for some discoveries not of his own making, still the total is astonishingly great. I shall adduce here briefly five sets of inventions, amounting to fourteen important individual inventions in all, that are in addition to the inventions of the Ark, the calendar, historiography, the alphabet and several others hitherto described.

The first set is national: Moses invented the idea of a new nation, the concept of Israel, and the plan for it to come into existence - the Passover and Exodus. Surely there was insurrectionism in Egypt and among the Hebrews; surely the name of Israel-Jacob was known as a grand patriarch of old; surely there was a plethora of desires and schemes to win independence or set up a colony somewhere; perhaps a vague notion of the Promised Land existed. But Moses alone, so far we can tell, confirmed that all of these things could be planned and carried out, and he directed the operations. That he met with a response adequate to the occasion, and could rally the people and find the resources, that he could evade a crushing preemptive suppression were effects of his workable scheme. The outcome was the republican confederation of Israel.

A second set of Mosaic inventions is religious: the new Covenant of Yahweh with Israel which he "negotiated;" the idea of a Constitution of morality: the Decalogue of Commandments; and the Code of Laws [62]. Of these, the Decalogue is outstanding, both as to form and to contents. Let me abbreviate these commandments of Yahweh [63]:

> 1. I am your god-ruler. 2. Do not experiment with other gods. 3. Do not employ me needlessly. 4. Rest from labor to celebrate my being. 5. Respect your parents. 6. Do not kill amongst yourselves. 7. Confine sex to your spouse. 8. Do not steal. 9. Do not slander. 10. Do not covet.

The first four are intended to protect Yahweh. The six that follow are for the protection of the community. All are designed for the circumstances of life then and there. They are designed for people moving among disasters and disorganization. That they have been considered to be for all time and have been proclaimed as eternal simply proves that mankind has been forever in a state of disaster and disorganization, one step, two steps, but ever hardly more, from the Israelites in the desert.

They are almost entirely negative, a criminal code, rather than positive, and punishment for their violation is intended to be heavy. To contemplate god; to sympathize with the gods of other people; to wish divine help for all who need it; to enjoy one's rest from labor; to love and respect one's parents in the measure of your maturity and their worth; to respect human life everywhere; to give a full measure of intimate love; to guard the possessions of others as your own; to be benevolent and generous to others; to wish all people well: these are hardly suggested in the Decalogue, nor are many other positive virtues. The Decalogue is a hard-hitting, explicit set of solutions for survival, brilliantly conceived and promulgated by Moses (though almost frustrated by the preemptive apostasy of the Golden Calf).

Even with this explanation, modern exegesis has presented a hurdle to believing that this Ethical Dialogue is of Moses. Winnett [64] assigns the Ritual Decalogue [65] to the times of Moses and the Ethical one much later, to others. Judging its linguistics, it is, he argues, of a more cultivated age. The question can hardly be solved by stylistic considerations, inasmuch as, throughout the history of the Old Testament, we have a condition prevailing whereby, alongside what has found its way into writing, there runs an oral tradition that has not been written down and a problem of lost written pieces that had later to be recomposed.

Moreover, the Ritual Decalogue is heavily agricultural. It contains instructions on how to make an altar, to sacrifice, and to cultivate; on attending to Yahweh's words but to mention no other god; it defines the Sabbath and feast days, and prescribes dietary practices.

If my analysis is correct, Moses was quite able, and indeed more likely, to have produced the Ethical than the Ritual Decalogue. The catastrophe of Exodus would not have destroyed Moses' cultivated and managerial mind nor those of the elders. The Ethical Decalogue would have been the more useful one in the wanderings. The Ritual or Cultic Decalogue would have emerged as a product of post-mosaic times, when the culture of the leaders would have slumped for several centuries.

The third set of Mosaic inventions treats of anniversaries and history; the change of the Sabbatical Year (from, I should say, a Saturnian-Elohist baseline to a Jovian-Yahwist baseline); an intense revival of the Sabbath day with the purpose of serving Yahweh; the possible inculcation of the second creation myth, that of Adam and Eve (which again I attribute to Jovian Yahwism), to follow the Saturnian-Elohim creation myth of Genesis. These are innovations, rather than heavy inventions. The Yahwist creation myth, like Mosaism in general, is sin-obsessed, punitive, and vengeful. It tells of an age of fire rather than water. It must have come into existence thousands of years later than the Elohim myth of creation.

The fourth set of inventions, more important here, deals with social organization. Moses created a new organization of twelve tribes that he called Israel, counted the people by tribes, and had them organized by tribes and by military units within tribes. The military units were based upon the decimal system, not upon families or clans. At the same time, he created a separation of powers between the priesthood and the security police (Levites), and defined their

The Charisma of Moses 233

functions; these men he placed over all the tribes, and then created an apparatus of state: the Ark, centralized worship, the Tabernacle; and provided (at the instigation of his father-in-law Jethro) a means of instituting complaints and pleas in the tribes and carrying the more important cases before Moses himself.

Finally, there is the religion itself: Yahweh and Yahwism as an integrated religion. The Elohist tradition "quite unambiguously states that Yahweh was a newly received god for the Israelite war confederacy received through Moses" [66]. So far as we can tell, Moses invented the name "Yahweh." Merely to imagine that this is possible is amazing. The Egyptians had not heard of the name, nor probably had the Hebrews. Both groups used Elohim until Moses brought Yahweh from his exile. Later on, this point will be argued further.

Although I believe that I have proven Yahweh to be in one sense an electrical engineering system, in the broad sense Yahweh stands for an integrated social system, a religion replete with a tradition in *Genesis,* a priesthood, a mobile cathedral, and a host of ordinances. This last achievement of Moses may also be considered as the invention of an integrated system of law related, of course, to the Decalogue. Thus Moses belongs with Confucius, Buddha, Jesus and Mohammed as an inventor of religion. There can be no question but that mosaism was as far from Elohimism as from Christianity and that these two latter manifestations may be closer to each other than to mosaism.

TALKING WITH GODS

Among the many thousands of Israel, there must have been a hundred who talked with god, the holy spirit, or angels - some once, some many times, some with every authentic sign, others lacking all substantiation. No one but Moses talked with god authoritatively: there is the difference. One has to earn the right to be believed to talk with god. Moses had every right to do so. Practically everybody admitted this; and almost all thought it fitting and proper that, as the Pharaoh of Egypt was himself a god, so the leader of the Hebrews might bear the Lord upon him like a crown.

When one claims to be talking to supernatural super-powerful beings one is "talking with gods." Such behavior is not at all uncommon and is engaged in sometimes by most contemporary people. One "prays to god" and god "answers one's prayers." In cases of disaster, such behaviors are normal. About ten percent of a western population in non-catastrophic times experience visual or auditory hallucinations, or both.[67] Many of these talk to the "other." When there is great physical and nervous stress and difficult decisions must be made, tendencies to hallucinate increase sharply. The environment, then afterwards the person, is deranged. Thus, a Dutchwoman on Java, when Krakatoa is exploding, flees in terror and arrives in complete distress and agony among people, where she hears her own voice as someone else talking [68]. An "Evil One," to quote one survivor, is everywhere causing confusion and driving people mad.

In ordinary times, persisting delusionary behavior is

The Charisma of Moses

deemed unjustified and therefore a symptom of mental derangement. When the behavior is part of a syndrome of activities and attitudes adjudged antisocial or personally deleterious, it is grounds for special repressive measures against (on behalf of) the person. When the behavior is associated with "beneficial" attitudes and activities, the person is tolerated and even promoted in esteem and encouraged to develop.

From culture to culture, or (which is to say the same) from one epoch to another, talking to god is deemed more or less possible and more or less rational by the therapeutic rulers, who are theologians, psychiatrists and politicians. The role of ordinary people in relation to the therapeutic rulers is generally similar to their role in relation to the elites of other areas of social rule.

In the case at hand, that of Moses and the politico-religious environment of Moses, there is every reason to believe that the situation was highly favorable to exceptional cases of talking to god. In the Egyptian setting the general power configuration was a theological bureaucracy, with a rationalized god-man ruler whose divine qualities were part of the law and did not have to be frequently demonstrated by charismatic acts: such was Pharaoh. On the same side, the Egyptian people may have been inefficiently coordinated to the ruling religion in that they were prone to accept wayward actions and ideas connected with religions. This, again, is not uncommon. It may be presumed that the present populations of the secular regimes of the world are also prone, though not to the same extent, to expect "true" and "real" divine manifestations, including talking with god.

Further, in the Egypt of the late Middle Empire, the Hebrews were generally a separately organized, ethnically distinct, and geographically concentrated element of the Egyptian population. It is precisely among groups of such special distinction and traditions that deviant religious manifestations may appear, often in connection with political movements arising out of perceived grievances. Numerous instances may be located in the history of protestantism and heresy in the Christian empires and among American Indian tribes of the past century. If, under such circumstances, a figure like Moses originates, the grounds are prepared for manifestations of charismatic leadership.

In such cases, talking to god is one of a number of attributes, though a key one, that are attributed to the leader, here Moses. Indeed, given the circumstances, so fertile for charisma and dedicated believers, it is to be remarked how widespread was the scepticism and opposition faced by Moses among the Hebrews. One may speculate that, if there had been an Egyptian policy of promoting an alternative Hebrew leadership and if the Egyptian elite and mass had not themselves been subjected to immanent tendencies to religious deviations, and, most importantly, if natural disturbances were not mounting in intensity, there would have been no real chance of Moses' assumption of power and successful leadership of a mass insurrection. Moses himself realized this and returned to Egypt when he deemed conditions to be favorable.

On the question of to whom Moses was talking and the functional analysis of this relationship, we are led to several conclusions. Although it is by no means clear how long Moses had spent in the psychically incompatible

Midianite environment, probably a period of some years is involved. He is granted a family. One legend has him spending forty years as King of Ethiopia before arriving in Midian to begin his period there. These stories indicate at least the passage of some time, and the development of a character which while basically operating with a mind that knows intimately the Egypt of the high courts, of polyglot areas, and jealously competitive theo-sciences, would have suppressed much and fixed upon a relationship between the old life and new life over the years.

Moses is an originally internalized rage type; his renowned humility rides upon a deep inner belief in his superiority both of origins and of mind. He would therefore be prone to hallucinating and projecting with great conviction this deeper level of his personality. Finally it became what was so obviously offered by the relatively devout and unidimensional shepherding culture - a god who discussed issues with him and who alternately browbeat him, cajoled him, and seduced him. Biblical historians have wrangled over how much of Yahweh Moses brought from Egypt and how much he brought to the Hebrews from the Midianites. The one critical export to Egypt was the talking god.

The pattern of hallucinatory projective development is so obvious that one would have to believe either that many thousands, perhaps millions, of characters in similar etiological circumstances have spoken to their god, or else that Moses was talking to himself, employing a spectacular set of media provided by natural events. Once more we recall the theory based on tradition and on evidence that Moses was a great magician and derived much of his political power from his successful competition with other renowned contestants in this sphere. Yes, we say, Moses was a successful competitor in contests of the marvelous. But his magic was the expression of a condition much more profound than magic.

Those scholars who are inclined to attribute magic to phenomena such as were played upon and excited by Moses and magicians, are usually ignorant of the intrinsic, embedded place in the history of religion and politics of persons possessed. The magician is, at least in the most common usage of the term, a person who is in rational and cynical command of a limited number of media of obscuration and symbols. The sincerely dedicated person of magical powers who acts consistently in matters of political and religious organization, negotiations, and leadership has to conduct himself in affairs that, intermittently magical, are ordinarily replete with pragmatic judgements of reality, heartrending failures, dull routine, and practical communications to mobilize human action. Agonizing self-appraisals, fits of disbelief in the capabilities of his associates and the possibilities of the situation, and divine discussions in both dysphoric and euphoric moods are not marks of the specialized and self-aware magician, but of the charismatic leader. The leader can be relied upon for responsible hallucinations. Thus was Moses.

THE CENTRALIZATION OF HALLUCINATION

The Holy Tabernacle and tent of meeting was not a public place. Moses had exclusive rights to its use and

The Charisma of Moses

extended that right to Aaron and other carefully supervised personnel. "When Moses went into the tent of meeting to speak with the Lord, he heard the voice speaking to him from above the mercy seat that was upon the ark of the testimony, from between the two cherubim, and it spoke to him."[69]

Hallucinations were exclusively his right, and were rarely delegated, Aaron was permitted them from time to time. The occasion of the visit of the seventy elders to see Yahweh on Mount Sinai was a command invitation from Yahweh conveyed by Moses to them. It was to be a visible visitation, not a talk, and certainly not a roundtable, and was not completely successful. The "footstool" of Yahweh was manifest in the gleaming sapphire rock and it is said that the visitors saw Yahweh but not how or what they saw of him.

A more extensive visit with Yahweh was achieved later. For he commanded Moses, when the people were desperate for meat, to bring seventy elders and "officers over them" to the Tent. "And I will come down and talk with you there; and I will take some of the spirit which is upon you and put it upon them; and they shall bear the burden of the people with you, that you may not bear it yourself alone." So they came and were placed around the Tent. "Yahweh came down in the cloud and spoke to him, and took some of the spirit that was upon him and put it upon the seventy elders; and when the spirit rested upon them, they prophesied. But they did so no more."[70] It was their first and last "pep talk" from Yahweh. That Moses and his aids were managing an electrochemical sound and light event here is manifest.

Meanwhile, in the camp, two invited elders, Medad and Eldad, did not come and were prophesying on their own account. A young man ran to tell Moses about them, and ever-ready Joshua said: "My Lord Moses, forbid them." But Moses, in a surprisingly benevolent mood, replied: "Are you jealous for my sake? Would that all the Lord's people were prophets, that the Lord would put his spirit upon them." Needless to say, precious little of this occurred; Joshua's posture was the official one. Talking to Yahweh was centralized.

Suppose that Moses had no god, as perhaps was the case before his revelation at the Burning Bush. Suppose that he had otherwise all of his genius and driving energy. Might he not have been accepted to lead the Hebrews out of Egypt and in the years of wandering? Could he not have established his authority and held his power out of sheer ability to solve their problems?

With all due regard for the pragmatism of people and for the effectiveness of sheer force (which was not originally available to Moses), there must be an identification with a god, a constitution, a popular will, or a possession by long inheritance to lend enough authority to a person to rule a people. The leader may then monopolize the source of authority, but he must rule in its name. The most obvious, striking, immediate, effective identification in this case was with a god. Moses found the god and established the ruling formula: Yahweh, through me, governs you for your own good. Moses could never have achieved his great tasks by his admittedly great energies, genius, and artifices. Yahweh, his companion, had to be acceptable to others, so that he, Moses, might be believed.

But how could such a stern god be acceptable to a people? It would not be Moses' Yahweh of course if he were anything but rigorous and stern. But, again, if Moses could perform the impossible feat of inventing a benign, good-humored, tolerant god, would not everyone be happier (everyone, that is, except Moses!) and the god made more acceptable?

The answer may very well be that Yahweh was not so acceptable. We shall soon look into the matter of revolts against Yahweh, but meanwhile we might try to visualize the Israelites and the state of their beliefs. Truly we are dealing with a practically unknown situation and there is nothing to be done about it, no public opinion surveys to call upon, no interviews of people to determine the degree of charisma in their relation to Moses.

Nevertheless, it is more useful to guide our thought with a model of the people's beliefs than to rest forever in a vague and confused cloud of ideas or to insist on some impossible idea such as that Moses was faithfully served by the Children of Israel unto his death. As soon as such an idea is abandoned, and one forces himself to roam with the help of an instructed imagination over the square mile or more of the Israelite encampment, one begins to appreciate how limited Moses' charisma must be.

AN ISRAELITE OPINION SURVEY

Granted his greatness and energy, given the need to believe in authority, given the marvels of manna and water and quail, given the glorious Ark, prescribed by a god to follow, nonetheless with all of this, strong forces work against the total harmony of convictions and behavior under the formula: 'Do thou as I say because I am uniquely assigned to your salvation': the nearly impossible situation of the people out of Egypt - beset on all sides by enemies, without a fixed territory, victims of repeated natural disasters, composed of diverse ethnic and religious elements, holding little realistic hope for the future, death on all sides. It is a charismatic setting, but by the same token, it is a setting for disenchantment, despair, and opportunism. Gressmann thinks that Aaron and many others were anti-Yahweh [71].

I have supplied a table of what may have been the situation. If my analysis falls anywhere near the true situation, then it is sharply evident that Moses had plenty of reasons for his dyspeptic view of the people of Israel. It would require altogether too many pages to discuss the numerous cells of the table. To repeat, it is presented so that a reader of the Torah may realize the importance of thinking of the whole people of Israel and so will not abandon them to the good graces of Yahweh and Moses.

TABLE I.
Attitudes of Israelites **(grown males)** *Encamped at the Holy Mountain (Hypothetical)*

	% of Egyptian Hebrews (7,000)	% of Mixed Multitude (2,000)	% of Midianites (1,000)	% of Total Elite (500)
True Believers				
in Yahweh (neutral or opposed to Moses)	8	10	20	15
in Moses (neutral or opposed to Yahweh)	8	10	5	15
in Both	10	20	10	10
Self-Servers				
support Moses	5	10	3	10
oppose Moses	10	2	2	5
avoid commitment	5	15	5	7
ApatheticsI (Tied to group by family or accident; nowhere else to go; taken care of; etc.	20	20	35	3
Disbelievers				
in Yahweh (neutral to Moses)	10	6	5	10
in Moses (neutral to Yahweh)	14	5	10	20
in Both	10	2	5	5
TOTAL	100%	100%	100%	100%

See Chapter VII first section, for the population in Exodus. Here the total population (with grown males in parentheses) is taken to be 25,000: 15,000 (7,000) of (A); 5,000 (2,000) of (B); and 5,000 (1,000) of (C).

To take one case, those who believe in Moses and are neutral to or opposed to Yahweh, and those that believe in both amount to 18% of the male Hebrew Egyptians, 30% of the Egyptians and other ethnics, and 15% of the Midianite and Kenite proselytes. This would total 2010 grown males who were the "true believers," the hard core of Moses' support, his charismatic followers. They would amount to about one-fifth of the potential warriors, and since the women and children would be inclined more than the males to be true believers, perhaps a somewhat larger percentage of the total population of 25,000. I believe that political scientists who are experts on elite theory would regard this as a robust basis for a tough and even despotic rule. The core of the opposition would be the 1970 disbelievers in Moses or in both Moses and Yahweh.

For the hard core of true believers, the charisma of Moses is evidently based upon many proofs: that the Israelites survived due to Moses was the main proof and incessantly, compulsively repeated as a soldier tells of a dud bomb landing next to him; then the litany of his miraculous infancy (Did you know, too, that Yahweh sent a plague of boils upon Egypt just then ?);[72] his immense erudition; his princely connections; his works with divine fire; his halo; his tablets written "with the finger of god"; his escapes from two Pharaohs; his rod; his forty days and nights on the fiery mountain without food and drink; manna, quail, water; his knowledge of healing everything from snakebite to leprosy; the strong and deep men who obey him; his silence and aloneness; his speaking in tongues; his amazing timing of when to move, when to stay, when to fight, when to evade; and all the laws that keep the camp from anarchy and

The Charisma of Moses

licentious chaos. He talks "mouth-to-mouth" [73] with Yahweh; Yahweh lives through him; Moses does nothing without Yahweh; who is against Moses is against Yahweh, and if you don't believe in Yahweh, you must all the more believe in Moses who knows how to pronounce himself in the "court language," the divine jargon of earthly rulers.

ROUTINIZING CHARISMA

I doubt that Moses was author of most of the as yet undeciphered rituals of the *Books of Moses*. A brief "Decalogue" may be traceable to him. The "safety rules" for handling the Ark and altar which extend to a danger zone beyond the tent are his. There are certain organizational ideas that would have been instigated by him. And, certainly, much else that was attributed to Moses in the Bible was his in fact.

But the veritable avalanche of rules and taboos that have fallen into the Torah are the work of people who needed to lay the heavy hand of god upon every detail of existence in order to give themselves occupation and power. Moses gave them certain concepts - national pride, ethnocentrism, law, written records, fear of Yahweh, circumcision, repression and suppression, punishment. He opened the door to mosaism. They entered and took possession in his name, and dwelled there forever after.

They routinized the charisma of Moses. Mosaism without Moses, like Christianity without Christ, or like Leninism without Lenin, brings about a different social order; behavior, and even the teachings change. However, the process began early, with Moses himself. He personally took charge of digging up and carrying the coffin with the bones of Joseph - traditional Hebrew authority - on the Exodus. Poor Moses, says the legend; while others carried their valuable loot from Egypt, Moses was burdened down by Joseph. Not at all. The coffin was like a suit of armor against his Hebrew opponents. And there was probably more in it than Joseph.

It is another proof of Moses' genius - and the competence of the people around him - that hardly had they left Egypt when, with a greatly reduced people, in hunger and amidst disaster, he began to fashion ideological and social structures for the new nation. The central headquarters system, the reorganization of tribes, the provision of eternal slogans such as the curse against the Amalekites and the framing of laws - not despite the chaos of Mount Sinai, but taking advantage of that very chaos - all tended to move the nation into a future. Promises, promises: the people were fed upon these as well as miracles of springs and manna and quail, and were fed up with them. Yet there was always a developing system of rule that carried its own promise. Perhaps those people who survived ancient catastrophes best were those whose religions in some fundamental ways imitated the catastrophes and whose nations were born in the name of the disasters: it is a thesis we should like to develop sometime. It seems, at any rate, to have been the case with the Israelites.

Like all charismatic leaders, Moses had problems in delegating authority: Aaron was a superb assistant but not harsh enough, Joshua was too harsh and very young. The tribal heads had little legitimacy in their own tribes. Moses complains to Yahweh: "I am not able to carry all this people

The Charisma of Moses

alone, the burden is too heavy for me." Yahweh suggests an assembly of seventy elders come to him. Along with the Holy Spirit, they get executive responsibilities, by nearly direct divine authority, "nearly" I say, because Moses is explicitly tied into the donation of the spirit and power [74].

Jethro came upon Moses, his son-in-law, occupied endlessly with hearing disputes and advised him to appoint subordinate hearing officers. Moses promptly did so [75]. This probably was the institution of the elders [76].

As soon as he could, Moses institutionalized the Levites. They were given religious foundation, functions, authority, and a claim on the revenues of the tribes. Yahweh, in one of his most bloodthirsty moments, had claimed all the first-born of Israel for his sacrifices. Moses, speaking for a more moderate Yahweh, dedicated the Levites as surrogates for the infants. What better basis for the authority of this security police force than their having ransomed by their own persons the first-born of the Jews from infanticide?

The Bible implies strongly that the whole Jewish nation was to have one Ark of the Covenant alone. It would be at the seat of government, the principal town. In fact it was literally the "mercy seat" of the government of Yahweh. This was certainly true centuries later, when it was installed in Jerusalem.

More significantly, in the earliest period, when the population is divided by tribes and assigned regions in which to settle, the Levites alone are not given a special place but spread out as detachments among all of the fifty-eight townships. This would confirm the role of the Levites as special troops of the central government but would also indicate that each township was expected to have its own ark, if not immediately, then later. The Levites would operate it. I guess that after Moses, Israel decentralized, but had agreed in principle to keep a single ark which would be under central control.

If one could rely upon the tribes to construct, maintain, protect, and employ their arks properly, there would be no cause for concern. However, in periods of low ark activity, they might expect too much from their arks and abuse them or abandon them; further, they might hear Yahweh with different ears, and disputes about the voices of Yahweh would occur. So, splendid and edifying as might be the possession of twelve or fifty-eight means of hearing and seeing manifestations of the Lord, and using arks in local warfare and criminal justice, there were probably even more compelling reasons for letting there be only one Ark, one Voice, one Interpreter (Moses or the high priest), one weapon system to maintain and control at instant readiness.

THE MANIAC SCIENTIST

If what has been said here were presented to a personnel officer or an occupational psychologist for a determination of the true vocation of Moses, the reply might be: he was a scientist. Educated. Literate. He is slow in speech, apparently modest but prone to indignation. Does everything in the third person (laying it onto Yahweh). Uncircumcised (indicating that neither Egyptians or Hebrews who raised him thought the question important, and that would mean a secular environment.) Heavy on abstract ideas. Does not believe in immortality. Impatient. Likes everything

The Charisma of Moses

in writing. Handy and knows materials and tools. Weak on family life and sentiment. Marries outside the tribes of Israel. Needs help in political negotiations. Has an international reputation as a "magician." Is highly respected by establishment scientist. Although revered by many, never fully trusted by most people. Understands phenomena like electricity, manna, plagues, phosphorus, fire, smoke. Continually experimenting and inventing. Likes to number things and count people. Does not eat much or carouse; doesn't like people very much, and likes to see them well-ordered, serious. Does not believe the priesthood should have full authority. Keeps records. Was very open-minded on questions when young until he learned the "truth"; then he becomes dogmatic and insistent upon "the one right way" to do everything. Now he tends to be dogmatic from the first moment of a problem. Contemptuous of idols and images, though strongly object-oriented. Perhaps our imaginary occupational psychologist would agree, "Yes, the man's a scientist, one of these new-type administrative scientists."

The question whether Moses had traits of a scientist may not interest the reader so much as whether he was a madman. I should say that by every criterion of madness, especially the test for schizophrenia, Moses would appear to have been mad. My answer, however, is that Moses was mad in theory but sane in context.

Whereupon, of course, we become involved in the distinction between madness and sanity, psychosis and normality. Let me first recite the indications of madness and then afterwards explain my position. Not only may we arrive then at a determination concerning Moses but also at a better understanding of the perennial mad leader.

Taking Moses to be psychotic, his illness would be termed obsessional neurosis leading into auditory hallucinations and culminating in paranoid megalomanic messianism.

The disease begins with a weak early identity and a loss of self-respect, arising from circumstances such as I have already related in Moses' early childhood - a biethnic parentage with a confusion of attendants and conflicting messages from Hebrew and Egyptian attitudes playing upon him. He must suppress his speech and, in so doing, adds a physiological handicap of incoherent speech to his already diminutive self-respect. His drive to achieve intensifies and, because of circumstances, is repressed into autistic reveries of grand scope and ambitions. On both his Egyptian and Hebrew sides, his educators encourage him (build up his expectations) but at the same time his ideals are incompatible and unachievable, frustrating him when he seeks a clear realistic directive. He turns to scientific (and necessarily, in those days, partly magical) studies which reinforce his solitary and exclusive character while producing a value that both his sets of attendants recognize - priestly scientific magic.

When we apply the Hoskins-Boisen basic behavioral manifestations of schizophrenia [77] - lack of self-respect, delusional misinterpretations, the externalization of conscience, and the sense of compulsive behavior, we can surmise that Moses is potentiated in all of these regards even before he gets into trouble and must leave Egypt. He is already a trouble-maker in the Egyptian scientific-priestly establishment. Naturally, excluded from the semi-theocracy of the pyramid cult, he is developing cultist tendencies of a different sort, probably Hermetic (Thoth), for Thoth

The Charisma of Moses

(Hermes, Mercury) is the most ambulatory and earth-bound of the pantheon, and probably in the direction of experiments and machines that are excluded from the main career line of science. His quietness, incoherence, and seeming meekness are the outward cover for a demand-system that is really excessive, harsh, and incredible. The conditions of exile, as I have detailed them, reinforce Moses' traits. He does not forget Egypt; his obsessions are nourished by the quite incompatible silences and solemn, accepting unrelatedness of the wilderness. God-names with a sound even of "Yahu" are heard among the tribal Semites[78]. His cultic tendency is confirmed when he hears a force that he has long thought to be everywhere - electricity - increasing its activity and producing god-like sounds, even the name of god itself.

There is a decisive change, a worsening of his mental disease from a psychiatric standpoint, a move towards one of the most noble ventures in history according to another viewpoint. In the years to come, Moses exhibits the full range of schizophrenic symptoms. To those already suggested may be added those indexed by Paul Meehl [79]. Meehl describes schizophrenia as characterized by a deficiency in the ability to enjoy life or people (anhedonia), an aversion to other humans, a loss of control over certain kinds of perception including the introduction of a special logic, concerns about the abnormality of one's bodily organs and functions, ambivalent confusion of simultaneous love and hostility towards all upon which and whom his interest is centered, and a hypercathexis or superabundance of intellectual activity of a possibly fully rational sort.

The application of these mechanisms to Moses is

apparent. Respecting anhedonia, there is scarcely any passage to be found in the Torah respecting pleasure. In a negative sense, Moses berates the people for not enjoying their poisoned quail and endless manna. But the point is too obvious to belabor - sex, food, all is: "Be glad you're alive: Thanks to Yahweh!" Miriam leads a victory chant and dances one time, a pleasant surprise, though she sings bloody murder [80]. If a Harry Golden would appear and call to Moses a hearty "Enjoy!" he would be thrown out of the camp. But we know from Puritanism, a mosaic throwback, that pleasure is a sin.

I have commented already on Moses' inability to support affectionate human contacts. The loss of control over perception is the famous "talking with Yahweh" of which we have said much and more is to come. But note only how well-regulated Moses is in this regard; he disciplines his hallucinations marvelously, according to a special logic of schizophrenia. And the result is not only persuasive as to the reality of his discourses with Yahweh, but also fits into Moses' general psychological dynamics, and this too is appealing: thus Moses projects his immense aggressive superego or conscience upon a god; then creates a bad family of children for the great father, namely the Israelites; then has Yahweh play the strict father of this bad family, punishing them on every possible occasion. He, Moses, finds the spectacle edifying, while preserving a remarkable detachment.

This matter of "cognitive slippage" may contribute to the solution, also, of the great riddle of how Moses, the scientist, could give what a modern scientist would regard as an unreasonable and inadequate description and explanation of his intricate and ingenious works and of natural events. I said earlier that the answer may be partly for establishing the greatness of Yahweh and partly out of contempt for the popular intelligence. But one may perceive another reason: a schizophrenic need to satisfy only himself with explanations of why he is acting so and he is satisfied by bizarre or simple explanations. Further, when an applied scientist, here Moses, cannot explain whether in thought or in language the theory and causes of his scientific operations, he may satisfy himself by introducing the *deus ex machina:* Yahweh causes all things to happen - end of argument. Putting together the last two impulses with the first two reasons, a conventionally acceptable cognitive slippage will do great service.

In regard to concerns about his bodily image, we have little of Moses' physiognomy to go on. The legends say he was a beautiful young boy and man. Obviously, his speech difficulty is relevant, as is the circumcision issue, already discussed. Yahweh is supposed to be invisible, and Moses is accredited with the great religious invention of abolishing anthropomorphism. Yet a review of the Bible and legends in search of anthropomorphic passages discloses them in abundance. Yahweh has mighty ears, arms, legs, brow, eyes, nostrils, lungs, and everything as Michelangelo paints him on the ceiling of the Sistine Chapel in Rome. He also hates, loves as a father, threatens, burns with rage, gives, takes, instructs, commands, discriminates, plays tricks, tests, and of course, is jealous. And as with Yahweh, so with Moses who is living in his image of Yahweh, and - apropos - it is not Yahweh who is the jealous god so much as Moses in his other self as Yahweh. Obviously this metaphorical kind of imaging did not violate the Third Commandment, whereupon we think that Ziegler may be correct in that the most important meaning of the forbidden "image" and "standing image" may be the visible presence of Yahweh on the Ark of the Covenant [81].

Next we consider Moses' ambivalence, alluded to earlier on in this chapter in connection with the Israelites. In several specific passages, Yahweh is directly described as the source of good and evil. Moses had no need for Satan: why? Because Yahweh was the devil and in Moses' unconscious mind there could be no separation of god and the devil: he must both hate and love the same personage. Again, going back to the bad children of Israel, Moses uses them to express all of his hatred of Yahweh - their willful disobedience, their unfaithfulness, their whoring after false gods, their ingratitude, their forgetfulness of the past, their disregard of obligations, and so on. Then, reversing the ploy in a marvelously acceptable but mad logic, Moses displays his detestation of the Israelites by having them continually and severely chastised by Yahweh. Thus Moses safely hates both Yahweh and the Jews.

As for Meehl's final criterion - the hypercathexis of intellect among schizophrenics - Meehl makes it clear that in some cases the schizophrenic often pursues, alongside his rocky road of cognitive slippage and incoherent behavior, a straight path of intellectual hyperenergy and achievement. I have already advanced much evidence of the superiority of Moses in this regard. Such genius is already a sign that a most extraordinary emotional dynamic must be operative.

With all of this, how can one avoid concluding that Moses was a madman? I refrain not so as to appease the billion labeled followers of Moses in the contemporary

The Charisma of Moses 255

world. I refrain because Moses effectively managed the Exodus in ways that were the outcome of his character and depended upon his character. Given the disastrous conditions, the heavy risks and the loosely aggregated people, it is highly improbable that another man could have succeeded in any other way than that of Moses.

I see two major errors in decision produced by Moses' character. The first is that it may not have been wise for the Hebrews to leave Egypt at all, or it may have been wise for the people to return, even if Moses and the cohort of leaders might lose their new power. The second is that there may have been enough stability and responsibility among the elders and representatives of the people at the time of Korah's revolt, of which I shall speak, to convert Moses' tyranny into a federal republic, with the ultimate result of holding all the tribes of Israel together in times to come. Other errors of judgement occurred, none fatal to his mission. Other traits of his also made life difficult beyond necessity for the people of Israel.

There is another and imperative reason for not applying the term "psychotic" to Moses. Many of the biblically related events of the Exodus and its aftermath took place in a physical environment that was as chaotic as it was unforeseen. It was surreal. It was the substance, but the real substance, of which the visions of the schizophrenic are composed.

Quoting alternately the studies of Hoskins and Boison [82], we see in the mind of the psychotic what was the real world of Exodus:

> To the patient himself, his ideas and emotions are... the matters

of primary significance... To him they represent firm, terrifying, torturing, mocking, and fascinating reality. An initial feeling of strangeness is rather common. In the words of one patient, the subject is often beset by a 'flood of mental pictures as though an album within were unfolding itself.' Elements of the unconscious come into awareness and are interpreted as manifestations of the supernatural, often with devastating impact. In the new world into which the patient is thrust, previous principles and standards seem irrelevant. 'He sees strange meanings in everything about him and he is sure of only one thing, that things are not what they seem.' His new ideas and mental pictures become so vivid as to constitute the voices and visions that a large proportion of the patients experience.

'Very commonly it is as if the conscious self had descended to some lower region where it is no longer in control but is at the mercy of the terrifying ideas and imagery that throng in upon it. The eyes are opened so that one seems to see back to the beginning of creation. One seems to have lived perhaps in many previous existences. To the individual, the new experiences are so vivid that they seem to represent profound, new revelations and the marked sense of mystery is often associated with the more profound types of disturbance, with characteristic archaic symbolism, bizarre ideation, and often deep religious concern.

A second set of observations confirms this view of the world as catastrophe.

The latent schizophrenic must always reckon with the possibility that his very foundation will give way somewhere, that an irretrievable disintegration will set in, that his ideas and concepts will lose their cohesion and their connection with other spheres of association and with the environment. As a result, he feels threatened by an uncontrollable chaos of chance happenings... The dangerousness of his situation often shows itself in terrifying dreams of cosmic catastrophe, of the end of the world and such thoughts. Or the ground he stands on begins to heave, the walls bend and bulge, the solid earth turns to water, a storm carries him up into the air, all his relatives are dead, etc.[83]

Here again, notably, is the *Weltanschauung* or cosmic image, this time observed by Carl G. Jung. It corresponds to the real images of the external world during natural catastrophe and the feelings normally inspired by the images. In the case of Moses, and generally in the psychology of catastrophe, the real and the unreal confirm and reinforce each other; they interact, but so much in tandem are they, that when the real pulls ahead of the unreal (or mental), it drags it along and vice-versa.

This is what I mean when I say that Moses, with a character appropriate to an environment "gone mad," is not himself of chaotic and disordered mind in the framework of the surrealist natural and human behavior he was experiencing.

Although Moses was beyond madness, the question of whether his life-work was "good" is swamped by "ifs" and "buts." Certainly he helped a small population to survive. However, the good in the survivors has consisted in the greatest degree of aberrations from, conflicts with, and transformations of mosaism. I shall explain this line of thought later on and in the light of more information about the revolts against Moses and the character of Yahweh.

Professor James Breasted wrote that Moses was "cognizant of all the wisdom of the Egyptians."[84] But he was a creator, too. He was a type of Leonardo da Vinci in the variety of his scientific and military inventions, although we would have to reconstruct his tabernacle and clothing designs to evaluate his aesthetic ability. He was a ruthless monotheist who slaughtered his own charges, the "Children of Israel," to keep them in line. He was a hallucinatory genius, without his own father (his own father being practically unknown to him and powerless, and the Pharaoh unaccepting and remote), who made the voice of god his father and everyone else's father in a pure patriarchal absolute form spelled out in a system of laws and political organization of which he was the dispassionate proponent. He was a George Washington (even to his inarticulateness and the combination of arrogance with humility) who fathered a nation and led it through difficult years. Moses was even a kind of adventurer, clever and unscrupulous, who conceived a scheme to fit the times and pulled it off successfully, giving Israel the most sophisticated weaponry of the Middle Bronze Age and thus ensuring the capture and holding of a considerable "Promised Land" against a ring of powerful enemies for centuries. All of this was achieved amidst recurrent natural chaos.

There was too much of Moses to make of him a god or a son of god: this at least all scholars and priests have agreed to and seen to. Moses was more than a man; he was many men at once. Yet he himself declined any relation to Yahweh other than being Yahweh's exclusive intermediary with Yahweh's "Children of Israel." From this one concept, which might be termed a legal fiction, ramified the structure of mosaism, then and thereafter.

CHAPTER SEVEN

THE LEVITES AND THE REVOLTS

The "Hebrews" of Exodus were of various degrees of Hebrew-ness. Many were quite Egyptian. Many others were assimilated to Egyptian culture. The most important larger group were traditionally loyal Elohists. Few could have been Yahwist, inasmuch as Moses was only then expounding the new cult.

In what would have been Goshen, at Tell ed-Dab'a, a town of the Middle Bronze Age has recently been excavated. It reveals a heavy non-Egyptian, Palestinian aspect. Skeletal remains, etymology, and artifacts disclose a heterogeneous population of Semitic and other backgrounds [1]. This would support our theory that the proto-Israelites were a geographically separate and autonomous people, to some degree maintaining their old ethnic identity, living among Egyptians and other peoples from East and West, intermarrying, holding a full range of occupations, but now caught up in a xenophobic, "anti-semitic" period and forced to supply corvées and employ birth-control. It is not surprising to learn that the *Book of Exodus,* as befits a historical work of those times, has much in it of the popular Egyptian language [2].

The some three million souls that the Bible asserts left Egypt are far too many. It is not that aggregated tribes of 500,000 or even more have never moved long distances; they have. The Cimbri and Teutons migrated in this number over a period of years at the end of the second century B.C. from the North Sea region to Southern France and Italy; after seriously threatening Roman power, they were annihilated by the Roman legions of Marius.

NUMBERS LEAVING EGYPT

The number of persons in Exodus has been estimated variously from 2,000 to 6,000,000 [3]. The great range of figures adds confusion to the theory of Exodus. We should at least estimate, if we cannot know, how many persons left Egypt and how many were alive to muster for the handing down of the Ten Commandments at the Holy Mountain a couple of months later. Avoiding such estimates, although usual, leaves many questions open and lends an air of unreality to the grand project of Moses and the Israelites. Therefore, reasoning from what little is known and what would have been possible, I shall try to establish how many people were involved at the several stages of Exodus.

The conditions of Exodus, as we have described them, were peculiar. The Exodus of three millions in one group in a few days would imply a line of marchers stretching from Goshen to Horeb; ten abreast with beasts of burden or one wagon, three meters apart, say, would produce a column 900 kilometers long. The flocks and herds would flank the marchers. If so many did leave Goshen, perhaps as a horde fleeing from the disasters, believing that the Israelites possessed secret knowledge of an undestroyed "Promised Land" (as likely a reconciliation of Bible and reality as one might conjecture), the refugees would have dropped to a figure nearer the one out of fifty that a rabbinical source says completed the march.

Even in this case, I would distinguish between the two types of persons abandoning their region, and allow for only 60,000 or so organized marchers at the end of the first two days. I would assume that of the three millions of refugees, some 300,000 may have been affiliated to the Exodus movement, but turned back on the vague promise, half-welcomed, of making up a second wave of Exodus at a later time. This has happened often in tribal migrations and in the wagon-train movements of the American western settlements. Another 240,000 Hebrews more or less would have refused to go from the very first [4], and it would have been with these that the departing Hebrews had their rumored conflicts.

The 60,000 who arrived at Pi-ha-khiroth near the frontier would include more warriors than is typical of a tribal migration. Many would have left their families. Men of working age would be the most anxious to leave. But when the pursuing Egyptian army was espied, many, especially of the Egyptians and physically weaker elements, would have deserted and fled to all quarters during the long bright night. A drop of some 10,000 persons would be expected at this critical point.

Next came the crossing. Here the legends, as well as logic, would dictate another serious loss, perhaps another 10,000.[5] The panic would be extreme, the time very short, the waters appearing from all quarters of the compass in cross-tides, the muck deep in places, exhaustion general.

The many days of march between the "Sea of Reeds"

and Mount Sinai (or Horeb) would have cost another 10,000 lives from weariness, thirst, starvation, and illness. And the assaults of the Amalekites would have cost yet another 10,000 lives, first from the slaughter of Hebrew rear elements and then, much less, of warriors in battle.

The survivors of Exodus, then, would have numbered 20,000 of which probably a full 10,000 were warriors. This figure of 10,000 is one out of sixty of the figure of 600,000 males of battle age carried, as "planned hope" and "lost vision," in *Exodus* and the *Book of Numbers*. The Bible mentions that the Israelites did not march as a single body but in phased stages; too large a number were involved to proceed in a single, or even in two, marching units.

These would then be reinforced by the followers of Jethro, a tribe, or part of one, of the Midianites, who had been struck by their own disasters, and who accepted Yahweh and little else in the way of conditions for becoming Children of Israel. Perhaps 5,000 were thus joined to the 20,000 from Egypt.

The 25,000 would still be a considerable and formidable people. Most were warriors, too. It would explain the prompt organizational step that Moses and the Levites took. The twelve tribes of Israel were filled out around cadres of the same name, in almost every case greatly outnumbered by the new elements - Egyptian, Asiatic and non-tribal Hebrews. The tribes were then assigned quotas of fighting men, organized by the decimal system, which would be called upon by Moses and Joshua when the hour for battle struck.

The Levites and the Revolts

IMPEDIMENTA

I have already explained, in Chapter One, that the Exodus was not a pell-mell flight of a horde of slaves, but that it was well-organized, with a highly competent and determined Hebrew leadership under Moses, Aaron, Joshua, Hur, and others [6]. As soon as he had finished his last session with the Pharaoh and Egyptian councillors, Moses hurried to Goshen, a few hours away. He may have cut across to a planned rendezvous with the advance elements already moving out. So far as he could tell, he had done his job well; the Egyptian forces were under orders not to interfere with the movement.

The people of Exodus were carrying all that they could. The headquarters materiel transported by Moses and the Levites consisted of more than one ordinarily imagines. On the wagon and in the coffin or ark-box carrying Joseph's remains would be the most secret and precious items. It would not hold much. They would also have collected and carried a complete collection of tools, including construction, metal working, medical and sculpturing instruments; metal rods; gold, silver, bronze; copper and lead, and preferably alloys of lead and copper already smelted; perhaps meteoritic iron or even iron from the Caucasus or Anatolia; levers and ratchets; nails; amber or a substitute; glass rods; magnets; surveying instruments; sun dials; water clocks; straps and ropes of various kinds; various small wheels; buckles and pills; artificial and volcanic glass; drugs; poisons; phosphorus (white and red); flint; a large quantity of papyrus; clay tablets; styluses; bales of cloth, especially canvas and wool, and skins of animals; cut hard and soft wood, especially cedar and shittum; written tablets and papyri, containing history, formulas, and instructions; military equipment including tools for its repair - swords, lances, slings, and missiles; staves; possibly some apparatus and models that Levites were working on or knew about; plus a variety of then known and now-forgotten implements and provisions, various idiosyncratic fancies and expressions of ideas of varying utilitarian possibilities, and, of course, rations for weeks of time, including tons of unleavened bread.

The collecting process had gone on for months. The Bible mentions almost none of this effort. In a number of passages, both in the Bible and the legends, we are offered a strange picture - of the Hebrews first borrowing valuables from their Egyptian neighbors for the trip and then being given them, with a strong implication of blackmailing and looting the frightened people - both Egyptian and Hebrew - who were staying behind, and stripping the ruined houses and settlements.

The implication, too, is that these activities were ordered by the leaders for the purpose of supplying the expedition. It would be in accord with the Bible's mode of expression, also, to lay the activity upon the departing people, whereas, in fact, the Levites and their helpers probably engaged in the work systematically, going to the known sources of the required or desired materials. Livestock was probably rounded up from wherever it was corralled or had strayed, the clip of the ears notwithstanding.

Calculating solely the transportation of the materiel of the headquarters and of the special assault and guard troops, perhaps a hundred carts, a hundred mules, donkeys and horses, and many litters would be needed. After the

The Levites and the Revolts   265

Levites, the Judah tribe seems to have been organized and of high morale. Moses and the Levites would march in the vanguard preceded by reconnaissance patrols of Levites and Judahs. The throng of followers was too great to organize properly and probably a detachment of Judahs was used as a rear guard, with a small Levite staff, under instructions to delay and hamper any pursuit or harassment but not to fight uselessly for the unorganized crowd of followers.

In the passage of the Red Sea, by which is meant the tongue of waters and lakes extending north of the Red Sea, the headquarters detachment and the special troops, with Moses, would move through first, hoping that some or most of the people would pass before the waters returned.

The sight of the heavily loaded caravan marching out would have been impressive. Reports and rumors of it and its contents would have been immediately relayed to the Egyptian armed forces headquarters and the Pharaoh at Memphis from road guards and small military posts that were not overrun before they could flee. Most unnerving of all might have been the sudden intelligence that a number of trusted officials and technicians had decamped with the Hebrews. The astronomers would have been quite discredited by events; the military would call the next move; logically, it was to pursue and recapture the materiel and slay or take prisoner Moses and the elite element. The pursuit was launched.

When the pursuing force and head of the Empire were lost, the regime of the Middle Kingdom collapsed and the Hyksos entered immediately. They would become aware promptly of the mass exodus when they found the land of Goshen stripped of valuables, livestock and goods. Soon afterwards, the Jews found a detachment of desert warriors at their rear, slaughtering the lagging elements. They showed knowledge of the Jew's history in Egypt. Moses detailed his best troops to engage them and accompanied them. I think that these Amalelite-Hyksos were not encountered by chance; they were on the same mission as the Egyptian forces, to retake the spoils of Egypt.

Moses took part in the first battle, standing on a prominence with Aaron and Hur, holding his rod of Yahweh aloft to encourage the Israelite fighters; before the day was over, he needed their help to keep his arm up. His staff would be the famous staff that performed before the Pharaoh. The three men may have been able to induce an electric charge from the ground and bring about a discharge into the clouds and dust that hovered very low above them. An effect of this kind would tend to intimidate the enemy and revive the Israelite morale. It would be especially effective because the troops were battling in near-darkness under the cosmic clouds. Every time Moses lowered his arms, the enemy gained an advantage, it is said [7].

TECHNICIANS AND SECURITY POLICE

More practically, now, we can consider the nature of the Levi's, the Levites, who were critical in the management of Exodus and the succeeding wanderings and conquests. Not a tribe, not priests, the Levites may have included representatives of all the tribes, says the article in the *Encyclopedia Britannica* [8]. I said in the first chapter, too, that the Levites may have been assimilated Hebraic Jews, many or

The Levites and the Revolts

most of mixed ancestry.

What is a tribe, and what is a nation? The Hebrews of Egypt became in basic ways the Jewish Nation in Exodus. A tribe is sovereign; it may be part of a confederation of tribes, but it can go its own way when it feels it must. Moses put an end immediately to any pure confederation.

It would have been exceedingly difficult to mobilize and lead the Hebrews from Egypt, and organize them into the masters of a promised land, without strong central leadership. This implied a group to wield the central power and carry out the central plan. Such were the Levites who had in many cases developed their skills under the Egyptian imperial administration. Only among the Levites were Egyptian names found in later times[9]. The Exodus marked the end of the dynasty. In Egypt, the other Hebrews were terrorized and driven to work without pay, "all except the tribe of Levi who were not employed in the work with their brethren...Since they had not been with their brethren at the beginning" they were not disturbed. [10]

The Levites appear in modern terms as a kind of technical police and fire brigade. They seem to be in families, yet not a blood clan. They served as individuals. They are competent. They are not as beloved or revered by the people, I think, as were the priests. At first, they are not permitted priestly functions. They have orders to "shoot to kill" should anybody approach the holy premises. In fact, they turn out to be something like the special forces that the Department of Defense organizes from time to time with high technical qualifications because of the special weaponry involved. They were indeed handling deadly equipment. They were in charge of the mobile worship-weapon system: the tabernacle, tent, altar, and ark. Various wagons were assigned to them for transporting this national equipment [11].

"Historians are still unable to explain satisfactorily such problems as the relationship that existed between the Levites and the hereditary priesthood."[12] Moses developed the Levites as a special arm of Israel. Satisfied that his older "half-brother" Aaron should have the priesthood and guarantee its security, he appointed the Levites, the best educated secular element of the Hebrews, many of whom had served the Egyptians along with Moses himself, to manage the Tabernacle with its equipment and the most precious goods of the people. No wonder there was puzzlement about the Levites centuries later as the environment became more orderly, uniform, and electrically balanced. Why should the Levites have shaved from head to foot, for example, if electric shock were not a danger? From elite troops, the Levites became property and stage managers, with a right to read the Torah following upon the preeminent right of the Kohens or priesthood. However, as one reads in *Deuteronomy* [13], during some lengthy period, after Moses, the Levites performed the duties of the priests themselves.

Moses decided, in the name of Yahweh, of course, that death would be visited upon a priest who approached the Ark with unclean hands - death by accidental or deliberate electrocution in some instances. Down to today, significantly, the Law does not get read in the Synagogue before a Levite washes the hands of the Kohen who is to begin the reading. A psychiatrist's reasons for this ritual purification (and individual problems of the genre) in an uncontrolled liberal society are usually adequate, but shaving one's body completely, wearing special clothes, removing

The Levites and the Revolts

one's shoes before the altar, and washing one's hands begin to make up a complex that primordially might have to do with precautions against unwanted electrical connections. And the technical expert is he who insures precautions.

Thus the Levites were to serve, but also to control the priests and their equipment. Exceptions from their control were Aaron, of course, and Aaron's son, Eleazer, subsequently High Priest. The reason is given in one place "that there may be no plague among the people of Israel in case the people of Israel should come near the sanctuary."[14] Here the intent to avoid a dew of dangerous chemicals and radiation seems clear. The plagues would be widespread outbursts of skin lesions and sores (mistakenly called leprosy), but would include plagues of vomiting, diarrhea and eye diseases, all of which occur with radiation poisoning. These are related in turn to the plagues of Egypt preceding the Exodus, when the red dust poisoned the water and covered the land. The natural excitation, emergence and proliferation of frogs, insects and vermin that would also be lifted and dropped in the cyclonic winds would be connected by observers with the chemically caused plagues.

Yahweh exempted the Levites from the Mobilization and Census of the people because they were his retinue, says a legend [15]. Only Levites from 30-50 years of age were called to active duty. They were divided in eight sections.
Levites were to consecrate themselves to Yahweh in lieu of the consecration of the first-born. The implication is strong here that the Jews were supposed to sacrifice their first-born, of all children and animals, to Yahweh. The Levites might always impress upon the people that they and they alone were responsible for and to be credited for removing a great

load of sacrifice from everyone else. Too, one may consider whether there is a threat contained in this relationship, in the fear that the Levites may renounce this surrogation and ask Yahweh for a resumption of the obligation upon all.
Yahweh spoke to Moses and said:

> I myself have chosen the Levites from among the sons of Israel, in place of the first-born, those who open the mother's womb among the sons of Israel; these Levites therefore belong to me. For every first-born belongs to me. On the day when I struck all the first-born in the land of Egypt, I consecrated for my own all the first-born of Israel, of both man and beast. They are mine; I am Yahweh [16].

Yahweh said to Moses:

> Take a census of all the first-born among the sons of Israel, all the males from the age of one month and over; take a census of them by name. Then you will present the Levites to me, Yahweh, in place of the first-born of Israel; in the same way you will give me their cattle in place of the first-born cattle of the sons of Israel.

As Yahweh ordered, Moses took a census of all the first-born of the sons of Israel. The total count, by name, of the first-born from the age of one month and over came to twenty-two thousand two hundred and seventy three.
Then Yahweh spoke to Moses and said:

> Take the Levites in place of all the first-born of Israel's soils, and the cattle of the Levites in place of their cattle; the Levites shall be my own, Yahweh's own. For the ransom of the two hundred and seventy three of the sons of Israel in excess of the

> number of Levites, you are to take five shekels for each, reckoning by the sanctuary shekel, twenty gerahs to the shekel; you must then give this money to Aaron and his sons as the ransom price for this extra number.
>
> Moses received this money as the ransom for this extra number unransomed by the Levites. He received the money for the first-born of the sons of Israel, one thousand three hundred and sixty-five shekels, sanctuary shekels. Moses handed over this ransom money to Aaron and his sons, at the bidding of Yahweh, as Yahweh had ordered Moses [17].

From first to last Moses depended upon the Levites for maintaining his absolute power. According to legend, the Levites were the most faithful to Yahweh in Egypt where so many of the population lost their religious ardor. (I think that they may have had the most skilled and curious religious cultists.) They passed Yahweh's test at Massah ("proof") and at the waters of Meribah ("contention") where they rallied around Moses when rioting began over the shortage of water and before Moses had had time to discover it beneath the rocks [18].

Nevertheless, leadership in domestic security and war went to Joshua, son of Nun, of the tribe of Ephraim, not a Levite. He was Moses' personal bodyguard from the beginning of Exodus.

His devotion, diligence, and aggressiveness were all that Moses could ask for, and sometimes more. He had neither sons nor daughters; when spies were sent to survey Canaan and report back whether Israel should then and there descend upon the Promised Land, Joshua was criticized by the other spies for having little to lose by going into battle [19].

Legend gives several surprising comments on Joshua, more consistent with this book's findings than with ordinary opinion. Joshua grew up without knowing his antecedents; he was raised by strangers, and his father's name, "Nun," means "fish," because, the legend says, he was cast into the waters, and swallowed by a whale, then spit up. "The government appointed him to the office of hangman. As luck would have it, he had to execute his own father."[20] He was called a fool because of his general ignorance and the spies called him a "head-cutter."[21]

BLAME THE PEOPLE

At first, Moses, Yahweh and Aaron were concerned that they would not be able to assemble and march out the mass of people. The Egyptian taskmasters were instructed to demand more work of the Hebrews for their unruliness; there was a general uneasiness, a feeling that the Exodus might not come off, and that all Hebrews would suffer severe discriminatory penalties. Moses and his following prevailed; the plagues were most impressive.

When Moses and the Levites could not control the situation, blame for it is projected upon the people. Because of their unseemly complaints to Yahweh, "His anger was kindled, and the fire of the Lord burned among them, and consumed some outlying parts of the camp." The people cried to Moses, who prayed to Yahweh, "and the fire abated."[22] Moses no doubt consulted the Ark and recognized that a temporary excess of electricity was leaving the Earth via tent poles and metals and exposed rock

The Levites and the Revolts

floorings. The electrical fire would travel to and enhance cooking-fires in or by the tents.

Having practiced several tricks with Yahweh at the Burning Bush - using an electric jumping rod and phosphorus - Moses employed them on a group of Hebrew leaders at a conference arranged by Aaron. They were impressed enough to hear his proposition, and liked it. But he had other difficulties from the beginning with organizing the people for Exodus. A change seemed gradually to come over him.

When the people cried in terror at the sight of the pursuing Egyptians and reproached those who had brought them out of Egypt, Moses spoke to calm them and to "see the salvation of the Lord which he will work for you today."[23]

The problem of bitter water three days into the wilderness from the Sea of Passage caused murmurings against Moses that he stopped by casting a certain tree made known to him by Yahweh into the waters, which made them potable [24].

When the people groaned with hunger and talked of returning to Egypt, Moses and Aaron addressed them, saying that all was the work of Yahweh:

> "For what are we, that you murmur against us?...Your murmurings are not against us but against the Lord."[25]

Quail fell in great numbers, as did manna, that could be baked into bread. Moses became angry when people tried to hold the manna overnight and, as he had warned them, it turned foul and wormy.

Then thirst assailed the Israelites. To their reproaches and threats to stone him, Moses retorted "Why do you find fault with me?" and, upon the advice of Yahweh, found water beneath rock. The Levites, we learn, earned high praise for helping Moses to suppress the protesters.

When a protest was raised, the complaint was turned against the people. To strengthen their own position, Moses and Aaron displaced responsibility upon Yahweh, let the people know how sinful they were to attack the Lord, and then punished them whenever they could.

The *Books of Moses* are generally unfair to the Jewish people, giving little credence to their opinions, requiring of them self-abasement, piling up rites endlessly, dwelling upon their "unfaithfulness" and exalting the wrath of God. As I labored to fix my mind and feelings within the mental, social, and physical state of the Exodus and Wanderings, I was often diverted by free associations to find myself once again amidst the English dissenters of the 17th century, the American colonial puritans of the same age, and the westward movements of the New Englanders. All of these, which I had studied when young, were attempts by groups to relive the Pentateuch; in some ways they are better analogies than the anthropological and historical comparisons of the Mosaic Jews with other semitic and nomadic groups, which are so common, for we have more information on precisely those matters which are left vague in the Bible - namely the reasons for the resistance to mosaic theocracy, the limits of the theocrats as nation-builders, and the souls and aspirations of the common men and women who were caught up in the new Israel.

Despite the considerable successes of the Jews in

The Levites and the Revolts

surviving as a people within the Mosaic framework and despite their occasional successes, under David and Solomon, for example, in setting up a larger national state, they could not establish an enduring nation over the centuries. It used to be believed that the position of Israel between great nations such as Egypt and Assyria made their military position difficult. But this is *post facto* reasoning; military history reveals a Roman Republic that wrested central Italy from numerous apparently stronger neighbors; a revolutionary France surrounded by enemies, which defeated them all; a Germany surrounded by enemies that required a concerted alliance including overseas America to contain it; and a contemporary Israel that has had to be restrained by distant great powers from conquering an empire in the Near East.

I am permitted, therefore, to think that the dominating influence of mosaism in Jewish history was a principal source of Israelite misfortunes over many centuries. By way of analogy, it was only the breaking away from mosaic theocracy - the taking in of other peoples, the revolt of democratic sects such as the Baptists of Roger Williams in Rhode Island, the coming of new democratic sects such as the Quakers, the rise of free science and a commercial life free of religious and state regulation - that permitted the explosive expansion of American culture in the eighteenth and nineteenth centuries within a unified and great domain. Because the people of Israel were downgraded and thwarted and kept as Children of God and Moses, the Jewish nation labored between an absolute monarchic vision and the squabbling tribes. The change in Moses, from a supplicating organizer of a loose aggregate of new believers to a religiously inspired autocrat, occurred in the first few weeks of Exodus and might have been predicted from his character. He was afraid at first that the people would not follow him, but once in control of the people, he set about becoming their absolute master.

It was no doubt Moses who led the Israelites to believe that they had been abominably enslaved in Egypt. This was required to counter-balance the call of Egypt to which many of the Israelites responded wistfully and by rebellion over many years. It was also a useful myth to inspire gratitude for Moses and Yahweh. The slogan is dinned into their ears: Yahweh (and Moses) led you out of slavery in Egypt. Obey them gratefully.

As soon as possible, Moses proclaimed a "Royal Covenant"[26] to replace the implied covenant with Pharaoh. A new authority, Yahweh, had to replace the old. (Thus were the mosaic Puritan covenanters of New England, who were fracturing their bond with the royal authority of England.)

About a dozen insurrectionary crises are registered in the Bible and legends[27]. In organizing the Exodus within Goshen, Hebrews clashed amongst themselves and with gentiles. A legend goes so far as to say that all Hebrews who refused to leave Egypt were massacred under cover of the plague of darkness. The leaders wanted no one to know of the dissent in the Hebrew ranks. The Bible gives only a hint of this; Moses and his cohort are opposed by many doubters and realists.

Next, Pi-ha-Khiroth; fights break out as so many desert the Exodus. The Levites acquitted themselves well here, but there was no way of avoiding a great many desertions. The sea was crossed and a great feast of singing

The Levites and the Revolts

and dancing by all, led by Miriam and including angels, took place. But after the ball was over, Israel petitioned Moses for a return to Egypt. The legend recites the story in a reasonable way:

> Hardly had they seen that the Egyptians met death in the waters of the sea, when they spoke to Moses, and said: "God has led us from Egypt only to grant us five tokens: To give us the wealth of Egypt, to let us walk in clouds of glory, to cleave the sea for us, to take vengeance on the Egyptians, and to let us sing him a song of praise. Now all this has taken place, let us return to Egypt." Moses answered: "The Eternal said, 'The Egyptians whom ye have seen today, ye shall see them again no more forever.'" But the people were not yet content, and said, 'Now the Egyptians are all dead, and therefore we can return to Egypt.' Then Moses said, "You must now redeem your pledge, for God said, 'When thou hast brought forth the people out of Egypt, ye shall serve God upon this mountain.'" Still the people remained headstrong, and without giving heed to Moses, they set out on the road to Egypt, under the guidance of an idol that they had brought with them out of Egypt, and had even retained during their passage through the sea. Only through sheer force was Moses able to restrain them from their sinful transgression [28].

Might this indeed have been Moses' greatest error, that he did not turn his expedition around, and, leaving a force to repel the oncoming Hyksos-Amalekites, go back to conquer Egypt in the name of Yahweh?

Then there are protests and demonstrations when the first crisis of thirst occurs, only several days into the desert. The word "murmuring" in the Bible must be distrusted; it means protest, demonstrations, a crisis requiring defense and resolution by Moses and the armed forces.

Next comes the food crisis. It lets one imagine that most sheep and cattle were lost in the first week of Exodus. Now came the quail - a gift and a punishment from Yahweh. Great flights of the birds fell - probably not quail alone. But the high doses of pollutants to which they had been subjected and which helped to bring them to earth poisoned many of the people. The Anger of God rose and "he slew the strongest of them, and laid low the wicked men of Israel."[29] Quail can carry a viral infection, it is argued, but a legend says that they came in a great wind, and the results were dramatically sudden.

The manna was certainly a godsend; it was not only nourishing but probably contained a specific antidote to radiation poisoning as does honey [30]. Next came the second crisis of thirst. Here, on the rock at Mount Horeb, Moses produced water with his rod.

In the third month of the Exodus, Israel was encamped below Mount Sinai. Moses ascended the mountain and, upon his long-delayed return, was greeted by the spectacle of the Golden Calf. This revolt will be described shortly. Then came the mysterious fire of Taberah, so unconnected with a specific misconduct of the people that the most general explanation is required; the Wrath of Yahweh was kindled and burned down portions of the camp. It was an electrical fire. Dissent and complaint were blamed. A legend speaks persuasively on the subject of the fire. The fire wrought havoc upon the idolatrous tribe of Dan and upon the Egyptian and foreign mixed multitude [31]. Yet we learn that as a result of this dissent and fire, Moses decided upon the election of the new elders by means of a lottery.

Then Aaron and Miriam personally remonstrated and

The Levites and the Revolts

demanded a showdown with Moses. Yahweh called Aaron and Miriam to the tent. Miriam emerged a "leper." Moses was appeased and kept both at their appointed functions. The people could see that not even the close-in family could affect the bond of Yahweh with Moses.

A legend says that Miriam and Aaron "talk against Moses" because his wife is a foreigner, a Kushite, hardly true, since Zipporah was from Jethro, the Midianite, not out of Ethiopia. Perhaps it is his second wife, we suggested earlier, also a foreigner. Perhaps Miriam wants Moses to begin a hereditary line of seers of Hebrew tribal extraction. Moses refuses and has Yahweh punish them. A foreign wife is preferable to a Jewish wife; she is without familial and tribal support, without hereditary linkage to Jacob. Moses is not interested in a succession; perhaps he does not foresee the survival of Israel, as we imply later on. He is not "a family man" as we have already indicated.

Next came the Report of the Spies [32]. All who disputed Moses' intimation that the time might have come for an incursion into the Promised Land were executed. Many others died in a plague, for once again harkening to the Call of Egypt. "Let us choose a captain and go back to Egypt, they said." Further, all must now wander a full forty years and never would those who had departed from Egypt live to see the Promised Land except Caleb and Joshua, who had refused to agree to the majority report.

According to legend, when the people thought that Moses was going to go against the Report of the Spies, "in their bitterness against their leaders they wanted to lay hands upon Moses and Aaron, whereupon God sent His cloud of glory as a protection to them under which they sought refuge." The crowd even cast stones into the cloud in trying to smite them [33].

Moses here does something only a true Machiavellian ruler would do; he punishes the spies for their pessimistic report and punishes the people for believing it. But he believes it himself, and he tells the people that now they must continue wandering because of their lack of faith in him and Yahweh. He also talks Yahweh out of exterminating the Jews for their general pessimism and nostalgia for Egypt.

Later on occurs the serious revolt led by Korah. For this episode, we reserve ample space a little later on. After Aaron's death, bitter civil warfare broke out again, between those who wanted to return to Egypt and those, especially the Levites, who insisted upon continuing toward Palestine [34]. The legend says that they actually retreated eight stations to Moserah. The Tribe of Benjamin lost most of its warriors and six other tribes lost heavily. Several divisions of Levites were mauled and did not recover until the time of David, some centuries later. Peace was made in a great mourning ceremony for Aaron.

Once more there is a grave insurrection, this time at Beth Peor, just before Moses' death, and of this too we shall shortly speak. When Joshua assumed command before the entry into the Promised Land, he instituted severe measures to unify the Israelites. He had all households destroy their god-images, masks, and other sacred representations [35]. And he ordered by command of Yahweh a general circumcision; the Bible says that those born in the desert had not been circumcised [36]. This is odd, coming so long after Moses had appeared to demand it; it does indicate, I think, that circumcision was a relatively new practice without heavy sanctions of opinion and tradition or else that a great many non-Hebrews had joined Israel on exceptional terms, or both. The population was now consecrated to the Holy War in Palestine.

Ringing in their ears were the words of Moses' last address to the people of Israel: "You have been rebellious against Yahweh from the day that I knew you."[37] True words, spoken by Moses-Yahweh, implying once more that Moses and Yahweh came late to know the Hebrews. Moses was not born and bred a Hebrew.

REVOLT OF THE GOLDEN CALF

Moses had gone up to Mount Sinai, at the command of Yahweh, and there received for the first time the Law and the tablets engraved by the finger of Yahweh. Returning from the lengthy isolation on the mountain, he discovered to his consternation that in his absence the people had melted down their gold and fashioned a calf of it, and around this marvelous image were worshipping, eating, dancing and singing.

For they had beset Aaron, demanding: "Up, make us gods, who shall go before us; as for this Moses, the man who brought us out of the Land of Egypt, we do not know what has become of him." So Aaron asked for their gold jewelry and melted it and fashioned it into a molten calf. And the people said: "These are your gods, O Israel, who brought you up out of the Land of Egypt." Whereupon Aaron "built an altar before it" and declared a feast day for the Lord.

> The people then betook themselves to the seventy members of the Sanhedrin (the ruling council of elders) and demanded that they worship the bull that had led Israel out of Egypt. 'God,' said 'they, had not delivered us out of Egypt, but only Himself, who had in Egypt been in captivity.' The Sanhedrin remained loyal to their God, and were hence cut down by the rabble [38].

This legend indicates that the Revolt was even more bloody than the Bible depicts (as well as testifying to the cometary bull).

In his fury, Moses cast down and broke the tablets given him by Yahweh. He seized the calf. Aaron blamed the people: "You know the people, that they are set on evil."[39] The people were scattered all about; the military aspect of the camp was quite lost. Moses stationed himself at the gate of the camp and called: "Who is on the Lord's side? Come to me."

The sons of Levi gathered around and Moses' orders were brief and harsh: "Put every man his sword on his side, and go to and from gate to gate throughout the camp, and slay every man his brother, and every man his companion, and every man his neighbor." Within the day, the Levites slaughtered three thousand men of Israel. Moses had the image of the bull burned and ground into powder. Then, mixing the gold powder with water, he forced the heretics to drink it. Order was restored. Moses spoke to the people, reproaching them but promising to intercede with the Lord regarding their great sinning. But Yahweh sent a plague upon the people because of the Golden Calf[40].

Although the Golden Calf disappeared into frightful memory, this was not the last of non-Mosaic Judaism, and most Jews were lost to Israel and Yahwism for the worship

The Levites and the Revolts

of Baal and other gods in the centuries to come. The Northern Ten Tribes, breaking away from the united kingdom to found a Northern Kingdom of Israel "worshipped all the hosts of heaven and served Baal." King Jeroboam founded at Dan and Bethel sanctuaries that rivaled the Temple of Jerusalem. He set up in each a golden calf image to Yahweh, and appointed non-Levites as temple custodians [41]. They were destroyed in 723 or 722 B.C.

Similar events occurred in the Southern Kingdom under Manasseh. Then, shortly before the Babylonians descended upon them and carried them off into exile, Josiah restored Yahweh against much popular opposition. Many Jews fled then and later to Egypt, where they worshipped Anat-Yahweh, Venus, "Queen of Heaven."[42]

What did the Golden Calf represent, if not Anat-Yahweh (as it is called in a Psalm)? It was the child of the comet Venus-Baal-Ishtar-Athene-Minerva-Isis-Devi and a hundred other names from all over the world. The same calf became the sacred cow of the Hindus who were moving just then into India.

The young bull was the apparition of the great comet at some points of its approach and retreat from near collision with the Earth, when it looked like a cow, bull and calf. "Only if we realize the planetary-cometary significance of the *egel* (meaning 'young bull', but also 'roundness'), do we find any sense in the reaction of the People of Israel to the calf." "... and... they cried: This is thy God, O Israel, which brought thee up out of the land of Egypt!"[43] One legend says that, while passing through the Red Sea, the people saw the Celestial Throne and most distinctly the ox among the four creatures around the throne (lion, man, eagle, ox) and therefore they thought to worship the ox as the helper of God in the Exodus [44]. Another report, already cited, says that the bull was inscribed on the chariot of the Lord as he drove across the skies in aid of the Hebrews.

The comet was regarded as the offspring of the greater god Jupiter-Zeus-Marduk-Amon-Yahweh in many places, and confused with these divinities, who were universally fire-and-thunder gods.

Moses would not have it so: His Yahweh spoke from heaven and mountains, true, but was a god of electric fire. He filled the heavens but not visibly. He was among his chosen people, went with them in those days in an awe-inspiring physical sense. Still, apparent in the verses of the Bible is the fright of Moses that somehow Yahweh would not act for him in the aftermath of the revolt. He pleads for assurances; he has to repeat the whole act again, returning to the mountain and descending once more, this time in a subdued triumph.

No Golden Calf could fight for the Jews like the Ark of the Covenant. No astrology could have provided a people with so personal a god as did the electrical science of Moses. Yahweh was always moving, always up to something new. All, even in the remote outskirts of the camp, had their attention focussed upon Moses and the Tabernacle.

Moses had every reason to become furious. The shock of betrayal was great. The people were ungrateful, too. They must have hated him to think him dead and become so happy. The fragility of his charisma was apparent. All of his plans seemed wrecked, the designs of the sacred machinery and of the religious center, detailed even to the priestly clothing and ornate draperies. The gold that the leaders had caused to be begged, borrowed, and stolen in Egypt was now unclean, and could not be reused for the instruments of the sanctuary. If the dancing and singing were not enough, a mere glance at the young bull exhibited its sexual connotations. Why was it a young bull - to replace Moses, the old bull? (Moses had already designed an altar with four corner-horns of undesignated species fashioned of wood in one piece with the altar.)[45] Many of his subordinate leaders had been massacred in the attempted coup d'état. For it was such; Levites, among others, were involved. A cometary image would replace Moses as the center of sacramental behavior; half of his power would be gone. His electrical science would be demysticized, desacralized.

The reprisals of the counter-revolution were severe. Perhaps thousands were slaughtered. All weapons were seized[46]. The gold-poisoned drink killed many. The legend says it was a form of "capital punishment."[47] A plague of Yahweh raged among the guilty people, until all who were involved were dead or had fled into the desert; Moses exterminated all those who had been unclean. As for the loyal and the non-participating, and for himself, he discussed seriously with Yahweh the question whether they too were unworthy to survive.

After the Revolt, Moses had his tent removed from inside to outside the camp. He posts Levite guards before it and says it is a tent of coming together. Actually it marked a new phase of reaction. He needed greater personal safety. He felt more strongly than ever in isolation from and aversion to the people. Perhaps he thought, too, that one day Yahweh would set the whole camp ablaze with a fire from his "Mercy Seat" and strong winds.

KORAH'S REBELLION

A 13th century English painting of the Rebellion of Korah [48] shows the rebels being assailed from the heavenly canopy by many pointy little tongues of flame. "These tongues remind us of 'little quadrants of light... constantly jumping' along a wire at the Harvard College Observatory at Pike's Peak, Colorado,' as described in a report [50].

Korah's revolt posed a grave threat to Moses' absolute rule. The boldness with which the rebels moved in upon Moses and close-in loyal supporters indicates a large confidence in their chances of success. It happens at the semi-permanent encampment at Kadesh, whence a short time before the spies had been sent out. Korah, himself, is rumored to have been Treasurer to the Pharaoh of Egypt. He was both a Levite and a Kohathite, therefore of the division of Levites directly responsible for the management of the sanctuary, except that the most critical jobs were given to Aaron and his priesthood. Legend has it that Korah was angered at having been passed over by Moses for the leadership of the Kohathites. Moses probably had already had trouble with Korah.

Top leaders, at least 250 says the Bible, were openly lined up with Korah. They had a large popular following, which Moses appreciated. And when the leaders confronted him at the Tabernacle the day after the rebellion began, they brought with them their popular following. Moses invoked the crowd to disperse, and it did so, possibly because he threatened them with a plague and also because he seemed to be striking a deal with the rebels.

The Levites and the Revolts

The philosophy behind the rebellion was well thought out. The rebels declared to Moses: "You have gone too far! For all the congregation are holy, every one of them, and the Lord is among them; why then do you exalt yourselves above the assembly of the Lord?" Notwithstanding that he is the one accused of exalting himself, Moses transfers the problem to a grasping for the top offices: Isn't it enough, you Levites, says Moses, that you do special services for Yahweh and are near him. "Would you seek the priesthood also? Therefore it is against the Lord that you and all your company have gathered together; what is Aaron that you murmur against him?"[51]

Moses promptly changes the grounds of debate. He does not address the main charge that he, Moses, acts as alone holy, whereas the doctrine of Yahweh is that all Israel is holy, each man in his own special relationship to God, as the Covenant with Yahweh would imply. Moses points out that Levites are in fact privileged and separated from the people of Israel. Thus he begins to isolate them from the people and limit their demands.

Moses then, I think, carries out a secret plan which he had held in abeyance for just this eventuality. No doubt he had conducted experiments with animals, and, I would guess, with prisoners who were caught in holy wars and brought to receive judgement within the courtyard or even before the "mercy seat" of Yahweh[52].

He announced to the rebel chieftains that, since they claimed equality before Yahweh, they should arrange to present themselves fittingly, lighted bronze censers in hand, with Aaron, before the Holy of Holies to see whom Yahweh would select to receive a sign of his favor. The decision would be up to Yahweh; this is repeatedly stressed. And they must not bring their weapons.

The rebels consented and repaired to their tents. Moses, Aaron, Joshua, and their most faithful assistants went to work. They set the Ark to accumulate its maximum charge short of sparking. Given both the atmospheric charge held by the cherubim and the ground charge gathered by the outer golden sheath of the box and focussing in the rod that extended above the outer box at the rear center of the mercy seat, a voltage of from 20,000 to 100,000 could be accumulated.

The total Tabernacle area was about 15,000 square feet, and was fenced off and guarded. The area enclosing the Altar of Incense before the curtain of the Holy of Holies was some four hundred square feet. Many, perhaps all, of the rebel chieftains, could press into the inner sanctum and the rest would crowd at the entrance. The tent would have been pitched originally on all area where ground currents of negative ions could readily be attracted.

Lightning is the discharge of the electrical potential (termed "voltage") between two points of different charges, when the setting is between air and ground or is air-to-air. Average amperage (current) may be about 20,000[53]. Electrical charges are measured in coulombs. Current is measured in joules or amperes. Resistance is measured in ohms. Electrical discharges can peel a sapling, undress a person, and pluck chickens. The effects of electroshock upon the human body depends upon the individual constitution, both genetic and acquired, and upon the intensity of the current (amperage) which enters the body and where it passes in relation to the heart or brain. "Fatal traumas from

The Levites and the Revolts

potentials of 10-24 V are described in the literature."[54] The current in such cases is perforce low, even under 100 Amperes. In most deadly instances, voltages of under 400 are involved. "As the great majority of electrical fatalities are due to currents passing between an arm (usually the right) and the legs, the current passes through the chest and affects the organs within it."[55] The longer the "juice is on," the greater the danger.

> Earth current can be a source of great danger. If a current of 50,000 amperes enters the soil at a point and spreads out uniformly in all directions, the current density, and hence the voltage drop, along the ground surface will be appreciable even at a considerable distance from the flash. The furrows which sometimes radiate from the point actually struck show that the voltage-drop may be sufficient to produce actual discharges through the soil. The voltage between two points on the earth separated by the length of an animal's stride might therefore be quite sufficient to pass an appreciable current up one leg and down the other. There are many cases of cattle-killing which can be explained in no other manner. When 126 sheep out of a flock of 152 are killed by a single flash, it is hardly conceivable that they were all hit by the main channel [56].

But we need not speak only of lightning. Closer at hand and more controllable was the artificial lightning of Moses. Granted that an electrocution of a herd of livestock is possible by lightning, we may surmise that a deliberate mass electrocution of humans would be possible, especially 3400 years ago, when electrical conditions of nature were disturbed. In the earliest beginnings of modern electrical science, and in a mood of dangerous play that forms an ironic and tragic contrast with the Old Testament setting, we find enough ideas and procedures to understand the behavior of Moses and the Israelites. It is worth citing in detail the new scientists of the mid-eighteenth century in connection with Korah's Revolt.

> Mr. George Graham shewed how several circuits for the discharge of the Leyden phial might be made at the same time, and the fire be made to pass through them all. He made a number of persons take hold of a plate of metal, communicating with the outside of the phial; and all together, likewise, laid hold of a brass rod with which the discharge was made; when they were all shocked at the same time, and in the same degree [57].

Scientists elsewhere produced similar effects:

> In France as well as in Germany experiments were made to try how many persons might feel the shock of the same phial. The Abbé Nollet, whose name is famous in electricity, gave it to one hundred and eighty of the guards, in the King's presence; and at the grand convent of the Carthusians in Paris, the whole community formed a line of nine hundred toises (1754 meters), by means of iron wires between every two persons (which far exceeded the line of one hundred and eighty of the guards) and the whole company upon the discharge of the phial, gave a sudden spring, at the same instant of time, and all felt the shock equally [58].

Joseph Priestley's own experiment is especially worthy of attention. It is contained in an essay entitled "Entertaining Experiments performed by means of Leyden Phial."

The Levites and the Revolts

> A great deal of diversion is often occasioned by giving a person a shock when he does not expect it; which may be done by concealing the wire which comes from the outside of the phial under the carpet, and placing the wire which comes from the inside in such a manner in a person's way, that he can suspect no harm from putting his hand upon it, at the same time that his feet are upon the other wire. This, and many other methods of giving a shock by surprise, may easily be executed by a little contrivance; but great care should be taken that these shocks be not strong, and that they be not given to all persons promiscuously.
>
> When a single person receives the shock, the company is diverted at his sole expense; but all contribute their share to the entertainment, and all partake of it alike, when the whole company forms a circuit, by joining their hands; and when the operator directs the person who is at one extremity of the circuit to hold a chain which communicates with the coating, while the person who is at the other extremity of the circuit touches the wire. As all the persons who form this circuit are struck at the same time, and with the same degree of force, it is often very pleasant to see them start at the same moment, to hear them compare their sensations, and observe the very different accounts they give of it [59].

Priestley's happy sublimated imagination was far removed from mosaism. (He was, in fact, a founder of Unitarianism.) He could go on and on with games, given a few basic electrical principles.

> This experiment may be agreeably varied, if the operator, instead of making the company join hands, direct them to tread upon each others toes, or lay their hands upon each others heads; and if, in the latter case, the whole company should be struck to the ground, as it happened when Dr. Franklin once gave the shock to six very stout robust men, the inconvenience

arising from it will be very inconsiderable. The company which the Doctor struck in this manner neither heard nor felt the stroke, and immediately got up again, without knowing what had happened. This was done with two of his large jars (each containing about six gallons) not fully charged [60].

A number of drawings of mass shockings are to be found. The one in figure 18 from Japan is chosen precisely for its lack of explicitness. Made far removed, culturally and geographically, from the scene of the experiments, it would inform or persuade us of nothing scientific. Therefore it suggests how the memory of Moses' electrical operations might be distorted, sublimated, and finally misunderstood over the centuries. The drawings we possess of Korah's rebels show them dying mysteriously, victims of the invisible Yahweh.

In the deep shadows of the past, grim real games were going on. We can watch them only half-understanding. We imagine only the simplest devices and system, even though the applications may have been more sophisticated. Moses and his officers, early in the morning, poured water over the rock floor of the tent, wetting it thoroughly to make it as fully conductive from the earth as possible. A copper wire was laid down and around the floor of the area. Then the carpets ordinarily covering the floor were replaced, hiding the wire [61]. The wire connected at the Ark on a metal rod extending from the outside golden plate of the Ark. Thus a very large negative charge could gather and be prepared to discharge if contacted or approached close enough by a positive charge.

The Levites and the Revolts

Figure 18. Mass Electroshock.
(Source: Figure 13.2 from Heilbron. op cit)

The positive charge was in fact gathering from the atmosphere on the golden cherubim and inner lining of the Ark. The whole inner metallic complex of cherubim and lining were separated by a screen of wood or glass from the stored negative charges of the outside lining and its upright rod.

It is apparent now that the Ark is charging up heavily but is being prevented from discharging upon itself by the insulation. We recall that the wire beneath the carpet is disconnected, so we imagine that it was carried around to the Ark and affixed to a heavy metal bar. The movement of this bar is controlled by the priest Eleazer, son of Aaron, who can push it into a lock against the positively charged wing tip of a cherub. He is insulated by gloves, masks, heavy clothing and non-conducting wood tongs. This is usual equipment for tending the Ark.

The rebels assembled the next morning, lighted censers in hand [62], before the Tent. Their large following had come as well, and Yahweh was enraged. They were threatened and dismissed by Moses. The sight of Joshua and many armed men frightened them, too. But also and even before the test of the rebels with censers, Korah and the two men who were rebels but refused to appear with the assembly at the tent had been killed dramatically at the instance of Moses. These two men had called out to Moses defiantly: "Are you going to bore the eyes of these men?"[63]

Aaron stood beside the Holy of Holies on an insulator, with insulating footgear and clothing, out of contact with any of the possible lines of electrical charge. He welcomed the rebels, who crowded, elbow to elbow, into the tent. They prostrated themselves before Yahweh, head, arms, knees, feet and censers touching the ground. Eleazer pushed the bar into the wing lock. Most, if not all, of the rebels were promptly electrocuted as the charges raced towards each other and coursed through each man, striking upwards at the brain and heart. Those merely stunned and shocked would be dispatched by the swords of Joshua's guards, moving in from their insulated corners, after the charges were spent, or the connecting bar was pulled out.

"Fire came forth from Yahweh and consumed the two hundred and fifty men offering the incense."[64] Thus the Bible. "The souls, not the bodies of the sinners were

The Levites and the Revolts

burned..."[65] Thus the legend.

Perhaps this method of mass execution was not followed [66]. The Ark might provide a second method by individual sparks. In both is involved the ancient and primitive means of administering justice through the trial by ordeal. Such is the trial of a woman for adultery, for instance, in the Bible[67]. The accused is traumatized, and is deemed guilty or innocent depending upon the outcome of the test or ordeal: "Yahweh will show who is holy, and will cause him to come near to him."[68]

Electrocution by the Ark of so many, individually, would be much more difficult. Since each leader was to be judged by Yahweh, each in turn would be marched to the altar and struck down. Men who were physiologically resistant to fatal shock would be dealt with by sword. (The Abbé Nollet in 1746 "gave the shock with porcelain, and observed that some persons were much more sensible to it than others in whatever part of the circuit they were placed.")[69] Those who refused the test would be dispatched by the sword; for the refusal was taken to be a confession of guilt. A ring of guards around the tent prevented any break-out of the group.

From a rubbed and electrified jar, Von Kleist, dean of the cathedral in Camin, in 1745, took "a nail, or a piece of thick brass wire" that carried a charge; "it throws out a pencil of flame so long, that, with this burning machine in my hand, I have taken above sixty steps, in walking about my room."[70] Around the same time, Monnier discovered that "the Leyden Phial would retain its electricity a considerable time after it was charged, and to have found it do so for thirty-six hours, in time of frost. He frequently electrified his phial at home, and brought it in his hand, through many streets, from the college of Harcourt to his apartments in the King's gardens, without any considerable diminution of its efficacy."[71]

Heilbron sums up this development: "Physicists soon learned that an electrified phial need not explode to be intriguing: when doing nothing at all, innocently insulated, it unaccountedly preserved its punch for hours or days. Even when grounded it remained potent, provided that its top wire was not touched."[72]

The English experimenter, Wilson, equally early (and all of these experiments and many more occurred before Franklin's discovery of positive and negative charges), found that the first discharge of a simple Leyden jar was the most explosive and dissipated the load quickly. "Whereas, when water was used, the subsequent explosions were more in number, and more considerable; and when the phial was charged with nothing but a wire inserted into it, the first explosion and the subsequent ones were still more nearly equal."[73]

Aaron, of course, came out well from the ordeal. The manner of Korah's death, by turning into a ball of flame that rolled into a cleavage of the Earth, is not too far removed from what might have happened in several cases, with help from the special police, and could have been a report displaced from these to Korah, the most important figure, as often happens in the garbling of news reports.

Now Eleazer was told by Yahweh "to take up the censers out of the blaze; then scatter the fire far and wide."[74] Afterwards, the censers were melted down and fashioned into a plate for the altar. Thereafter nobody save

The Levites and the Revolts

of the seed of Aaron would dare to "come near to burn incense before the Lord ," lest he die. This grim reminder was an endless source of sorrow to the families of the deceased, the legend says [75].

The next day a mob approaches the tent of Moses, "murmuring" as was their wont, whereupon the cloud of Yahweh appeared dispersing them. "Wrath has gone forth from Yahweh, the plague has begun."[76] Some 14,700 people were killed in this manifestation, says the Bible, before Aaron, with his blessed censer, could move out and halt the plague. The implication is that the cloud was directed into the crowd of people, for Yahweh told Moses to get out of the way before he consumed them. The cloud was of some type of poison, evidently, probably white phosphorus grenades cast into their midst by Moses' soldiers. Faced with declaring this, or assigning the action to Yahweh, the Bible, as it commonly does, simplified and moderated the action by laying it upon Yahweh; ruthlessness becomes justice when done by him.

To confirm the end of the three-day tragedy, another contest is rigged. This time a beam is split into twelve rods, Aaron receiving the rod of Levi, and the tribes a rod marked for each of them. After a night by the Ark, Aaron's rod has grown blossoms and almonds. Let us say that it has been sundered in a most interesting fashion, which we have already described. Thus Aaron receives one more sign that he is to remain High Priest; Yahweh does not fear nepotism as did Korah and his rebels.

Following Korah's rebellion, Moses dowses, after Miriam's well dries up.

> "Moses then fetched out of the Tabernacle the holy rod on which was the Ineffable Name of God, and accompanied by Aaron, betook himself to the rock to bring water out of it."

He refused to find water from any random rock, despite the jeers of those who said he knew how to find water not because of Yahweh but because he had once been a shepherd. He insisted upon a chosen rock and succeeded in two attempts [77].

FREUD AND THE MURDER OF MOSES

Sigmund Freud, inventor of the psychoanalytic method, and principal creator of the theory of psychoanalysis, could not resist, in the last years of his life, the temptation to publish his highly speculative book, *Moses and Monotheism*. Correctly he foresaw that he would offend Christians and Jews - and, of course, the world of biblical scholarship.

Brave intellectual that he was, Freud offered frank answers to several moot issues. First of all, he claimed Moses to be Egyptian. So were most of the Levites, the retinue of Governor Moses (for Freud placed Moses most likely as the official in charge of Goshen, with its unruly Hebrew population). Moses was a devout follower of Pharaoh Akhnaton (Freud calls him Iknaton) and, upon the overthrow of this great reformer and monotheistic sun-worshipper, Moses aroused the Hebrews and others in his bailiwick to follow him out of Egypt to a land where they might worship Aton instead of Hammon or Amon or the solar identification of Aton, for Moses was more enlightened,

The Levites and the Revolts

and derived the first abstract god. For his pains, Moses received death in the end. Following the biblical scholar, Ernst Sellin, Freud argues that a rebellion overthrew Moses and he was killed.

The curtain then drops upon this hapless abrogation in the desert. Perhaps a century later, the same group, with the now assimilated Levites, make a religious and political pact with their ethnic relatives, the Midianites. If the Midianite "Jews" of Kadesh agree to a watered-down version of monotheism that takes in the ancient patriarchs such as Abraham and Isaac and accept, without mentioning his name, their one god (Aton?), and upgrade the history of the Exodus, then they - the Egyptian faction, now practically a tribe - would agree that Yahweh, a local volcano god who hovers about Mt. Sinai, become their special god, too, and lead them in a totally chauvinistic, ruthless career of expansion to the north and west. As token of their good will to their Egyptian brethren, the Midianites must also accept circumcision, which Freud, particularly in this case but also in general, believes to originate as a form of mutilation carrying on from generation to generation the punishment of the young for the murder of the father. The leader of this new Israel would be known in the future rewriting of history as Moses (number 2) and the intervening century or so would be forgotten.

Having concocted this scenario, Freud, a Jew, has brought the Jewish nation to an all-time historical low. They were, in the days of which *Exodus, Numbers, Leviticus* and *Deuteronomy* chant, mere barbaric Semites, acknowledging the memory of a single Egyptian god, guilty of murdering their greatest leader, and set to follow a frightful marauding God,

Yahweh, whose main claim to fame was that he was better than any other god they were likely to encounter in the course of their bloody wars. As for the Exodus, while not a stroll in the desert, it was a group departure when conditions in Egypt were unsettled.

Freud does not hesitate, in this forceful little book, apologetically presented, to promote three of his older scientific theses: religion as a collective neurosis; the unconscious collective memory of humankind as having begun its guilt-laden career with the murder of the father of a horde by the sons for possession of the womenfolk; and the slow release of the load of guilt upon tribes as well as individuals by a suppressed traumatic incident of early times or early life.

Freud uses the Exodus as a kind of unreliable case study in which the three concepts are displayed. Moses, says Freud, proclaimed a good god, a universal god, and became identified in people's minds with him. Although, to be sure, every attack upon a father or father-figure repeats the primeval prototype patricide, presumably the more meaningful and great the figure (e.g. Jesus Christ, Julius Caesar, Abraham Lincoln), the greater the burden of guilt thereafter. The killing of Moses was the greatest historical shock for the Jews and they have lived ever since in the guilt of this recollection, which they suppressed and denied even a few years after the rebellion against him.

But over many centuries this guilt has worked itself out by an increasing devotion to the ideals of Moses the First: an ever purer monotheism, a dedication to philosophy and intellectualism, a renunciation of instincts to violence, and an obsessive claim to the lion's share of the early history of universal religion. Little by little, they strove to eliminate the Yahweh in themselves in favor of the unknown universal god. They cannot help but feel the chosen people of God; their unique guilt goes to prove this.

It might be thought that, having gone this far, Freud would bestow his blessings upon Christianity. For Christianity, he points out, is founded upon the murder of the son who is also the father. As grateful recipients of this favor from Jesus, who stands for all sinners and who dies for their sins, the Christians are relieved from the very heavy burden of guilt carried by their fellow-Jews (speaking now of the earliest Christians who were all Jews): Freud offers this possibility. But, he argues, it does not happen so. For, the relief from the burden of their sins only permits Christians to behave badly with less troubled consciences. And especially badly towards the Jews who raised the issue in the first place in this particular form.

Hence Freud ends where he began - and where most scholars feel that he should have stayed - in the anthropological perspective that regards all religions as a more or less uncomfortable treatment of neurosis. But a great mind, like Freud, or Picasso, or Plato, or Leonardo, or Marx, or Dewey, is incapable of a work that is all bad. In the present instance, Freud does not labor under the compulsion of biblical scholars to cover up for Yahweh. He makes Judaism a part of the anthropology of religion. He reveals, by his very errors and wild speculations, the flimsy foundations of biblical exegesis that are made to seem solid by the silent consensus of biblical experts to assume or ignore them.

But there are a number of improbabilities and impossibilities in Freud's study of Moses and the beginnings of the Jewish nation. For some of these he was responsible, such as various exaggerations, as when he exaggerates the unconscious guilt felt by Jews for the "murder" of Moses; it is most doubtful that the average Jew has, since the Romans became Christian, been more guilt-laden than the average Christian. And one must challenge, too, whether a group-trauma operates in the group over the millennia just as an individual trauma functions in a single lifetime. The old bulls are disposed of in many a mammal group without guilt-feelings. There had to be an interposition of conscience, which would require a more fundamental genetic or environmental change than a repetition of an act that had been going on long before humanization occurred.

Freud's official biographer, Ernest Jones, provides illumination: Freud had thought of his idea for many years. Nearly thirty years earlier he was looking upon Carl Jung as his successor and referred to him as "son and heir." Further, "Jung was to be the Joshua destined to explore the promised land of psychiatry which Freud, like Moses, was permitted to view from afar. Incidentally, this mark is of interest as indicating Freud's self- identification with Moses, one which in later years became very evident."[78] I pointed out earlier how, when in Rome, Freud was drawn to Michelangelo's statue of Moses and contemplated it for a long time.

So the "truth" which Freud revered was hidden from the master of unconscious truths. When the time came to analyze Moses, his genius failed him, for he was talking about "himself." Moses was not to have the traits that are strewn about the biblical record for the edification of the psychoanalyst, nor commit all of the horrendous acts that are described or to be inferred. Moses the First was a good man, like Freud; rather flat in profile, to be sure; and Egyptian, not Christian, because of some inconvenient lapse of time. Moses the Second was the Bad One and the Jews had become unhappily stuck with him and his Yahweh.

For two additional errors in his scenario, Freud was not completely responsible, but they are fatal to his work; they are errors of the same biblical historians who denounce him. The first is the false and evasive notion that the Exodus was not a journey through catastrophe. There was nothing in the experience, Freud believed, to determine Moses' behavior or a people's character or the events of history or a peculiar religion.

The second error that the professional establishment handed Freud was that Akhnaton lived before Moses. Velikovsky has demonstrated the opposite: Moses came first.[79] This of course is logically fatal to the thesis that Moses was a devoted disciple of Akhnaton and led a utopian community to the practice of his religion. The *Encyclopedia Britannica,* to exemplify what confronted Freud, even in 1974, some sixty years after Freud got his key idea, gives the reigning dates of Akhenaton (their spelling) as 1379 to 1362 B.C. and calls him "possibly the first monotheist in recorded history." (Freud uses the dates 1375 to 1358 B.C.) The same work accords Moses the date "fl(ourished) 13th century B.C." and reports that "Ramses II (1304-c.1237) was probably the pharaoh at the time." Freud puts the Exodus between 1358 and 1350 B.C., dates that he regards as shortly after the death and obloquy of Akhnaton. Hence Moses is supposed to have followed Akhnaton, and closely enough so that the fluid dating might even have permitted Moses to have personally known the guidance of Akhnaton.

Freud, the iconoclast, followed the great majority of traditional scholars on the key fact and went wrong. But how was he to know? Velikovsky had not begun to work on the problem. Freud was one more victim of the chaotic Egyptian chronology. The other psychoanalyst gone egyptological, Velikovsky, had discovered the weak point in Freud's psychic armor, and knew "in his heart" that Hebrew and Egyptian history must be synchronized. So he proceeded with an iron will, indefatigably, to disassemble the "unassailable" structure of ancient Near East chronology. In the process, and with the help of an unsupported, unpaid, self-disciplined, polymathic group of scholars, he ended up engaged in an assault upon the belief system of modern science as well [80].

BETH PEOR

There is usually a suspicion of foul play when a person disappears. Moses, says the Bible, went off alone to die and was buried by Yahweh in a gorge below Mount Nebo whence he had looked out over the Promised Land. (See figure 19) Strangely, it seems, he was buried facing Beth-Peor, where the last of the collective disturbances that marked his rule had occurred [81].

There the Israelites in large numbers had united with settled Moabites or Midianites in unauthorized religious festivals - particularly, recounts the Bible with some indignation, fertility rites encouraging free love in the fields in the name of the local Baal, with the purpose of inspiring nature to greater productivity.

The Levites and the Revolts

Freud cited Ernst Sellin, a German scholar, as proving Moses died in a revolt, but gives little detail on the occurrence, referring only to Hosea, a prophet of six centuries later, as insinuating the events. As I read this on a remote island, far from a copy of Sellin's book, I sought to follow the hypothesis by myself, in anticipation of ultimately locating the work.

Hosea writes a diatribe against the Israelites, which he acts out. Imitating, so he says, the behavior of Yahweh towards the Jews, he takes in marriage a prostitute. The history of his relationship to the prostitute whom he has freely and firmly wedded then comes to stand for the history of the wedding and marriage of Yahweh and the whoring people of Israel. I thought that Hosea or Yahweh here could as well be Moses, speaking as he often did for the Lord. And I thought of how Moses might have acted in the circumstances of Beth-Peor.

I concluded that there was a possibility that the old man, Moses, would have met his death in a murder or under undignified circumstances - a stone thrown, a stroke - in the course of suppressing the Baal-Peor heresy [82]. He was fearfully agitated and may have been fatally strained in dealing with the heretics and their Moabite seducers. Moses' loathing of sexual deviancy, his strenuous efforts to keep Yahwism free of sexual imagery (No Zeus bull rapist of Europa he! No Baal bull here!) and his severe attitude in general towards breakdowns of law and order, made him more ruthless than ever: the peoples' chiefs were hanged, murders were committed and sanctified, and plague carried off thousands of Israelites, 24,000 says the Bible. Moses directed, further, the extirpation of the Midianites [83], first the men in battle followed by massacre, then cold-bloodedly the male children and all women who were not virgins. Their camps and cities were burned, and their livestock and valuables taken as booty.

The verses on executing the Israelite leaders carry a grim double meaning 1) "Take all the chiefs of the people and execute them in full sunlight before the Lord so that My blazing wrath will be turned away from Israel" and 2) "Cut off the heads of the leaders of the people and impale them in the courtyard before My Holy Tent so that my blazing wrath will be turned away from Israel." Further, Moses ordered his officers: "Each of you slay those of your men who attached themselves to Baal-Peor."

The crowd before the court of the Tabernacle was full of grief and rage. To the many deaths occurring with the raging plagues of Yahweh there was added to their grief this harsh remedy to propitiate Yahweh which would also strike down many of their loved ones.

At this juncture, there passed before their eyes the noble Zimri, with his Midianite companion, the lady Cozbi, as they went into his family tent. Phineas, son of Eleazer and grandson of Aaron, in a fury, seized a spear and followed them. He drove the spear through their bellies. Moses approved. The plague ceased. Moses heard from Yahweh that Phineas' zeal for Yahweh's honor had saved Israel from extinction. Phineas earned the perpetual right to the priesthood for his family by this action. But what Moses had said was good in the eyes of Yahweh was perhaps beyond the sufferance of the people.

It was Moses' last battle on behalf of Yahweh. He knew that he was to die and perhaps wished to leave things

The Levites and the Revolts

tidy [84]. We note in Hosea, moreover, a repeated violent denunciation of the tribe of Ephraim, to which Joshua belongs, and which took for itself perhaps the richest section of the Promised Land. Possibly, Ephraimites accompanied Moses on his last journey.

No matter how Moses met his death, the Bible would adorn it with some elements of the legendary. Founding heroes of a nation are not permitted to die ignominiously or even ordinarily. Romulus, founder of Rome, was reported to have been swept into the skies where he joined his father, Mars. But, as Freud says, a murder by his own people would be shameful, considering what role Moses must be given in the founding of Israel. Hence what would be in any case censored and elaborated for the sake of the sacred egoism of the tribe would in this case invariably result in strong guilt feelings. Proportionately, as the return to Mosaic rule and law would be demanded by the prophets and priests, the guilt feelings would be restimulated, and work their way out in an even more frenzied and dedicated mosaism or Yahwism. This, then, would be the effect of a murder of Moses upon the history of Judaism. It is to be expected that the verses involved are considered as some of the most confusing and esoteric of the Old Testament.

So much was surmised by me from the normal open lines of the Bible. Three months later and five thousand miles distant, a microfilm copy of Sellin's work at the New York Public Library was consulted [85]. What had Sellin discovered? First, in various places the Bible refers to a Messiah, a servant of God, who is to deliver the Jews from their enemies; this person, says Sellin, was Moses. Moses was once the Redeemer and would return again to save the Jews

Figure 19: Myth of Moses Blessing the Tribes, and His Death.
(Bible of San Paolo Fuori le Mura ca. A. D 870., folio 49v)
ed [85].

The Levites and the Revolts

and establish in Jerusalem "a Kingdom of God for all nations."[86] In line with Hosea, Moses was considered by tradition, writes Sellin, to have been the atonement victim of the Baal Peor heresy. Long before, Moses had asked Yahweh to kill him in atonement for the sins of the people. This was during the Golden Calf Revolt [87]. The tradition of a second coming of Moses persisted into the third century and is even to be located in the New Testament, in the Gospel of Matthew (17:1-13).

The major thesis is summarized by Sellin: "Moses, in Shittim in the Holy place of his God was killed by a trick of his own people after they turned to Baal Peor and Moses had called them to repent or in any event had called down punishment upon them. Maybe his sons encountered death with him as well."[88] Sellin derives this scenario from three places in Hosea's book, and relies upon a reconstruction and some rearrangement of lines at ambiguous points; in these respects his ability is unquestionable and I would accept his new rendering. I repeat the verses here:

> "*They have dug a deep pit-trap in Shittim.*"*[89]*
> "*The days of terrible ordeal arrive; now come the days of reckoning.*
> *Israel shrieked:*
> '*A fool is the Prophet, a madman in his mind,*
> *Because of the enormous guilt and the great making of enemies.*'
> *Ephraim skulked by the tent of the Prophet and laid snares on all his*
>   *paths.*
> *In Shittim in the house of his God they have dug a deep pit.*
> *Like vines at the panicle I found Israel, like an early fig on the fig tree.*
> *They came to the Baal of Peor and gave themselves up to shame, and*
>   *became abominable fornicators.*
> *I have seen Ephraim as a poisonous plant. Ephraim chose as its hunting*

> *game the prophet*
> *and Israel led his sons out to be strangled,*
> *The people shall disappear beyond sight like birds .*
> *May it be the end of child-bearing, of conception, of pregnant bellies.*
> *Even should their sons grow, I shall take them away until there will be no one left.*
> *But a curse upon themselves as well, when I come skulking upon them.*
> *Give them, o Yahweh, what you can and will,*
> *Give them a childless belly and withered breasts." [90]*
> *"But through a prophet I brought Israel out of Egypt, and, it was shepherded by a prophet.*
> *Ephraim aroused his anger. Israel made him better.*
> *So long as Ephraim read my Torah the prophet was preeminent in Israel.*
> *Though he made atonement because of Baal he was killed.*
> *I will leave his blood upon you and I will make you pay his shame." [91]*

From the new rendering emerge certain clues. A great crime has been committed. The prophet who is involved was certainly not Hosea and is not any prophet before Hosea but Moses. Ephraimites are most involved in the sin and the crime. The people are enraged against Moses, a "fool" and "madman", burdened with the guilt of massacring his charges and hated for it. The conspirators hide themselves on the approaches to his tent, seize him, take him to the Holy Tent where stand the altars, and there dig a pit and bury him in it. They kill his family as well. Not since the original sin of Adam and Eve has such a sacrilegious act occurred. Ephraim (and by implication Israel) repeats the original sin; it is the original sin of the history of Israel from its founding to Hosea's time [92]. For it, Israel and especially the Ephraimites are cursed and must pay in days of terrible ordeal and reckoning. The worst curses of Hosea are in these lines. He would have the land and the people return to the

The Levites and the Revolts 311

desert so that Yahweh might rule as of old.

The Biblical scholar, Gressmann [93], and others, among them Sellin, believe that the judges refused to carry out the orders of Moses for the killing of all the people implicated in the Baal Peor orgies and rites, and that the Levites, obeying Moses, began to carry out the massacre. I think that these deaths must be the 24,000 who were scourged by Yahweh, as the Bible reports. The scourge or plague now was of the Levites' swords.

My theory is this: While the Levites were dispatched and dispersed upon their murderous mission, the Ephraimites trapped Moses, killed or disarmed his guards, killed him, buried him, and held prisoner Joshua of their own tribe. When Joshua agreed to recognize the coup d'état and to take command, as was his right, and as Moses would wish, he was released, and he ordered the Levites to cease operations. The killings by Phineas are passed over in arriving at the new ruling formula, and his sacred role is confirmed.

We note in connection with Joshua's role a legend educed by Elie Wiesel [94]:

> "When Moses refused to die, says the Talmud, God made him jealous of Joshua... God's explanation to Moses that he must die, to allow Joshua to take over, meant to Joshua that so long as he himself would not take over, Moses would go on living. For him to rule, his beloved teacher had to die."

One perceives here what could be a rationalization of Joshua's conduct and a hint of the killing of Moses.

An impressive network of authorities stress that Moses' death took place in public. It is witnessed, or almost witnessed, or circumstantially witnessed, even though the Torah and Bible assert that he finally died alone. Ginzberg [95] thinks that the legendary assertions originated to combat the vulgar demand that Moses not die but be made to ascend to heaven. A typical scenario has all of the people following him until they were dismissed; then the senate followed him until they too were dismissed; then finally a cloud descended over him and he was lost to the view of his last companions, Eleazer the priest and Joshua the generalissimo and heir apparent to Moses' authority.

 Can we decipher this legendary scenario? Only within strict limits. Suppose an alternative hypothesis; not Ginzberg's, but one in keeping with the theory of these pages, is suggested: if a great hero is killed and secretly buried by some of the very people to whom he is and will remain a hero, he must in legend either "really" not be killed and/or ascend to heaven. Thus Jesus is said to have been voluntarily killed and to have ascended to heaven. If he had been killed by his own people who had continued to believe in him, he would have ascended to heaven when his mission was completed without having being killed. But the Christians' discrimination against both Roman and Jewish authorities permit them to assert that he was killed; they need not cover the fact.

 A second point may be induced from the scenario. The public is asserted as a witness of Moses' death, at least down to the very last moment, when the two witnesses are left standing outside of the cloud enveloping Moses. If, on the one hand, the Bible has Moses dying quite alone, and the traditions have Moses dying in public, the contradictory insistence now upon the one, and then upon the other,

The Levites and the Revolts

implies that neither is correct and that both are straining for their own kind of credibility. If the solitary death admits the public, it must explain what kind of public was present and what it saw. If the public death admits the solitary, it must implicitly allow the belief that Moses was secretly killed. So the two legends exist in eternal uneasy partial contradiction, The legends of Moses' death dwell pathetically upon his desire to live, particularly to live to lead Israel into the Promised Land. The legends seem to feel an injustice is being done. We weep in sympathy with the grand old man's frustration and importunities to Yahweh. Why, too, must he die so alone? Why does Yahweh harden his own heart so, we wonder? Then, in a start of realism, we recall that Yahweh is Moses, and lives after Moses in the minds of the tellers of the story. Moses is condemned, dies, and is buried by Yahweh no more than the sons of Aaron are electrocuted by Yahweh for approaching the Ark in an improper frame of mind. Moses is killed by his enemies and his remains are disposed of. Both murder and burial probably occurred within the sacred precincts. Foes and friends join thereafter in a conspiracy to cover up the deed and refashion its circumstances into a sacred lie. Soon the sacred lie transforms itself psychologically into holy myth.

When the Israelites had crossed over the dry bed of the Jordan, Joshua did not immediately press on to attack Jericho. Instead, following the order of Yahweh to "circumcise the sons of Israel again, the second time,"[96] Joshua performed the ceremony and "when they had completed circumcising all the nation, they kept sitting in their place in the camp until they revived."[97] Yahweh, satisfied, said "Today I have rolled away the reproach of

Egypt from off you." In these passages, the Bible explains that all the circumcised men out of Egypt were dead but "all the people born in the wilderness... had not been circumcised."[98] Max Weber believes that the operation was performed so as to emulate the circumcised Egyptians and "allegedly in order to escape the scorn of the Egyptians."[99] Neither reason is correct, I think; rather the mass circumcision was an atonement for the collective guilt in the death of Moses, and a fresh affirmation of loyalty to the army of the confederation in preparation for the campaigns ahead. The location of Moses' grave was taboo to all except the High Priests and his attendants. In a sense, and as it would appear, Moses died by order of Yahweh. The Bible's insistence upon the unknown grave, while declaring it to be nearby, seems needless unless it is an unwitting confession that Moses was deliberately put into a grave that should be unmentionable and unknown (except in this metaphorical sense). And, as the Bible says, "his eyes had not grown dim and his vital strength had not fled."[100]

CHAPTER EIGHT

THE ELECTRIC GOD

A famous figure of the French Enlightenment of the Eighteenth Century, Voltaire, reduced the miracles of the Bible to a laughing stock of the French salons. Voltaire nevertheless believed in a god. In a world then bemused by the technology of clocks, with clock-makers and clock-philosophers everywhere, he examined the astronomical system of the Earth and the heavens and pronounced it a clock. With all of this clockwork, said he, there must be a clock-maker somewhere. So Moses and his men will be readily understood when, in an environment that exhibited electrical effects in many places, they found, behind the grand *son et lumière* show, a great electric god, Yahweh.

It may be that Moses, in ways unsuspected by the psychohistory of science, has infiltrated the lives and work of Newton, Darwin, Edison, Einstein, and others; by his tenacious insistence on the single god, he made all things dependent on a single system incorporating a key machine assembly, and therefore made an integrated philosophy of nature imperative. In one legend, Moses cannot get the great natural bodies Sun, Moon, Earth, Heaven, Stars, Planets, Sea, Rivers that is, all the gods of the Greeks, to intercede on his behalf with Yahweh because, they said, they were but

Yahweh's helpless creatures [1]. Possibly Yahweh's invisibility was a model of the ordinary invisibility (immateriality) and omnipresence of electricity, and of its appearing as incorporeal "fire" when it was visible. I think it no coincidence that among the enthusiasts and practitioners of early electrical science were numerous mosaist clergymen, both Catholic and Protestant. G. Beccaria, pioneer of electrical field theory, was a Piarist; John Wesley, founder of Methodism, wrote copiously on electricity.

By one cause or another, being mortal, Moses died. But Yahweh did not die. Even in the technical sense of "the name of the Lord," he did not die, because the Ark and Altar remained in the Yahwist repertory for some centuries. He was no longer, thereafter, much of an hallucination; he joined the ranks of the gods as a pure collective delusion. With the ups and downs typical of divine careers, he has come into the present.

Moses' greatest triumph was to bequeath a portion of his mind to posterity by means of Yahweh. Unfortunately, it was the wrong part, the conscience-loaded superego, but so it must go with the birth of religious cults. Since it was the hallucinatory and delusionary operations of his mind that were handed down, these would in some ways not be truly Moses. They would be idiosyncratically Moses, but not completely him.

Moses stopped far short of placing all his religious impulses into the hallucination of Yahweh; he seems to have been previously what might be called a liberal Hermist, a devotee of Thoth-Hermes-Mercury.

His invention-conversion to Yahweh did not eradicate the Hermetic qualities that took deep root during

The Electric God

his Egyptian years. His great and versatile skills gave him a reputation throughout the ancient world for being a veritable Hermes.

Julian Jaynes has developed a theory that the human race, for a period of time extending up to the classical period, was of two minds, one rational and pragmatic (corresponding to the traits of the left hemisphere of the brain) and the other mind hallucinatory and occupied by gods who talked to men and appeared before them (corresponding to the traits of the right side of the brain) [2]. Moses, he said, was an archetype of this type of mind. The hallucinations are of a type well-known in psychiatry, often if not always associated with a diagnosis of paranoid schizophrenia. This is true, I think, and also Moses was much more than Yahweh, and maintained a pragmatic balance that brought him great and justified fame as a scientist and leader,

There is much to be said for Jaynes' theory. Its analytic side is in line with what is advanced in these pages, and I have elsewhere pointed out that the complex membrane dividing the two lobes of the cerebrum, the corpus callosum, may well be the site of schizoid behavior; in fact, I have hypothesized that behavior which is specifically human has occurred because of a possible physiological-psychosomatic microsecond block in transfers of information and impulses through the corpus callosum; this delay would constitute an instinct block and therefore would promote human self-awareness, reflection, and the feeling of talking to oneself, whence one hallucinates others as well [3].

Jaynes was not able to cope with the historical materials, largely because he relied upon conventional ancient history and chronology. As a result, he was put into a position where he had to perceive just the opposite of the actual process. He says that the "bicameral mind" as he terms it, finally broke down because world-conditions became unsettled and the gods that had satisfied the needs of the hallucinators such as Moses lost face. In reality it was the catastrophes of the world whose terrible stresses made hallucinatory leaders out of borderline cases and staunch believers out of normal people. (And elsewhere Jaynes makes this very point.) There is every reason to believe that long cycles of history occurred before the time of Exodus and Moses when there were "golden ages" of Saturn and Elohim, whose central and celebrated significance was the reduced role permitted to mosaic characters, that is, reduced schizotypical behavior.

Yet, as one studies Moses as a person, it is plain that his peculiarities as a human being are remarkably well reflected in Yahweh as a god. If Yahweh were given a worldly childhood and experience, like some gods and god-heroes, instead of being presented full-blown, they could be like the childhood and experience of Moses. If Yahweh were extinguished from Biblical history as a god and became a kind of sequestered ruler speaking only through Moses, he might appear inexplicably incoherent, stupid, non-revealing of his motives and reasons and of his knowledge of the world. Moses would be continually besought by his people to seize the name and authority of the hidden power.

One is placed in a tight logical-psychological corner here. Speaking now for persons bred in cultures colored by mosaism, one's conception of a father is Moses' conception and is also, in fact, Moses. So when one says Moses is like a father, and is also like Yahweh, who is the father, one is measuring a standard by the standard itself.

One has to make a very simple statement, which sets up a very different anthropological perspective, namely: "I would not want Moses, hence Yahweh, for my father." When asked "Why?" one responds in the pragmatic manner: "Because I do not like the consequences." Then one lists those experiences that emanate from fathers like Moses-Yahweh. Those that evolve from other kinds of fathers are possibly better; in any event, one rejects the mosaic consequences.

THE NAME OF YAHWEH

Recently circles of biblical scholarship were agitated by some newly uncovered tablets of the ancient city of Ebla in Northern Syria that were reported to contain the name "Ya." If this were a contraction of "Yahweh," it might be Moses' Yahweh, and place the god several centuries earlier than we have him here. One of Moses' inventions would be struck from our list. More lately, it appears that the syllable might have had several usages in the Semitic languages, and that no single tie with Moses' Yahweh has appeared [4].

There is some likelihood, however, that Moses derived the name from the Midianites or another tribe thereabouts when he was in exile. Buber, for instance, says that Yahweh may be related to "Ya-hu," that is "O He!" of the Dervishes and that this cry occurs once in *Genesis* during the blessings of Jacob [5]. The name is not foreign to *Genesis;* Abraham uses it, but more commonly used is Elohim, and most likely, Yahweh was implanted in the *Book of Genesis* by Moses or Yahwist editors [6].

A suggestion can be made that would lend integrity to such an assertion. In the years of the grandson of Adam, "men began to call upon the name of Yahweh." I make the identification, as have others elsewhere, of Yahweh with gods of lightning and fire, such as Zeus and Jove, and I place the beginnings of the great electrical gods around the time of Adam and Eve, replacing Elohim and Saturn. Yahweh may have been inserted into *Genesis* to claim his own from times long past.

Ziegler maintains that "the original god of the Hebrews at the Exodus was Zeus." The Greeks change H to E and final H to S. (Jeremiah is Jeremias). The "Y" was originally a "Z". Thus YHWH becomes ZEWS or ZEUS, and with the erroneous transliteration of Y for J, "Jews." The Etruscan-Roman case, "Jove," pronounced "Yowe" is so close to Yahweh that the Roman Jupiter may be considered as basically the same entity [7].

Another theory holds that Moses framed the word from Egyptian roots, meaning "I am." Egyptian was familiar to all Hebrews and was Moses' native tongue. A Jewish legend says that Yahweh's first word when he announced the Decalogue was Egyptian: "Anoki!" ("It is I") [8]. The Bible has Yahweh announcing the well-known "I am that I am" from the Burning Bush. The phrase has been played upon endlessly, which is what a religious phrase should be and do for people. Moses is given to understand this when he asks Yahweh for more concrete identification, and it is denied him.

Let me now assemble the name of Yahweh in the

The Electric God

context of this book. Moses, learned as he was, had known the syllable "Ya"; he heard it, and also other compound words including it, in Egypt and then in Midian among the Kenites and the nearby tribes. It was a godword, part of various sacred epithets. He heard a sound very much like "Yahweh" streaming with light from the Burning Bush. This is the essence of god, he thought; it is the name of god and is hinted at in all the "ya" syllables that I have heard.

Now he asks what it is, and "Yahweh ehweh" is heard. This makes sense. "I am that I am." "I am the great I am." I am It!" "I am the essential principle." Not the principle of light alone. It is already sound and light. It is the activity of the skies and earthly nature. It is the main and primary manifestation. It is connected with the old gods as well.

Yahweh tells Moses: "Say this to the people of Israel, I am has sent me to you... Yahweh, the God of your fathers... has sent me to you: this is my name forever and thus I am to be remembered throughout all generations."[9] Then Yahweh tells Moses that his plea before the Pharaoh is to lead the Israelites thither to worship him. Unless Moses convinces the Hebrews that they should worship Yahweh [10] and that this will be the way that they will be able to break through to freedom, and unless he is ready to give the Pharaoh a good reason for their leaving Egypt, after so many years of sacrificing within Egypt, his plan will not work. He must therefore tie in Elohim, whom both Hebrews and Egyptians acknowledge, with Yahweh. So Yahweh is a very new god of special manifestations and with a concrete task to perform: getting Moses through the specific obstacles on both sides to an Exodus.

Hence, Moses was the inventor of Yahweh in every meaningful sense of an invention, no invention ever being unprecedented and quite new. Merely to imagine that it would be possible to propose a new god to the world was audacious and brilliant. Yahweh is explicitly new, yet another name, as Yahweh says, for the old god of the Hebrews. His name dwells most precisely on the mercy seat of the Ark, and then in the place in the temple chosen by him. With negligible exceptions he speaks only to and through Moses. Moses invents Israel as well, in the sense that he takes a nickname given to Jacob after Jacob has wrestled with God, or the Angel of God, and attaches it to the descendents of Jacob and the initiates into the new Yahwist Israelite group led by Moses himself. The term is translated variously as "the god-fighter " "God fights,"[11] "the god who battles," or "god rules." [12] Israelites were then "the people of the fighting god." Yahweh is of course a bellicose god, so the name is apt, and both "Israel" and "Yahweh" become battle cries of the newly founded nation.

The idea that the Jews never spoke the name YHWH seems to me preposterous. The name was inutterable simply because its authentic voice came only from the Ark of the Covenant. When the time came that the Ark was rarely functional, the name became secret. The name of "Amen" had the same history; presumably the Egyptian pyramids, too, were no longer displaying or sounding the god's name; whereupon it was said that Amon hid himself - not of course from all prayers and enunciations to which the response is "Amen."

Does not the idea that YHWH has the electric name of god when he spoke through the noise of the ark

The Electric God

contradict the very Third Commandment that says: "You shall not take the name of the Lord your God in vain?" Of this, Ziegler says, "with the idea of YHWH as an electrical discharge, there are at least three possible reasons for the commandment. First, there might have been a danger of injury to those using the power indiscriminately. Second, its use might have allowed the enemies of Israel to obtain this secret, Third, a frequent use of the power might discourage the worship of it."[13] Or at least, so Moses thought at the time. Actually the ark ceased to speak as YHWH when the electric age ended - around 600 B.C. - and the substitute notion arose that the commandment referred to the human voice not uttering the word YHWH, because it was the name of God[14].

Moses was concerned with law and order, and therefore with blasphemy. The Douay (R.C.) Bible adds abruptly to the Third Commandment: "For the Lord will not leave unpunished him who takes his name in vain."[15] The Jerusalem Bible (also R.C.) renders the verse as banning utterance of the name of Yahweh to misuse it (that is, maliciously or for unholy purposes).

Ziegler argues that "we are warned against effecting the sign or signature of the powerful YHWH. More specifically here, the Third Commandment forbids us without good reason to discharge an electric arc with its accompanying flash of light and noise. It is believed here that this discharge is the name of God, YHWH."[16] Later on the sound becomes a word and then a secret word, for the sound has gone.

Cassuto gives this version of the Commandment: "You shall not take up the name of the Lord your God for unreality, for the Lord will not hold him guiltless who takes His name for unreality."[17] I think that Cassuto's version gives us the clue for expatiating fully the commandment. The word is the thing. We face here the crux of the ancient philosophical debate between the "realists" and "nominalists," Platonists and Aristotelians. (Primitive, untrained thinkers and religious devotees are generally realists; the word is a sacred entity and not to be used as a mere tool, nor certainly for deliberate blasphemy.) The thing, by reverse (and incorrect) logic, is the word, and especially the sounded name, for the most ancient sacred associations of things and sounds came before the written word.

    The electrical discharge is the voice (as well as the vision) of Yahweh, and, in the Ark, the name of Yahweh. Blasphemy is any assertion that the sound of Yahweh is unreal and does not exist, and by inference that the name is an inconsequential incident; and by extension blasphemy is also any assertion that the name can be used for purposes other than harkening to the emanations from the sole source of the authentic God on the Ark. For common people, the sin of blasphemy is ordinarily a denial of the reality of the word, or ridicule of it.

    Bearing in mind this anthropological and psychological process, one can understand how the cult of the secret name of god developed and how the common sin and crime of blasphemy evolved.

    Does not the design of the Ark contradict the second commandment: it says "You shall not make for yourself a graven image, or any likeness of anything that is in heaven above, or that is in the earth beneath, or that is in the water under the earth; you shall not bow down to them or serve

The Electric God 325

them.." This is altogether strange since the Lord also commands that Moses make the Tabernacle and the Ark "after the pattern for them, which is being shown you on the mountain." And the Ark even carries two cherubim. The Ark itself was duplicated at a later time by a private person and carried off by the tribe of Dan. The answer is, of course, "I am a jealous god," who reserves the right to spot and destroy possible competitors, such as the Golden Calf

The cherubim were almost surely recognizable likenesses of living things, although Cassuto apologized that since they were composites of more than one being, they were not to be banned. He surmises that "on the *kapporeth* [the lid or mercy seat] there was not sufficient room for two images of quadrupeds, and it appears that the cherubim on it were erect figures, like the cherubim of Ezekiel's visions and those of Solomon's Temple [18]." R.W. Moss also believed them to be winged human figures [19]. The mention of quadruped is logical, inasmuch as many winged bulls and other animals are to be found of the same general period throughout the Near East. The word "cherubim" itself seems related to an Assyrian word for the winged bull.

Yahweh was a ground force sometimes exhibiting himself, but ruled the heavens invisibly. By keeping Yahweh as a heavenly god, under a new name, and invisible, Moses could avoid choosing among the specific historical heavenly gods. Moreover, Yahweh must not be identified with a heavenly body, for a good reason: the heavenly body could not be controlled or possessed uniquely by the Jews, that is, by Moses.

As time passed and the name of YHWH disappeared along with his image in electrical form and his burning of the altar-offerings, the Jews might have been expected to bring back images, especially of YHWH. But here we may call into play Freud's concept of instinctual renunciation which he applies to the self-denial of holy image-making [20]. This refusal of the strong urge to reproduce the forms of the deity was probably built up in the mosaic period and later on maintained by the compulsive repetition of the highly ritualistic religion, with discipline maintained by the priesthood. Referring to Max Weber's analysis of rabbinical Judaism, we may speculate that any image of

Yahweh would have to represent some other culture's image and therefore violate the "pariah" tendencies of the Jews.

Yahweh and Moses made the Jews a lonely people, isolated, not sharing other gods, as other nations did whenever they so desired for purposes of international amity and communication of sentiments. This was a source of pain to many Jews, as it was a source of pride to others. Many more Jews chose other gods than other people chose Yahweh. No wonder, then, that the Jews as a group never could fulfill the promises of Yahweh that they would multiply in vast numbers. Moses' deep aversiveness to humanity determined in the beginning of Israel that this should be so.

THE CHARACTER OF YAHWEH

Yahweh says and Yahweh does. What he says consists of describing himself, expressing his emotions, relating what he has done, instructing as to what must be

The Electric God

done, and foretelling what he will do. In describing the hallucinatory voices of schizophrenic patients, Jaynes stresses that they speak "often in short sentences."[21] They command, yell, curse, and consult. They are sometimes rythmical. The abrupt commands of Yahweh, his great noises, curses, and marvelously clear consultative advice enrich the verses of the Books of Moses. The lack of explanation is typical of both hallucinatory voices and of Yahweh's words. One must wonder whether the hallucinatory patients have learned through mosaism to speak like Yahweh or whether Moses is the prototype of hallucinators.

All that Yahweh says is in an absolutely authoritative mood. This includes those expressions which comment upon behavior that is against his will or interests; one learns of the crime when Yahweh refers to it and considers what punishment to meet out, without trial, of course. This last kind of behavior is presumably an exercise of "free will" on the part of Israelite believers or non-believers or on the part of gentile non-believers. They have the uniquely human ability to obey or disobey him. It is a totalitarian system in that no human act is done outside of his jurisdiction or without religious meaning. A secular sphere does not exist for him.

What Yahweh does, supplementing what he says, is to cause all things to happen, even expressions of disobedience coming out of "free will", in the sense that if he wished to do so, he could make people will what he wanted them to will. He is thus all-powerful, even against free will. Sometimes, as with Pharaoh, Yahweh plays a mean game with people, forcing them to be bad so that he can punish them more. "I will harden Pharaoh's heart, and though I multiply my signs and wonders..., he will not listen to you."[22]

He even asserts a power to be bad, to do evil. He is not bound by notions of good or evil. "Who makes peace and creates evil, I Yahweh do all this."[23] Speaking through the prophet, Ezekiel, Yahweh proclaims of Israel: "I defiled them through their very gifts in making them offer by fire all their first-born, that I might horrify them: I did it that they might know that I am Yahweh."[24] Nor is he bound by promises and laws, or a principle of consistency. Thus he is unlike Zeus, as Eliade Points out.[25] He is in this sense, like Moses, charismatic, above the rules.

Although he causes all things to happen, only selective actions of Yahweh are described. Yahweh acts in categories set up almost always by his worshippers, rarely by non-believers or opportunists outside of Israel. He rules the heavenly host, destroys nations, feeds Israel, punishes friend and foe, and so on; he wills all natural forces and especially great or unusual natural forces.

Particular actions are of the same kind, but deal with special cases that come to his attention, such as punishing a named person or giving a sign at a certain time and place or appearing on the mercy seat of the Ark, or sending down manna or causing all East wind to blow. As with his speech, all that he does is likewise in an authoritative mood.

Can one then slip in a substitute word for Yahweh such as "nature" and read the Exodus and wanderings as natural history? If one uses the word "nature" or "a natural force," can one then also eliminate all anthropomorphic or metaphorical references? Such would be, for example, reading only the first three words from "Smoke went up

The Electric God

from his nostrils..."etc[26] Perhaps, yet one must not dismiss metaphor. In a certain broad sense all language originated metaphorically, and further, one can often find a fact through the metaphor used to describe it. If Yahweh (Nature) melts mountains like wax, it may be that sudden eruptive thermal melting is occurring, producing the viscous appearance and softness of wax. Or, whenever Yahweh "appears," is it to be taken as metaphor? A god who is everywhere, omnipresent, cannot "appear" in one place; he was already there; or, logically, since nothing is beyond him, he can appear, even in seeming contradiction to himself.

No, Yahweh is not Nature animated. And he is not metaphor (unless hallucination is metaphor, which in a way it is but in a way that is irrelevant here). The activities of nature - especially the powerful, disastrous and brutal forces - are contained within the sum total of activities - moral, social, political, and military - of a hallucinated, all-powerful man.

But then, in the end, all words and deeds are but weak tools to describe one to whom the absolutes of presence, knowledge, power, and activity are assigned. One either makes of blind faith a virtue or brings to bear the tools of psychiatry. A logical exposition of Yahweh's mental labyrinth is impossible. It is the ghost of Moses' mentation. A religion cannot come to be without voices sacredly and definitively authorized to speak accurately on behalf of the god; therefore, it has to be presumed that Moses, who claims and is accorded such credentials, is speaking the truth about Yahweh. Yet Moses himself is but a delegate of limited instructions, and often repairs to Yahweh for further orders or clarification. But Yahweh, the absolute one, knows that, at best, Moses is only a superior human; that is, Moses is still a weak reed to lean upon for establishing godly rule among a portion of the human race.

And, as for the Jews as a body of people, Yahweh has little confidence or trust in them, and the grounds on which he has chosen them as his "peculiar treasure" are indefinite, to say the least. The choice seems to have been practically a random act of grace on his part.

An outside observer can scarcely be faulted, then, if he feels himself racing giddily in a circular trap, with his every attempt to question a fact or a cause being referred back to an absolute quality which respects neither fact nor cause. He can only cease his anxious circlings, he is assured, if he accepts to believe, or if he is coerced into non-believing acceptance. Accepts what? Authority, of course, and please do not begin circling around again in search of the justification of authority. That is merely another circle around Yahweh.

Are the words and actions of Yahweh such and only such as would emerge from the delusionary projections of Moses? Generally, yes, and nothing important comes other than through the screen of Moses or through the operations of nature. Are all the events that occupy the perceiving apparatuses of the speaker(s) of the Pentateuch - Moses and all the preceding rememberers, and all those who have worked upon the materials after Moses - possible or probable when appraised by the rules for testing the occurrence of events that are laid down by social and natural scientists? Again the answer is yes. The "unscientific miracles" that are left to explain are few and casual, not worth explaining, one might say. I am not here denying the great mysteries of existence, I merely assert that these are in no wise explained by the Pentateuch-Torah: Moses and mosaists are not theologians, much less philosophers.

Those who accept such scientific answers do not generally find themselves less in control of themselves and of the world about them, and less happy, than those who have accepted the authoritative complex of Yahwism or have resigned themselves to the coercion to accept the same. That this should be generally believed, even among psychologists after the manner of William James, does not make it so. It is ordinary to feel, when anxious, that "the grass grows greener on the other side of my fence." I would not deny, however, that one day a religion might be invented that would deliver a delusional system that would make humankind happier than even a dependence upon truth and consequences.

SIN VS SCIENCE

If Moses is a scientist, a great inventor, why does he not hallucinate a god who is recognizably a scientist? Yahweh writes; he organizes lists or rules; he keeps books; and little else that is technical; he is the product, not the fountainhead of the science of Moses. Yahweh, though, is an unlimited, ungoverned power. Being a great scientist is certainly sometimes a strong fantasy and even can be hallucinated, but the urge to know is subordinate to the urge of power. The urge to power was exceedingly strong in Moses, for reasons and in ways already put forward. Further, hallucinations generally fulfill a role that is absent in the person, not one that is satisfied.

Everybody had always said that Moses was a supremely intelligent person. But that was not enough. They also withheld from him, partly because his demands were so excessive, the power that he wanted. Only god could give him that, so Moses, the archetypical mad scientist, invented a god.

This invented god is full of instructions but is a perfectly bad model for a teacher. He rarely connects things causally. He rarely explains. He simply asserts and commands. That is quite satisfactory for Moses who has no love for his pupils, and, more and more, wishes them simply to memorize and obey.

Moses' Yahweh begins as a set of creative miracles coming out of Moses' science and his cooperation with and exploitation of nature. Then, owing to the rush of catastrophe, what begins as a fairytale ends in a monstrous takeover by wild natural forces. Yahweh becomes catastrophic. Yahweh symbolizes the most terrible memories. Moses is changing his own character, though in directions pointed out by his earlier character. Yahweh is accompanying this change with changes in his character. Every attempt is made by Moses, the Bible, the people, to assemble and reorder their minds in the process and aftermath of the natural catastrophe of Exodus. Moses' mind, and to a quintessential degree that of Yahweh, moves towards severity, punishment, and order. As much as must be forgotten and reassembled, that much is to be converted into sin, blame, and chastisement.

The invention of a punishing god is to help people to remember lessons of unity and ethnicity. "Early Israel was the dominion of Yahweh, consisting of all those diverse lineages, clans, individuals, and other social segments that, under the covenant, had accepted the rule of Yahweh and simultaneously had rejected the domination of the various local kings and their tutelary deities - the baalem."[27]

To recall the slogan: "Yahweh brought you up from Egypt," is to recall slavery and catastrophe. And it is also to recall simultaneously Moses. So the edifice of history and religion is the private property and power of Moses. In the famous formula of Harold Lasswell: the power-driven man displaces his private motives upon public objects, and rationalizes the displacement in terms of the public interest [28].

Moses needs a god of power - nothing very much else. Once Moses has his god, and that god has become identified with a catastrophe, then the god has to be the center of a cult of power centered around the expiation of disaster. For Moses, and therefore Yahweh, there is no other route, and for the people who became Israel there was no escape, no turning back to the call of Egypt, no popular vote on what type of character Yahweh should be, no fairytale religion except in the underground of their popular legends, no evasion of his rule. The continuous disastrous circumstances of nature and society, beginning in Egypt and ending generations later, reinforced the authority of the god that the people had taken, for better or for worse, as their spouse (as the prophet Hosea would call the relationship). Not even by turning whore (again using Hosea's image) could Israel escape the claims of its husband, and indeed suffered the mosaic penalty for adultery, death.

It is not hard to prove the primary obsessions of the Books of Moses. One can examine, even if summarily, the amount of declaiming about sin, guilt and compulsion that occurs in their pages. Should the reader at this point complain that everybody knows this to be true, I would grant that most may know it, but few have the nerve and stomach to bear it in mind. As their part of the general trend of scholars and ministers to make the Bible unthreatening, by erasing the natural catastrophes, and by "humanizing" Moses, they also downgrade or dismiss its obvious impact and look in it for sweet and rare words like "love." Buber's elaborate Index to his life of Moses contains no references to sin, guilt, blame, or punishment. Nor does the equally detailed Index of Daiches.

The major concordances of the Bible list references and passages to all except minor words. If we look into a concordance to see how often certain significant words are used in the Books of Moses, we shall find them in context. Should we count the references to sin, guilt, punishment, coercion and enemies, and then their contraries of love and friendship, we might test our impression that aggression in its various forms overbalances affection in the Books of Moses. And, as Table 11 shows, so it does. Overwhelmingly. In the two concordances, based upon two different translations, differences occur. But both versions agree emphatically at all important points.

The five books of Moses carry from eight to twenty times as many accusatory, demanding, punitive and hostile references as they do affectionate and friendly ones. If Genesis is removed from the calculation on grounds that it was mostly inherited by Moses from the earlier Hebrew religion and incorporated partly to bolster his claim to base Yahwism upon the "god of the fathers," then the extreme misanthropism of mosaism becomes all the more evident [29]. Love and friendship are absolutely wanting in Moses himself, if this statistical indicator possesses any validity.

To search out additional evidence, we can fashion another kind of sample, this time the first verse that appears on every upper left hand corner of every page of the *Oxford Bible*. Of the *Pentateuch,* there are 262 pages and therefore a sample of 262 verses. Statistically the sample approaches randomness and adequacy, so that what is represented in the 262 verses is probably close to what is contained in the whole. We judge in each case whether the statement does or does not directly involve sin, blame, or compulsion. Table III reveals the findings.

Sin is guiltiness and is defined as an ascribed quality of deserving punishment, implicitly or explicitly stated, and attached to an action. Blame is the assignment of guilt or sin or evil to a person or object involved in an action. Compulsion is a holy penalty established in the verse or referred explicitly to its being provided elsewhere for this described action.

Half of the *Books of Moses,* we would conclude, is devoted to alleging sin, casting blame, or inflicting and threatening punishment. Very few of the balance of actions are concerned with love, neighborliness, mutual help, sowing and reaping, or the like. The rest is mainly comings and goings. The catastrophes of *Genesis* such as the Deluge and others less definitely treated are long gone into thousands of years of tradition. Moses copied *Genesis;* he lived and wrote the essentials of *Exodus,* and the other books are in a way commentaries upon *Exodus* or extensions of it. Hence they reflect his character.

TABLE II

Affection and Aggression in the Books of Moses

	Strong's Concordance		Presbyterian Concordance	
Explicit words of Books of Moses	5 Books of Moses	*Genesis* only	5 Books of Moses	*Genesis* only
Love, Loved, Loves, Loveth, Loving	41	15	42	14
Guilt, Guilty	16	1	66	2
Must	17	4	24	11
Lest	64	17	22	1
Anger, Angry	43	7	66	12
Obey, Obedient, Obedience	21	3	12	5
Sin, Sinned, Sins, Sinning, Sinners, Sinful, Sinneth	204	8	179	6
Enemy, Enemies	58	3	64	6
Friend, Friends	5	3	12	5

Sources: James Strong, *Exhaustive Concordance of the Bible* (Nashville: Abingdon, 1963) based on the Authorized Version; and the *Living Bible Concordance,* J. A. Speer, ed., Poolesville, Md.: Presbyterian Church, 1973, based on K.N. Taylor's (Paraphrased) Bible, 1972.

We can observe that little place is left in mosaism for an honest mistake or an error in judgement. There are no means of discriminating between pragmatic and sacred action. This is truly primitive or, better, traumatized; practically everything is within the grasp of religion. It reveals, too, how profoundly Moses had changed from a scientific genius; to all intents and purposes, apart from his bag of techniques, Moses had become a wholly obsessed, hallucinatory, punitive theocrat.

Those who profess a Christian, Moslem or Judaic mosaism, or who are subjected to mosaic education in the contemporary world number some 1.3 billions, a third of the world's people. The history of Europe and the Near East has been deeply affected by mosaic conduct and ideas for 1900 years - since the Christians let them out of the bag, so to say. There should not be so many mosaists in history if the momentum of mosaism came only from Moses. That is, people have had within themselves, as a product of their genesis and ancient history, a capacity for grasping and becoming Mosaists and Yahwists. They can become something else - and obviously most people who have ever lived were something else - but not something so different that they are freed in utero or in culture from the possibility of lending themselves, as leaders or followers, to mosaism. The human is catastrophically constructed and prone to a kind of schizotypical behavior.

TABLE III.
Sin, Blame and Compulsion

Book	Actions involving Sin, Blame or Compulsion	All other verses
Genesis	18=27%	48
Exodus	32=58%	23
Leviticus	30=79%	8
Numbers	19=35%	35
Deuteronomy	26=53%	23
TOTAL	125=48%	137

What universally appealing features can make mosaists of normal humans? First there is the world out of control: the heavy anxiety in the face of disturbed nature and nations creates the need for psychological, if not actual, control and security. In ancient history, and still today, nations imitate nature. There is a constant interplay of metaphor between the two: rulers and winds are strong; saviors and suns bring illumination; and so on into hundreds of parallels. When we have "Gott mit uns," we feel a control over both our human problems and our natural problems.

Mosaism very clearly places gods on earth among us. It establishes a worldly god who is interested in the smallest details of our existence, so as to control us; but we are controlling him (little does he know) by occupying him with our problems. A jealous god, like a jealous lover, is a prisoner

The Electric God

of his chosen one. This limitation of, or demand upon, the divinity is most useful for the organization of primitive political power and of political power primitively. If people look elsewhere than within the fabric of their conscience for their god, the rulers cannot so neatly use him.

Further, the insistence upon a single god, monotheism, pyramids the possibilities of employing the one god for the purpose of absolute social control. There has been a great god in most cultures and the erosion of his powers is fought in order that power may be more concentrated in the hands of rulers. Monotheism simplifies the monopoly of authority and totalitarian rule.

Inasmuch as societies have not discovered how to exploit the mines of human energy without coercion and oppression, they may find in mosaism an ample and simple ideology of sin, blame, and coercion. Unconsciously, sincerely, and manipulatively, the power to speak in the name of a single, absolute, demanding and unbound god is a very great power; it leaks into politics, family relations, work groups, and every other sphere of life, with plenty of power to spare: it is theoretically unlimited.

When, to this power, is attached the logic of sin, blame, compulsion, and punishment, the power is greater and more effective. Thus occurs the formula: Yahweh has an interest in all your actions; all your actions are good or bad; that is, either demanded by or prohibited by him. If you fail to be good, you can expect punishment now or later, and punishment then is never a surprise, for the storing up of evil is great in you. If you do good and suffer, this is for a past misdeed, even as Moses was kept from the Promised Land by an obscure fault.

Even the most heinous deeds are in the name of Yahweh or are committed as a punishment by him. Sacrifice to Yahweh of the first-born of children and cattle was originally proclaimed as the price of his guiding the Israelites out of Egypt. It is avoided or discontinued by Moses by the expedient of dedicating the Levites as substitutes for the sacrifice, the cost being obedience to the Levites. The duty of such sacrifices remains as a holy theoretical obligation. Exceptional killings of offspring occur in the royal families of Judah and Israel, and elsewhere.

The gruesome passages on infanticide and cannibalism in *Deuteronomy* (28:53-75) are put into the future tense. However, it is not reasonable to believe that the prophets, in accord with what scholars say often, told history in foretelling events, whereas the Deuteronomist had no historical sense when foretelling events. Both recited history. The terrible memories of sieges and famines erupt in the present tense. We stress here that the people are assured that they were condemned to commit these acts because of their disobedience to Yahweh.

Again, as we said earlier, the concept of absolute, peak obedience to Yahweh makes all other crimes pale into insignificance, and all evil actions are capable of losing their criminal quality. Moses could commit his frightful actions because they were in the name of Yahweh. When any and all crime can be justified if attributed to a god, then secular authority will not lag far behind. Rarely is an action mentioned that is good, either pragmatically and socially or religiously; much less is it praised. A dreadful negativism pervades the Pentateuch or Torah.

All of this is helpful in controlling a population

The Electric God

without their consent. At any instant, the criminal or charitable or pragmatic (useful) nature of an action may be altered; the psychological bind in which a person finds himself is obvious, as is the inherent connection with schizophrenic training, where Moses is the trainer.

The connection with ritual becomes manifest here as well. One reaction to contradictory and inexplicable behavior of authorities is catatonism. The person dares not move in any direction. To reestablish control over this numbed mind, highly explicit and numerous behaviors are prescribed; life processes become ritualized.

Moses inaugurated an obsessive ritualism, that was to be perpetuated over the generations by the succession of priests. The signal quality of obsession, which can begin with the obsession of sin, is that it provides a compulsiveness to behavior. That is, once put on the treadmill of obsessive-compulsive conduct, the person cannot get off of it. If a population behaves so, the rulers know at any given moment where the people are and what they are doing. They will not become friendly with foreign people, as at Beth-Peor; they will not be running up to the high places and behaving licentiously, as the Yahwist prophets later complain. They will be working painstakingly, guiltily, and reserving the Sabbath for Yahweh.

There is this to be said on the positive side of mosaism, but only from a psychological and not from an ethical or religious viewpoint. By keeping people eternally in pain and guilt, with a sense of being continually observed by the kind of mean father that Moses conjured, there would be produced not only many mad-persons but also some unusual number of geniuses. For creative, driving genius is a kind of malady of deviance that can win freedom from mosaism but cannot win freedom from the watchfulness, self-consciousness, restless movement, and obsessiveness that had been inculcated by mosaic training.

Unfortunately for mankind, more humanistic and pragmatic forms of pedagogy, as in classical China and Greece, Augustan Rome, Medieval Islam, Renaissance Italy, the Enlightenment and the centers of nineteenth-twentieth century science - including always the formidable humanistic Judaic contribution - have had only small constituencies, and are always in danger, whether from some extended form of mosaism or another religiously founded authority-formula.

IMMORTALITY

In Yahwism, life after death is a matter for legends and rabbinical speculation. Moses is given a guided tour of all the wonders of heaven says one story, while he is supposed to be on Mt. Sinai elaborating designs for the Israelite camp and carving the tablets of the Decalogue. But the Bible, more correct as to Moses' mentality, has Yahweh visiting face-to-face, "mouth-to-mouth," with Moses on solid ground.

Yahweh does not grant immortality nor even comment upon it. Death is everywhere in the Books of Moses, and death is final. There is no intimation that Moses believes in heaven as an abode for the souls of the departed or as a place for terrestrial visitors, nor for that matter does Moses believe in a hell or a sheol, where the dead may receive punishment or purgation.

This lapsus on Moses' part is strange. First, one might think that so ambitious a man would find a place where he might continue his mission after death. Whether he would have received the inspiration from Egyptian, Hebrew, or Mesopotamian sources, he might have felt the need to project himself into a prolonged relationship to Yahweh. Further, it might have consoled his people "in the land... of the shadow of death"[30] to provide a place for at least the better among them in heaven, and it might have helped him to control the people were he able to assure them, as did later Christian mosaists, of burning in hell-fires for their wrong-doing to Yahweh-Moses while they were alive.

Various explanations occur to us. Moses was in need of immediate obedience, not in allowing a lifetime of choices to qualify for heaven or hell. "Obey, or be burnt now!" is rather obviously his theme, whether addressed to individuals or to all of Israel. On the annual Day of Atonement, one goat is burnt before Yahweh and another, the scape-goat, is heaped with the sins of all the people and loosed into the wilderness to find his way to Azazel, the evil demon. Atonement is earthly, too. Moses would have felt threatened with the loss of control of the people, if each had come to think of himself according to Plato's vision, as destined to occupy one of the myriad of stars.

Moses is intent upon conquering an earthly Promised Land where Israel may dwell in material comfort and seek to please Yahweh. "The God he discovered was eventually a protecting lawgiver who enunciated comments to the people in their own interests, not in the interests of their eternal salvation, for such a concept was quite foreign to Moses' way of thinking, but in the interests of their earthly welfare [31].

This nationalistic goal would be rendered vague and even unessential, if a heavenly goal and immortality were projected as well. Perhaps he believed in an eternal nation, with endless religious and blood descent, whose people would fulfill their need for immortality in the transmission of Yahweh along the lines of their descent as the Chosen People, "the Peculiar Treasure" of Yahweh.

There is another side to this matter of the Chosen People. Yahweh commands the destruction of all peoples who stand in the way of his "children." The limits of their territory, it may be argued, are those of the Jordan Valley and Canaan; but the directive is without limits, according to another argument. Since even related tribes come under the annihilating directive, thanks to the monopoly the Israelites allow themselves in the use of the Ineffable Name, one would have to conceive of a special heaven for Israelites only. This invites theological problems, and we know that, as Neher points out, Moses was adverse to such. Later on, Christian and Muslim sects would produce the theologians to invent exclusive heavens for their true believers.

Moses himself would probably not care for such a heaven, no matter how thinly populated by select yahwists such as Aaron, Joshua and himself, some of the people of Israel, of whom he has little good to say, might by some independent judgement of Yahweh, find their way there. He would not like his decision-making powers to lapse, and, if they were tendered to him ad infinitem, heaven would soon be cleared, and hell full.

These musings may not be in vain, because ultimately they lead us to a hard theory. Moses, we have stressed, possesses a catastrophist mentality and an earthly mission; he has no interest in preserving the souls of the people of Israel. If one were to judge by the many times that he prophesies for them, and threatens them with, total destruction for their failures in respect to himself and Yahweh, one might guess that he fully expected the world, or at least the world of the Jews, to go up in flames and destruction at any time. And certainly, he would believe that, upon his own demise, and deprived of his leadership, the chances of their prompt destruction would be greatly increased.

Can we go one step farther and say that Moses harbored the wish, not very deep below the surface of his consciousness, that the Chosen People be destroyed? Yahweh occasionally toys with the idea. In the Revolt of the Golden Calf, Yahweh says of Israel: "Let me alone, that my wrath may burn hot against them and I may consume them; but of you I will make a great nation."[32] But when Moses remarked that he would lose face with the Egyptians, and that he should remember his promises to Abraham, Isaac, and Israel [Jacob], Yahweh repented and forebore to kill them all.

Again, quoted by Ezekiel [33], because they profaned the sabbaths and walked not in his laws, Yahweh says: "I promise to pour out my fury upon them in the wilderness, in order to exterminate them." He withholds his hand: "But I acted for the sake of my own name that [it] might not be profaned before the eyes of the nations, before whose eyes I had brought them forth." Again, too, a vulgar regard for public opinion.

This catastrophic wish and its related belief disposes of the problem of immortality. Like many a sick and dying person, and like many otherwise normal persons, Moses wanted to take the world with him. Or, if he refused to entertain such a notion, he would expect and prophesy such an event. Then there would be no problem of immorality; the solution would be total. Neither Moses nor Yahweh, when they argue the question of extirpating the Israelites, wonders how to go about judging their merits and assigning them a place in the afterlife.

I would conclude, until otherwise instructed, that Moses carried like a great lump with him an obsessive idea: when Moses dies, Israel must die with him. Reinforcing his obsession was the unconscious appreciation that Yahweh also must die with Moses.

Moses did not grow kinder with age; the obsession would have become more and more difficult to suppress and conceal; it might ultimately have contributed to the cause of his death - by a flying stone, by shock, by accident, by abandonment, by physical removal from office, by execution. Then, despite his unconscious wishes, Yahweh, mosaism, and Israel did survive. As the psychological imprints of Moses, they survived.

The brand of Moses and Yahweh upon the character and history of the Jews carries this sadism into a corresponding masochism of self-destruction. No matter how successful in mundane terms, no matter how let to live in peace, they were haunted by the fear that they would be destroyed as a people. It is of course part of the tragic game that they should be encouraged by their religion and leaders to believe that this destruction is the desire and intent of the outside world, for they could not permit themselves to recognize that it was Moses and Yahweh who wanted them to die as a people. Yet, with unerring technique, they set themselves up time after time for destruction, expecting, in the end, to tell themselves: "You see now it is as it is written in the Law. We shall be destroyed for our sins." And they permitted their destroyers to say: "By your own profession, it would not happen, if it were not that you are wicked."

One after another national disaster is attributed to Yahweh - whether the instrument is some now-dead nation, whether the Egyptians, or the Neo-Babylonians; it happens because they have misbehaved towards Yahweh; the score of millennia amounts to an impressive collective masochism. Hardly is one disaster ended, than the prophets of new disaster arise, recalling to them all the previous disasters back to Exodus. Although it cannot be said that people behave as they say or believe, nevertheless, in the absence of a competing ideology - and the Jews have never permitted one in their midst - it cannot be argued that the dominating ideology has been without effect.

MONOTHEISM

Myth presents us with a cluster of ideas about Judaic-Christian-Islamic religion which are in significant respects untrue and harmful. The function of the myth (as is typical) is to make its believers feel well and superior to others. So it is with the myth that Yahwism is monotheism; further, that Yahweh is invisible; further, that monotheism is good for people and naturally reasonable.

Yahweh is very much anthropomorphized, in fact. He is portrayed as a magnificent man. He is, like Moses, exclusive and will not show himself to anyone in his true figure. Once he promised Moses to exhibit himself to the

Elders on Mount Sinai, but they were treated only to a smooth rock and bright light. "No prophet had anything to tell of a figure resembling the human until Ezekiel..."[34] He does reveal his presence by the light of the Ark and the column of smoke. He sits on the "mercy seat." He directs campaigns, promulgates laws, decrees punishment and in every way, save sexuality, which he treats almost entirely by restrictions, he is human. I have found it difficult to distinguish between Moses and Yahweh once Yahweh is assumed to be Moses' other self and his presence is otherwise manifested in forces of nature and in the good and evil fortunes of people. Then, too, he has the normal emotions of hate, love, anger, boastfulness, jealousy, mercy, but not fear, because fear is the reciprocal of power, and power is the essence of Yahweh.

      Yahweh does not claim that he is the only god. Nor does Moses claim that Yahweh is the only god. He is content to quote Yahweh to the effect that Yahweh is the same god as the god of the Hebrews. At the Burning Bush we hear "I am the God of your father, the God of Abraham, the God of Isaac, and the God of Jacob."[35] And again, after Moses' first meeting with Pharaoh, "I am Yahweh. I appeared to Abraham, to Isaac, and to Jacob, as God Almighty *(El Shaddai)*, and by my name of Yahweh I did not make myself known to them."[36] Buber says that Moses saw the god of his wife's tribe but recognized him as the god of the fathers [37]. This is interesting but goes unexplained: how do you recognize a god as your own?

      It is perplexing. Surely the Hebrews of Egypt knew their god, Elohim El Shaddai, God-Most-High, well enough to tell whether he would permit himself another name.

The Electric God

Gressmann, among others, declares Elohim and Yahweh to be two distinct gods. "Yahwism, in mosaic times, suppressed the older religion of El."[38] "The legends treat the patriarchs as thoroughgoing pacifists. Their god is a god of peace-loving men," writes Max Weber [39]. Moshe Greenberg tells us so:

> The God of the patriarchs shows nothing of YHWH's 'jealousy'; no religious tension or contrast with their neighbours appears, and idolatry is scarcely an issue. The patriarchal covenant differed from the Mosaic Sinaitic Covenant in that it was modeled upon a royal grant to favourites and contained no obligations, the fulfillment of which was to be the condition of their happiness [40].

Perhaps the Hebrews had become Egyptianized and religiously indifferent, as legends indicate. Messianism is not specifically conceptualized in *Exodus;* but sociologically Moses would have to be understood by the Hebrews and related populations as a messiah coming with a representation of the old god on a specific mission of deliverance.

And always there were the looming catastrophe, the perceived comet and the plagues to validate a return to religion and messianism. With Moses there came another kind of god. With Jesus there came still another, closer to Saturn-Elohim than to Yahweh. The disciples and crowd of Jesus formed one more of the several splinter movements that took their devotees from Judaism. The Israelites had no sooner struck the deserts when they began building variant gods: idols of Egypt came out of the luggage; a new cometary Baal emerged in the Golden Calf.

Following the proclamation of the Covenant, Yahweh claims the whole earth; Israel is but his "peculiar treasure."[41] In Amos' prophecies, Yahweh asserts that he led other nations to safety at the same time as he retrieved the Hebrews from Egypt. He says that he punishes them all alike, including the people of Israel [42].

These seem but minor claims when contrasted with the striking verses that, along with much other evidence, put Yahweh in his place. They are the words of Moses, in a farewell address to Israel, as recomposed by a writer during monarchic times, six or seven centuries later:

> When the Most High [Eyon] gave to the nations their inheritance, when he separated the sons of men, according to the number of the sons of God. For the Lord's [Yahweh's] portion is his people, Jacob [43] his allotted heritage. The Lord [Yahweh] alone did lead him and there was no foreign god with him [44].

Clearly Yahweh here is one of the sons of god, to each of whom a nation of the Earth's people was distinguished and allotted. Yahweh receives Israel, and is free of interference from any foreign god.

"The sons of god" are "the divine beings who belong to the heavenly court," and when god speaks of them he uses the term "us" and "our."[45] It is a very old relationship, encountered in the first chapter of Genesis. The resemblance here to the Olympian family of gods under Zeus the Father is notable; the Greek gods take up the sides of different nations as in the *Iliad;* have favorite countries as Athene with Athens; and so onto other conformities.

A god is usually an idea of a people about a being

The Electric God

that controls their destiny. The people establish a religion to control their god by being in step with him. The more out of control their destiny, the more they look for and seek to control a god. The god takes on traits that are appropriate to their problems: if fire is threatening to their world, a fire-god occurs; if sheep are critically important, god will tend their flocks. The worse the problem, the greater the status of the god attending to it.

Stabilizing the universe is a most common trait of the most powerful gods. Therefore we reason that the unstable universe has been the most important problem when the greatest of gods came upon the scene. The moral dogmas of humans are avocational pronunciamentos of the great gods; try as may the philosophers and theologians of another, later age, they cannot get rid of the essence of divinity, the bringing and removing of catastrophe. Yahweh saved the Hebrews from catastrophe: specifically, he brought them out of Egypt and through the years of wandering; but these events are formal history, the idiosyncratic chronology moving on top of the informal history of the catastrophe.

Elohim (God-in-Heaven) would appear to have preceded Yahweh in the Hebrew theogony. He is frequently mentioned. He is securely identified by a number of writers as the Osiris of the Egyptians, the Saturn of the Romans, and the Kronos of the Greeks. Other god-names in *Genesis* are El Shaddai, El Eyon (God Most High), El Olam (Eternal-God), El Bethel (God of Bethel), and El Ro'i (God of Vision) [46]. The word "Elohim" denotes a plural entity in Hebrew. Isaac Asimov, in his commentaries on the Bible, discussing this point, concludes that an original polytheism existed; we would agree.

Cyrus Gordon in all analysis of Psalm 82 shows that Elohim is regarded as the "President of the gods."[47] The gods let rulers be wicked. Whereupon "all the foundations of the earth totter." Elohim then says:

> Ye are gods And all of you are deities. But ye shall die like mankind, And fall like any of the princes. Arise, 0 God [Elohim], rule the earth; For Thou shalt take over all the nations!

Gordon finds a parallel to the Psalm in the Ugaritic epic of Krt. We would again see in Elohim the great god Saturn whose recall of the world's people to his Golden Age is longed for. The character of Yahweh, like Indra, as well as Zeus, is bound up with catastrophe and war. Max Weber writes [48]:

> Yahweh, like Indra, is fit to be god of war because, like Indra, he was originally a god of the great catastrophes of nature. His appearance is accompanied by phenomena such as earthquakes [49], volcanic phenomena [50], subterraneous [51] and heavenly fire, the desert wind from the South and South East [52], and thunderstorms. As in the case of Indra, flashes of lightning are his arrows [53] as late as the prophets.

Yahweh includes insect and snake plagues, and epidemics in his repertoire.

> The connection of the qualities of Yahweh as a god of frightful natural catastrophes, not of the external order of nature, preserved down to the time after the Exile, [that is, for a thousand years] was, beside the general relationship of those processes with war, based historically on the fact that God had made use of his power first in battle...

We have seen in this book that what Weber says of Yahweh as god of catastrophe and battle is exactly correct. But we have also seen that Weber is quite deceived by a Biblical reductionism of the Exodus environment so that he reverses the order. Yahweh, in fact, historically made use of his power first to create catastrophes, then to bring wars. His pugnacity, Moses' pugnacity, and the bellicosity of the Israelites, Hyksos and many other nations followed, both in time and as effect, the natural disasters whose turbulence destroyed the social order.

Gressmann, like Weber, committed "the four sins of modern biblicism": confused chronology; reductionism; primitivism; and uniformitarianisin. He too observed that catastrophe was connected with Yahweh. "The catastrophe of the Sea of Reeds," he declares, "laid the basis for the Yahwist religion."[54] He treats this event as a local disaster caused by a volcano and tidal wave at the gulf of Aqaba, far from Egypt; the plagues are to him relatively meaningless. Therefore he is in no position to make the correct statement, which is that cometary Yahweh brought the ecological catastrophes of Yahweh, which incited Yahwist aggressiveness among people, and all of this laid the basis for Yahwism.

But, if Yahweh is just coming upon the scene, and Elohim is Saturn, how could Yahweh not be known to the Hebrews before Moses, since Yahweh is like Zeus and Jove, and Horus-Amon? And these gods have been heavily worshipped for perhaps 2500 years. There is a gap. A god of the Hebrews is missing.

Perhaps, unlike other peoples, they clung to Elohim from the first creation of the world in *Genesis* and through the flood and thereafter, disregarding candidates for a Jove-type god until Yahweh was introduced. Then Elohim would be given an additional name and, with this new name, certain new qualities,

The early Hebrews moved long distances, had many skills, were not bellicose, and lived among many nations. Their religion shared many legends and features with other peoples. Perhaps their monotheism had its origins in an innocuous name that was not objected to by their neighbors, not a source of contention.

That is, Monotheism may be a pantheistic device. We tend to think of it as we see it in Moses, as a parochial, exclusive, anti-polytheistic device. It may not be so.

But if Moses were the Messiah, coming upon a people in distress with a new version of god, there would seem to be good reason why a universalistic uncompetitive god should suddenly acquire the traits of a nationalistic jealous god - keeping monotheism constant.

Still this would presume that Elohim, and also El Shaddai, were plugging the gap. However Elohim-Osiris-Saturn, while still a great god in Egypt, had long given way there to Horus-Amon and Thoth. "From the sixth dynasty on, Horus alone appears as the true patron of monarchy" until the end of the Middle Kingdom.[55] Then Seth, who can be identified as the perennial antagonist of Osiris, Horus, and Isis (Venus), becomes the principal divine monarch of the Hyksos until their overthrow by a combined Israelite- Egyptian army.

But Thoth is not to be neglected. He is the Egyptian Hermes or Mercury, who bear a caduceus like Moses' Brazen Serpent. Just as Hermes served under Zeus in Greece, Thoth

The Electric God

might have served under Horus in Egypt. His cult in Egypt was huge. His character is singular. In Egypt, Rome, Greece, Phoenicia, India and Mexico, he is powerful and gives judgement on the law; clever; rebellious; electrical; inventor of writing, expert scribe and linguist; magical; a wizard; a healer; mundane; instructor; guide of wanderers and roads; equivocal; he hides himself; but never so great as the greatest on high, never El Shaddai (God Almighty), never Jupiter. But when Horus resigned his earthly power, Thoth succeeded to his throne [56]. The cult of the ram followed the cult of the bull in Egypt [57] that is, Thoth followed Horus.

It is conceivable that Abram when he changed his name to Abraham, was adding the Egyptian god Ra to the name of his Hebrew capital city of Ramah. Ram is Thoth and its totem animal is the ram. In this case, one might investigate whether the god of the fathers may not always have been a Saturn or a Jove, but a Mercury.

Moses would have been familiar with Thoth - the sophisticated man's god - in Egypt. Perhaps when he began to hallucinate Yahweh, the traits of Yahweh became a combination of those of Jove and Mercury, Horus-Amon and Thoth. The mundane Thoth is perhaps the strongest model. What he found the Hebrews enjoying was a composite of Elohim and Amon-Thoth, perhaps so indefinite as to be the source of legendary complaints that the Hebrews had lost their religion in Egypt.

Thoth, believed the Egyptians, created the world by the force of his word [58]. And the Gospel according to John says: "In the beginning was the Word." Whose word? Thoth's? We have noted how strong for the word were Yahweh, and Moses: "Write it down in your Book!" And how Moses has been inextricably identified with Thoth-Hermes by scientists of the occult over the ages. Biblical exegetes insist that "Logos," the original word in John, means more than Word; it means Life, Intelligence, Light, and metaphorically, Christ the Savior, present in the Word and in God from the beginning of creation. So did Thoth represent his Word, too, as life, intelligence and light striking upon mankind.

We must observe closely and speculate cautiously: Moses as a "rational" cultist was Thoth-Hermes; Yahweh was Zeus-Horus-Amon. That is, when it came to projecting a god, Moses' personal need was for a stern, heavy father-figure, connected with lightning and meteors [59], admittedly more powerful than Thoth. Moses does not introject Zeus as well as he does Hermes, Horus as well as he does Thoth. This may explain why Yahweh is such a crude and simple power-directed god, so unidimensional. He provides the strength and will, the compulsion, and the brute force. Thoth-Moses provides the brain.

The reasons why Moses chose monotheism are fairly plain. Not only was there this syncretistic monotheism to work with among the Hebrews, but Moses had only the technology for one god. If the god were to be wandering with, talking to, and working with a tribe, he should better be unaccompanied by potential competitors.

Moses did not have the ability to talk to more than one god at a time. He was a rigid person, and changed roles only with great difficulty. He could not be the executive secretary of a council of gods. He had in mind the concentration of power in his own hands: as on earth, so in heaven. A single god seemed logical, and could manage everything alone, with occasional messengers or angels. By the same line of reasoning, we may understand why there is no devil in Yahwism; Yahweh is his own devil-demon when necessary. Moses did not need to split his ambivalence into personalities. The destructive behavior of Yahweh gave Moses all the satanism that he needed.

To be possessed by two or more gods at the same time is not at all impossible; indeed, such is the case with most people and most of history: monotheism is claimed only for some few religions. The human mind compartmentalizes readily. Saturn, Mars, Jupiter and other gods occupied the Roman mind, and no one will say that the Romans were confused or impractical, at least not by historical standards.

Nor does personal development - although many imagine such - shunt all that is god's onto one's superego or conscience. Just as a boy will take several men as his models, believing, whether true or not, that these men possess abilities and traits that he must emulate, so he may take on several hypothesized gods as his inspiration for learning different skills and achieving different goals in life.

So it was that Thoth-Hermes could fill the developing Moses with desires, techniques, and traits, and then bow down within Moses to let pass the new god of the conscience, the aggressive and absolute Yahweh, who is exclusively to occupy the grand ballroom of world dominion in Moses' mind.

In this basic sense, Moses was a double religious personality, and thus, quite specifically, polytheistic. He was Thoth-Hermes in his ego and unconsciously, while he was Yahweh-Zeus in his superego and consciously. This, if nothing else, can explain why monotheism may never have existed in mosaism except as a formal, scholastic, linguistic construction, ex post facto.

This construction of monotheism, once it burst its priestly bonds, encouraged everyone from philosophers to mechanics to shave off strips of reality from the religious sphere. They might invest their conscience in Yahweh while inventing a realistic, objective, scientific world, as did Isaac Newton and a host of other workers. Or they might reinvest their conscience in Jesus, while dealing pragmatically with the scientific world. Joseph Priestley (1733-1804), one of the founders of electrical science and experimental method, was an early Unitarian leader. John Wesley (1701-1791), founder of Methodism, wrote on "Electricity made Plain and Useful, by a Lover of Mankind and Common-sense."

Such is the "monotheism" that the present world inherits and passes on. It is descended from the monotheism of Moses. It consists of concurrent and successive images of a single god, who is usually accompanied by a host of celestial figures. It is certainly not the logically sharp and eternally consistent monotheism, such as the human mind has conceived and maintained.

Monotheism belongs actually in the category of legal fictions, together with concepts such as "sovereignty." All the world may be persuaded of one god, with no single person agreeing within himself on the matter, and with no two persons agreeing between them. Nevertheless, the persuasion of monotheism will have substantial effects upon mind and conduct.

CONCLUSION

In what could be called his last sane moment, before he had ever talked to Yahweh, Moses was leading his flock and saw a bush that was alight and not reduced to ashes, and said to himself: "I will turn aside, and see this great sight, why the bush is not burnt."[1] This kind of "why" stood behind my undertaking this book and has, I hope, conveyed my reader rewardingly through its pages.

The work is now finished, with its details fitted into its major parts and there assembled into the whole. Some 3500 years ago, the area subject to the Bible came under an extra-terrestrial force, apparently a great comet, which, amidst the destruction that it wrought, set into motion the human characters whom we have come to know well: Moses, the Pharaoh, Aaron, and especially the Israelites, who were shaped into a chosen people.

The experiences of this people contained the material of a great and true story of disaster and survival. The story centers upon a scientific genius - Moses - and a new god - Yahweh. Yahweh is recognized as a great comet, as an electrical presence on earth, as the hallucinations of Moses, and as all cognate mental and social behavior in the times and places of Exodus, the Wanderings, and the invasion of Canaan. Of Yahweh, Vriezen has stated correctly: "If this God has to be typified in one word, that word must be: Power; or, still better, perhaps: Force. Everything about and around Yahweh feels the effect of this. He as it were electrifies his environment."[2] His electrifying force is more than psychological and metaphorical; "The Great I Am" is electrical in fact. The ideology of mosaism, a set of formulas for tying the aims of Moses to the purposes of Yahweh, proved to be adaptable from one restricted area and culture, the Judaic, to several grand civilizations - Byzantine, West European, Islamic, and American.

The Ark of the Covenant, "the Vehicle of Yahweh," symbolized, as well as played a critical part in, the whole story. Its electrical functions represented the achievements of the Egyptian theocratic establishment from which Moses, one of its luminaries and scientific managers, was expelled. The Ark was the centerpiece around which the aggregate of survivors of the flight from Egypt were organized into a new nation. The Ark gave voice to the new god, Yahweh, distinguishing him from related old gods, and lent credibility to his being one god, the great god, the most active god, a god who moved and rested with his followers, an invisible god, a god of explicit advice, a god who was independent of any sky body once he was defined by Moses.

Numerous miracles of the Bible have been shown to be based upon historical happenings: the escape from the enemy, the finding of food and drink, the punishment of sinners by god's fire, and so on to all significant miracles. They are demonstrable by ordinary rules of anthropology relating to a group interacting with nature to produce recognizable cultural behavior. Much of the non-miraculous but apparently nonsensical - the clothing, the taboos, the prayers, the rites, the devices, the social behavior, the attitudes of people - can be linked to the miracles, the setting, the motives and purposes of the leaders and people. All of

CONCLUSION   361

this invites a renewed attention to old problems under a new light. We may be in a better position to learn from the Bible and to know what is not to be learned from it. The experiences of Moses and Israel may be better guides through history than they have been in the past.

Yet even such generalities seem bland and anti-climactic following the outburst of arguments and propositions in the individual chapters. But rather than summarize all of these too, which are clearly signalled where they occur in the book, I should like to enter a plea on behalf of their implications. It is that Biblical scholars may join with specialists of other cultures throughout the world in reviewing materials of this electrical period of Exodus. It is, furthermore, that natural scientists, especially geologists and meteorologists, may lend their skills as historians of nature to the researchers in human history. I have no doubt that my book is to be corrected in many ways; I would, however, be gratified if the process of correction be managed so that all benefit in their own field of interest, rather than that I be loaded with the sins of all and sent into the desert to Azazel.

Figure 20: The Moses of Klaus Sluter, 1403-1406.
(Sculpture at "Moses' Well," at the Chartreuse of Champmol, presently an insane asylum, near Dijon, France)

APPENDIX

TECHNIQUES FOR THE ASSESSMENT OF LEGENDARY HISTORY

The *Book of Exodus* reminds one of the *Iliad* and other great epic poems. But *Iliad* and *Odyssey* chanted of much later events [1]. I am ready to believe, with Cassuto, that "one of the principal sources - possibly the principal source - was... an ancient epic poem, an epos dating back to earliest times, that told at length the story of the Egyptian bondage, of the liberation and of the wandering of the children of Israel in the wilderness."[2] It has numerous lyric passages still, also word and sound play, and formulas and fixed numbers to help remember its verses.

V. Cassuto points out various sacred literary harmonies through the text: the play upon threes, sevens, and seventies, for example; the repetition of words for emphasis; the use of expressions of salvation and deliverance in the 3rd episode of Moses in Midian, and so forth [3].

THE LIMITS OF DISTORTION

There was a major difference, however, between the *Exodus* and other epic accounts. The *Exodus* began in writing, under the authorship and direction of Moses, then was carried by epic tradition in oral form, and then was revived in written form in the tenth century at which time there was no Homer to reassemble it. So it came together afterwards piece by piece for five hundred years, as sacred history and in writing. In inception and conception, the Exodus was modern; it was to be a sacred written history.

Luckily for students of ancient events, the Exodus was from its beginnings a sacred happening so that no despot, no matter how powerful, could afterwards rewrite it with impunity. Apart from the theological miracles that the Books of Moses describe (which we translate into historical and scientific miracles), the book in itself represents a set of historical miracles. First there was Moses who believed in historiography. Then there was Moses' Yahweh whose imprimatur on the mosaic word made tampering sacrilegious. Afterwards, there was spawned by the new nation a priesthood, Aaronites, Levites, and popular priests and prophets that oscillated between centralized and decentralized federationism. These men were compelled to recite historical truths even when the truth hurt their interests; they could never erase it; they could only accent their own position in the process of history, swearing continuously that they were only repeating what had been historically said. The divisiveness of the Jews let this process go on for many centuries.

Then, in exile in Babylon and fortunately deprived of their own secular leadership, the priests crystallized their Torah, and upon their return to Jerusalem, decided once and for all that they possessed the sacred truthful history that must hereafter only be discussed, never changed.

APPENDIX 365

Thenceforth, no matter where they might be, those who claimed descent from the Exodus preserved with very little change the writings, while the Christians, who might have rewritten them, were from their own beginnings somehow persuaded that the Books of Moses were reconcilable with the teachings of Jesus and therefore sacred and untouchable. Thus happened the miracle of the Torah, that unique book.

As a result, we have found much history in the Books of Moses, and we shall find much more. But perhaps the moment has arrived to explain how this adventure in historical discovery is engineered. What logic and techniques am I trying to employ? I shall explain my procedures now, hoping that the reader has reached "the point of no return." First of all, we need some agreement on the composition of the Pentateuch. Who wrote or pronounced what in Exodus? Who says that they did so? When did they say so? And we begin by asserting that Moses himself kept the log of Exodus; he wrote, too, of his talks with Yahweh; he recorded as well the laws that he promulgated. We have already learned of his passion for the written word, which is integral to his character, and became part of the Jewish national character. The log is reported in the *Book of Numbers:* "Moses recorded their starting points in writing whenever they broke camp on Yahweh's orders."[4] We recall, too, that Yahweh refers to Moses' book and tells him what to write in it as well as helping him write the Decalogue.

Probably most scholars will agree that writing was indeed occurring in the wilderness. The major problems occurred subsequently. The writings were entirely lost. The period between the events, which in great part, no doubt, were not even originally recorded by Moses, but in vital parts were, and the canonization of the experience and its discussion consists of some eight or nine hundred years. "The final redaction and canonization of the Torah book... most likely took place during the Babylonian Exile (6th-5th century B.C.E.)."[5]

Hence the attempt to establish the authenticity of Biblical passages has depended largely upon linguistic analysis, and, to a lesser degree, upon internal consistency, comparative history and archaeology - all supervised by logical and anthropological speculation. Linguistic analysis allows an expert to criticize and perhaps rearrange passages in accord with what is known of the progress of the Hebrew language and of the style used by different individuals whose accounts have come down to the present.

Linguistic analysis is inadequate often not only because of the uncertainty of its data and of its premises, but also because it cannot discover the career of oral traditions. We know from general anthropology and ancient literature that an exact rendition of a large body of verse and prose (such as Homer's *Iliad* and other epic works) can be transmitted over generations and centuries. The same exactitude can be expected of a sacred written work which is committed to collective memory, then lost in written form. Even though the style and other minor changes may be introduced when the oral version of the original written version is written down, the substance of the account may be exact. In both cases, in the period of oral transmission, trained speakers can memorize and reproduce exactly thousands of lines heard from the lips of a teacher.

All along the line, a sacred duty to repeat the original faithfully encounters social interests to whose advantage

APPENDIX

certain changes might be made. In the case of the Bible, much effort must go into locating such interests, whether by internal analysis or by matching the known later political and natural environments with the suspected changes in the text over time.

We have to take it for granted that those who had the last word to say on the Old Testament said it the way they wanted it. Nobody knows the name of these gentlemen, but they were a group of Jewish scholar-priests living 800 years after Moses. We can assume that they were a corporate group and, therefore, the "very last word" would have been that of a "research director," namely a qualified priest with political and social engagements and contacts, more attuned to the mission of the Old Testament as he saw it than to the literal nuances of the text.

We know, too, that the period in which the last important editing was done was without general physical upheavals. Hence, the editing would lack the first-hand experience with catastrophe that marks the age of Moses and the age of the prophets and would not be conversant with strong references of the words, as compared to alternative weak references. Lacking direct comprehension, they would be tending toward using the name of Yahweh ever more promiscuously as a shorthand substitution for natural explanations or references. They would be uniformitarian ("conditions were the same then as now") and metaphorical ("what a fine analogy is implied in this language about angels.") Pari passu, the translations that are generally used now exhibit both tendencies of the text editors to a marked degree.

The editing, moreover, occurred in a parochial and

depressed period of Jewish history, the period of the Babylonian exile from which only some fraction was freed by the Persians and wanted to return to the Jerusalem area. The priest-scholars would be intent upon preserving their small ethnic and linguistic group, and would be without hope of expanding their realms, as contrasted, for example, with Jesus and Paul, working with the protection of and with the model of the seemingly universal Roman Empire before their eyes.

The unwritten directive that would guide their minds and hands would then be:

1) The "Chosen people" are a "select and exclusive people," and should preserve their religious heritage against any infiltration, expansion, or assimilation.

2) Establish the continuity of Yahweh with Elohim, i.e., between the gods of *Genesis* and *Exodus*.

3) Eliminate realistic and natural explanations of events in favor of the indefinite, all-explaining "hand of god."

4) Provide a maximum of ritual so that the priests must be involved in all personal actions: "Whatever is not forbidden, must be prescribed."

5) Let it be clear that all that Moses did, he did under strict orders from above, and further that he was the last man to be under such direct divine guidance.

6) Stress the undeserving character of the people; build up their guilt; establish, as the only route for the expiation of this guilt, renewed obedience to the Torah (the Law) and to the Priests and Levites who administer it.

7) Evade the secular, the political, and the contemporary environment of Judaism.

Then, of course, the last word to the people of Israel

would carry a meaning like: "now you have your inalterable sacred text. It is your first and last resort on all life's issues. And you have the priests to answer any questions. Lucky, undeserving people under Yahweh that you are!"

I would argue that something like this revisionary process actually occurred and needs to be watched for in educing history from the Torah. Nevertheless, one must not take the naive cynical view that anybody who handled Biblical material in the course of a thousand years could shape it to his whims and fancies. On the contrary, the great scandal of the Bible is its uncompromising confrontation of real human behavior which in modern "scientific" society is confessed to psychiatrists or kept secret at all costs.

The Revolt of the Golden Calf offers a case in point. Frederick Winnett flatly declares that the story of the Golden Calf (incident, affair, revolt, revolution - one names it out of prejudice often, just as modern scholars quarrel over whether the Korean or Vietnam conflict was a "war") was a product of the southern penmen of Judah after the Northern Kingdom had been destroyed in 722 B.C. and its inhabitants lost to Judaism [6]. The Northern Kingdom, reports the Bible, had two major places where images of golden calves were worshipped. Hence, southern blame-mongers had inserted the Golden Calf of the Holy Mountain into the story of Exodus to prove just how blasphemous and deserving of destruction were the idol-worshipping northerners. This intervention would have occurred shortly after 715 B.C.

However, as we have already evidenced earlier, we here take the Golden Calf revolt seriously, and fit it neatly into our total theory of Moses' character, of Yahweh, and of how the people really felt about religion.

Are we now to erase our theory and loosen one of the stones of our edifice? I think that the answer must be negative, for several reasons. The weakest of these reasons is that practically all biblical scholars accept and discuss the Golden Calf revolt in its place in Exodus. This is an appeal to authority; but it is the authority of linguistic analysis in which we ourselves are weak and impressionable.

The next reason, concerning which we feel stronger, treats of the minds of the vindictive writers of the Southern Kingdom. These men, scholars themselves, are caught in a bind. Just as rulers nowadays almost invariably reject rational advice to assassinate their political enemies, the priestly writers cannot violate the rules of the Bible, including that what goes into it must be sacred and true, and, further, must not violate a widespread appreciation of what the book ought to contain. Tampering with Moses was like playing with dynamite.

A third reason is a question: Are we certain that Jeroboam did indeed cause two golden calves or bulls to be erected at two principle sites of his Northern Kingdom of Israel? Or is this one the concocted story? Or were these images only rumored to be "golden calves," and were something else; or were they metaphors for the very word "images"? They might be arks, even the ark seized by Dan.

A fourth reason for maintaining the credibility of the Golden Calf Revolt is that, after the return from the exile in Babylon, a priestly group had occasion to make revisions in the Hezekiah recension that, says Winnett, had produced the story. They had good reason to remove the story if it were not true, because the Southern Kingdom itself had also been destroyed shortly after the Northern Kingdom and therefore

APPENDIX 371

the redactors may have felt less triumphant and scornful and more subdued. They let the story stand.

A fifth reason is that the Torah did not then and does not now include accounts of all that happened during the Exodus. The oral tradition was rich and exact. It is likely that the scholars who wrote down the story found as their basis something closely matching the act of elevating the image of the Golden Calf to worship among numerous stories of Moses' struggle to maintain an imageless Yahweh. With malice aforethought, they wrote up this story and inserted it at a most logical place, if it were not indeed the proper place. What more likely occasion for this act to occur than after a prolonged absence of Moses on the Mountain? Winnett advances this possibility when he writes that "the story was present... in the form of the [mosaic] tradition that reached D [the redactor], and, of all the incidents related in the tradition, that of Aaron's making an image of Yahweh in the form of a bull seems to have made the greatest impression on his mind."[7]

At this point, it may be proper to argue a scenario: the great revolt at Sinai (Horeb) happened; among the gods raised up was the golden young bull; Moses put down the revolt harshly; the people never could quite believe Yahweh was fully competent when invisible or that the whole outside world of bull-worshippers was wrong; the bull theme reappeared many times, usually tied loyally to Yahweh, and in the days of Jeroboam, images, including the bull, were well-received, just as Zeus, not a bull, could be represented as such on occasion, as when he kidnapped Europa.

Without question, the written *Books of Moses* expanded with time, as in this case, and usually, where a major affair is concerned, an oral historical tradition and a structure of truth are present. So it goes with the Moral Decalogue, the plagues, the confusing infancy of Moses, and other important elements; the written increments, uncovered by linguistic analysis, are founded upon ancient and authentic oral accounts and lost fragments. I think that more barriers to understanding the Bible have been erected by poor sociological and philosophical theorizing than by the more commonly criticized exegetes.

UNBELIEVING SCHOLARS

Theodor Gaster's book of *Myth, Legend, and Custom in the Old Testament* is a compendium of analogous actions performed by characters in a number of different cultures. His typical procedure is to take an act or practice from a passage in the Bible and to show that similar behavior is discoverable in several other tribal or folk cultures here and there in the world. Explanations are rarely afforded. As an example, he writes of the taboo on touching the Ark of the Lord [8]. As we have already told it, the unlucky Uzzah tries to steady the Ark when an ox drawing it on a wagon stumbles; he is struck dead. Gaster gives two parallels. One is from Troy, where Ilus tried to rescue the Palladium of Athene from the flames and was blinded. In the second, Metellus rescues the same type of object from the temple of Vesta and is also blinded. Both have their sight restored. Gaster then ends the discussion.

This procedure is purely descriptive and primitivist anthropology, even less sophisticated than that of Frazer on

APPENDIX 373

whose nineteenth century work Gaster's is founded. Human behavior must of course be analogous everywhere. People talk, eat, produce, have sexual relations, fight with weapons, and symbolize their actions, in basically similar ways everywhere. The resemblances of the three actions that he cites seem to be superficial. His implication here, as throughout his book, is that these are not events; they have no causes nor consequences; they are simply cartoon sketches coming off the brushes of long-gone legend creators. But our book is dedicated in part to showing that each and every legendary episode has a lesser or greater accumulation of characteristic symbolization centered around a core of historical reality; it is like the trillions of manganese lumps on the deep ocean bottoms that have accumulated around cores of shark teeth and other bones and stones; they are all alike but have a unique happening as a seed.

By way of contrast to Gaster, U. Cassuto's *Commentary on the Book of Exodus* (1951, 1959) uncovers a string of three stories of wells, with Abraham, Jacob, and Moses as the heroes, each obtaining a bride thereby [9]. In this case, however, the fact that wells were universally employed for meetings and rendezvous is made significant by a close parallelism of Jacob's story with that of Moses. The two plots, involving other shepherds and the damsels Rachel and Zipporah, suggest a deliberate embellishment to tie Moses to his ancestor Jacob. Nonetheless Cassuto explicitly denies that his book aims at establishing historicity.

In 1957, Greta Hort published two articles on "The Plague of Egypt,"[10] there tying together skillfully much scientific knowledge pointing towards the actuality and sequence of the plagues. Briefly she argues that an unprecedented rainfall in Ethiopia eroded the red soil basin of Lake Tana and the banks of the Blue Nile and sent red floodwaters causing down the some 2000 miles of river, carrying with them a red micro-animal *Euglena sanguinea* as well. This polluted flood killed the fish of the Lower Nile and drove the frogs ashore, where insects infected them with an anthrax. Infestations of mosquitoes and flies followed. Independently a fierce hailstorm from the North blew up the Nile Valley. Fire is not mentioned. Weather conditions were propitious afterwards for a massive locust invasion. The dried-out land gave up its coating of red powdered dust to the first *khamsin* or sandstorm of the year, bringing days of darkness. She advances plausible reasons why the Hebrews should have been spared, in their partial isolation, some of the plagues.

The plague upon the first-born is reduced to a ruination of the first fruits of the harvest that were ordinarily consumed in spring. The Israelites left then partly out of fear of being robbed of their harvests by the less fortunate Egyptians. Pharaoh was hard-hearted about letting them go; although prayer expeditions to the desert were not unknown, he would not chance the Hebrews leaving, because their god might answer their prayers and discountenance his god, and because sedition might be served with such moving about of people.

I cannot do justice to Hort's ingenious scenario here. By way of negative criticism, I would allude to the enormous distance the red dust and flagellates would need to descend. Also, the lack of repetition of the plagues in earlier or later times makes the Exodus still unique. Critical connections are missing between the other plagues and the hailstorms and

APPENDIX 375

locusts. The first-born killing is laid aside. The magic wand contest is evaded. So is the climactic movement of waters in the passage out of Egypt. Nor are the negotiations or the human movements incorporated precisely into her scenario. The actuality of biblical events is, of course, a provocative issue in scientific quarters. A few years later, Dorothy Vitaliano, in *Legends of the Earth* [11] stresses again a geological approach in attempting to restrain popular faith in ancient and folk accounts of unusual natural events. Vitaliano confronts causation directly, like Hort and unlike Gaster. She offers to explain the plagues as natural events, giving as much credence to the Bible as she can admit.

But she is operating with a weak instrument, the uniformitarian law that the same natural conditions of today have prevailed over millions of years. Consequently, there is not enough energy in the ordinary, terrestrial, natural forces she employs to deliver the quick succession of shattering blows to the Egyptian Empire. Nor are the forces integrated by a single, sufficient cause. Her a priori refusal to consider an extra-terrestrial force cuts short the explanation at an unsatisfactory point. The major concession that she makes to the literalness of the Bible is the connection (which earlier I have adversely criticized) between the explosion of Thera-Santorini and the tidal waters sweeping in upon the Egyptian army [12].

A much greater freeing of the intellect is required before the Exodus events can be understood. It is notable that upon the conclusion of her heavily researched studies, Hort qualifies the results by reference to research by Professor Bodenheimer "on the connection between solar activity and pests" and the hope for an ultimate explanation by "cosmic and terrestrial" connections [13].

The combination of uniformitarianism and disbelief in legend leads, as with Buber and Daiches and Gaster, to a general distortion of the Bible by reductionism. The result is a sugar-coating of reality by a questionable commonsense. Shrinking from the realities of Exodus, not one but most editors and scholars have painted its human and natural background, the wanderings, and the struggles, as a quaint nineteenth century romance. Martin Buber was one of the best of biblical scholars and a hero of resistance to the Nazis; but little of the madness that he experienced under Nazism ruffles his calm book on the life of Moses.

He is a rationalist - wrongly regarded as an existentialist - who ever so subtly deflates the rhetoric and propositions of the Bible, following a principle of maximal reductionism; at the same time, he is trying to keep his people, the Jews, bound together in a community, with the Bible as its glue. Perhaps the double task is impossible, or perhaps he is more an expert than a theorist; for his book is littered with disconnected, uncontrolled, and fallacious surmises.

At one moment he may be Machiavellian. Thus he thinks that Moses had no clear mission in Egypt but, when rejected by the Hebrews, got himself accredited as the representative of the Hebrew god at the Pharaoh's court [14]. Machiavelli himself might have approved this notion; he regarded Moses as a model prince, perhaps even better than Caesar Borgia: Moses formed a nation and led it forth to survival.

Then again Buber stretches time with an uncontrolled imagination; Moses is a kind of spook who haunted

APPENDIX 377

Pharaoh's court for years while the plagues went on at large intervals [15]. Buber analyzes the passover feast as an old shepherd festival of spring [16]. (Why each family should stay in its own home during a fiesta is rather strange.)

His scenario of Moses talking with Yahweh is a fine example of reductionism, himself, quite unbelieving, yet letting his reader believe:

> In our vision, we see this man Moses at times, following some new and wearing experience with his people, entering the leader's tent, sitting down on the ground and for a long time weighing in his soul whatever may have befallen; until at length the new comprehension rises to the surface and the new word oppresses his throat; till it finally darts across into the muscles of his hand, permitting a new utterance of the Zealous God to come into being on the scroll [17].

This is practically all that passes for psychiatry in the book. Is Moses, or is he not, talking with Yahweh?

Of all that is said and done in the Crossing of the Sea, Buber concludes: "It is irrelevant whether 'much' or 'little', unusual things or usual, tremendous or trifling events happened; what is vital is only that what happened was experienced, while it happened, as the act of God."[18] Here is your second greatest episode in Jewish history! (If the handing down of the Decalogue is the greatest.) "Miracle," he says, is "nothing but an abiding astonishment." But he cannot escape the urge to trivialize events: "It may be assumed that the frontier guards set out in pursuit of the fugitives."[19]

As for the greatest episode, at Mt. Sinai, "every attempt to penetrate to some factual process which is concealed behind the awe-inspiring picture is quite in vain."[20]

The principle of uniformitarianism leaks out now and then: "We must maintain the conclusion that, for times about which we have nothing more than reports impregnated with material of an obviously legendary character, it is necessary to assume the same fundamental forms of historical behavior as we know in periods which have found more sober chroniclers." This, regarding the Passover! Things were then as they are now, legend-analysis is futile! (Notwithstanding that in the aftermath of catastrophe, legend, rather than purely factual history, is more likely to be written and to survive.)

Gripped by philosophical confusion, he speaks of natural forces at the crossing from Egypt: "Here there is no Nature in the Greek, the Chinese or the modern Occidental sense. What is shown us of Nature is stamped by History."[21] And the history is stamped by wonder, he says, which produces cosmic exaggerations. "The defeated Egyptian 'dragon' grows into a symbol as vast as the world in the drama of rescue which serves as prelude to the revelation…" From what unconscious source did Buber conjure up the Egyptian 'dragon'? It can be none other than Typhon, the great monster whom Zeus struck down with thunderbolts at the time of Exodus, and the name of the first Hyksos king of Egypt whose forces were invading the country at the moment of Exodus.

If this be sheer conjecture about Buber's mind, let it pass as such. But let me nevertheless conjecture about a similar effect in the mind of David Daiches, for he, like Buber, dismisses any psychological approach to Moses. In

APPENDIX 379

the Epiloque to his learned and beautiful "coffee-table" book on the life of Moses, Daiches writes "For generations schoolboys have asked each other: 'Where was Moses when the light went out?' and replied, 'Under the bed, looking for the matches.' Thus he moved easily from the sublime to the ridiculous, a fate shared by many great names."[22]

Perhaps Freud, master of the theory of wit, a biographer of Moses to whom Buber gave only one demeaning sentence and Daiches gave two, quoting Buber approvingly, would have noted this remark. Also, that the remark is in the last paragraph of the book.

Why should schoolboys "for generations" (I remember well the joke) associate Moses with the light going out and why was he "under the bed looking for the matches"? Moses was the great leader of the times when darkness befell the world. Under the grim pall (pallet?) was it not he who was finding matches to make light?

I play this game only to show that it is serious. Humor is an escape from fear. When legendary characters or historical characters or identifiable substitutes for them are involved, not alone Freud, but also anthropologists generally nowadays suspect that a clue to something that happened in history is contained in the joke. That Daiches should choose these words to be among his last of the book, which tackles an awesome subject, is nothing more, I suppose, than a little giggle of unconscious self-depreciation. It confesses that he has not solved the problem of Moses and has hardly dared to address it.

THE PRAGMATICS OF LEGEND

Many scholars specialize in analyzing legends, but I do not know of a manual of their techniques. Whoever has not worked with legends is prone to believe that their analysis is a waste of time, baseless, or even fakery, like persons often believe who have not worked with the analysis of dreams, handwriting, or propaganda, or with the authentication of documents and paintings. On the other hand, some of those who have done so believe that rules of analysis are impossible to formulate and an informed intuition is the only resort. Nevertheless, I feel an obligation to announce what rules I try to follow, and to accept the critical consequences. Actually the rules are simple enough and can be practiced generally with fair success.

We can take as a first rule what was to some degree done earlier in this chapter: *locate and dissolve the editorial screen imposed later upon a legend by well-wishing, malicious, power-seeking, or unbelieving translators, reporters, or scholars.* An extra-brief example is the word "Noga" translated "great light" from Isaiah, without regard for the fact that the word has another meaning "the planet Venus." Now I think that the reader will wish to analyze my own book here in this way.

Read god-names as words performing specific functions. The fire referred to in the Pentateuch is of several varieties, and it is possible, although I have not studied the matter, that in a significantly high proportion of cases, the possessive "Yahweh" is appended to instances of fire other

APPENDIX 381

than ordinary combustion. The same may be true of natural phenomena other than fire, as for example, it was "Yahweh's wind," not simply a heavy wind, that brought down a massive flight of quail. It is ordinarily believed, in instances such as these, that the taking of the Lord's name is either to indicate that all things are caused by Yahweh, or else that any benefaction (or punishing act) is the work of Yahweh. That is, the grammar is to be read as, for instance, we might say that interference with radio reception can be caused by the Van Allen belts, meaning a special kind of belt, not that Van Allen caused the belts.

In the *Books of Moses,* the name Yahweh, when it occurs, can have six additional functions besides this first, which is a shorthand substitute for the cause of a variety of natural events or a confession of ignorance of such causes. "Yahweh" is a battle-cry; the Israelites attack or rally with the calling of a name, as in the old American song "Rally around the flag, boys!"

Yahweh is a collective, abstract fiction of authority, objectified in the minds of community members, giving binding force and security to their transactions. Yahweh is who is obeyed when obedience is demanded.

Yahweh is a label or designation of what is collectively sacred. A secular (slightly sacred) example is the label "Property of the U.S. Government." It joins hundreds and thousands of things, actions, persons in a commonalty. Yahweh is an attribution to a delusionary universal being of responsibility, accountability, or blame by people who wish to evade or avoid or are ignorant of such. "My son died by the will of Yahweh."

Perhaps the most important function of the word is

the dynamic for activating Moses and hence Israel. Yahweh is the inner necessity of Moses to objectify and reify his conscience and to spread his inner dialogue upon the official public record. "Yahweh says 'Do this' lest you die." Finally Yahweh is the inner necessity of other Israelites to objectify and reify their consciences in a privatized dialogue or collective sanctioned discourse, as limited by authority, sacred labels, and Moses' priority. They are discouraged save on rare occasions to place any hallucinations or delusions upon the public record or to discuss them in public.

Different Israelites, as I have explained elsewhere, would have various Yahwehs. No two Yahwehs are the same. Yahweh is a somewhat different component in each Israelite's mind, character, and behavior. No doubt many of the people neither perceived Yahweh nor believed in other people's perceptions, such as Moses'.

A corollary of this general rule about god-names is: If you accept an authoritative voice speaking for god, or talk with him yourself, then there is no point in your analyzing a legend; it is done for you, you are in a different kind of ball game.

A third rule is to *treat every legend as a confused and bothersome collective memory containing some truth and therapy for those telling it*. Yahweh's wind blew a great flight of quail down around the Hebrews when they were starving for meat. Thus he answered their need upon hearing of it from Moses. But then, because they had complained of him, he caused many to die of eating the meat. We expect and know of the destruction of the biosphere occurring in catastrophe. Violent atmospheric turbulence with heavy radioactivity would both bring the feast and poison the feasters. A legend says that the wind that downed the quail was terrible enough to destroy the whole world. Tornados, it is now demonstrable, have plucked chickens [23]. The bird was probably *coturnix coturnix,* the common quail of Europe, Asia and Africa and the only migratory gallinaceous bird.

If long ages have said so, respect a legend's claim to history. Persistent discussions of infanticide or cannibalism under extreme conditions merit belief. More broadly the intense conviction that the Exodus happened is some proof of it. But what of the intense conviction of Yahweh? The belief that Yahweh happened is true in relation to all the qualities that make him an historical god, and make many other divinities also "historical gods." He is a unique god, and says so himself, therefore historical, with a highly touted, historical mission as well.

Do not be arrogant about how scientific our age is, and about how much is known today that used to be unknown. One thinks of perfumes, mummification, herbal medicine, etc. The evidence of this book shows that, partly because of hyper-electrical activity in nature, Moses' generation knew more about electrostatics than did the modern world until perhaps 1850. I speak not alone of natural history but in some cases of pure science and applied science. Where not lapsing into oblivion, a great deal of material, and the literary evidence of it, has been destroyed. It is hard to believe that the many thorough and even brilliant scholars who have dug and delved into the Old Testament setting could otherwise have believed that the wandering and desolated peoples were ignorant primitives. But they have been seduced into following the excursions of anthropologists into primitive cultures. Robert Temple has recently shown how advanced is some astronomical knowledge of the Dogon tribe of Mali; they have known since time immemorial of the invisible dwarf white star, Sirius B, and it is important to them. Obviously they have held onto sound remnants of a lost scientific corpus [24].

Harken, also, to new scientific knowledge that may require old analyses of legends to be revised. Radioactivity was unknown or quite misunderstood until recently. The possibility of explosive meteoric "chemical factories" was ignored until recently and hence the manufacture of great quantities of manna in the atmosphere by natural means was not considered. Another area of recent scientific progress has been psychiatry. Even a century ago there did not exist the systematic, empirically tested categories of mental aberrations such as we here apply to Moses. Or, in the field of geography, it has been established that three large rivers once flowed west to east across the whole width of Arabia, and that there was a great lake, now dead, in Northern Arabia, and that, too, immense areas of blasting and burning are discoverable [25].

Bear in mind that, *within broad limits of individuality and broad limits of culture, human nature and behavior do not change.* People hallucinate today and hallucinated then, under similar conditions. By torture, starvation, a volcanic eruption, and fear, a great many people are compelled to hallucinate. "Angels" may be hallucinations but sometimes only in the limited sense of reifying incredible natural operations and events occurring in the atmosphere.

Neither believe nor disbelieve an event on the first reading of it. This rule applies to very many cases in the present work. The problem arises mostly, or course, in relation to disbelief, regarding the quail, the manna, the rod of Moses, etc. I first disbelieved the story of over three million souls joining the Exodus. Continually nagging the passages, I finally theorized that many people could have left Goshen, for various reasons, and only a small fraction accomplished the Exodus.

Judge a possible truth both by itself and by its context. The story of Miriam's rebellion against Moses and her punishment by leprosy is rendered believable in the context of many cases of leprosy that do not conform to medical definition today. Knowing what the Inner Sanctum contained and the meaning of the ominous cloud allows one to deem the story credible.

Transform the words of a legend to behavior. Words too are a form of behavior. Visualize them as real operations. Just out of Egypt, Moses holds up his rod all the long dark day in battle with the Amalekites, but needs to be propped upon a stone and helped by Aaron and Hur. Why doesn't Yahweh hold it up or give Moses the strength? The "self-reliance" imposed upon Moses lends an air of factuality; further inquiry leads me to regard the story as true. The darkness makes light a heavy morale factor.

Translate the legend into a story-form and a language that you read in the newspapers or watch in films or use in your ordinary work and days. I could not understand Pharaoh's actions until I displaced him into the setting of a contemporary head of state, interposed all I had come to know about the goings-on in, say, the U.S. Presidency, and then carried them back again to the Middle Bronze Age in Egypt.

Accept the possibility that *two legends may be talking about the same event in a different way*. Did Moses really spend two forty day-night periods on Mount Sinai, or was there so much material coming out of one episode that it was made into two? Nothing vital is at stake in either case. The first prolonged period has to stand, in order to make the Golden Calf Revolt and other matters plausible. The second does not. It may have been a brief return following the suppression of the revolt for prayer, supplication, and redemption of the wicked people, whereupon the halo and the message. It would also let people test themselves in Moses' absence and redeem themselves by passing the "faith and patience test." Another case, already discussed, is that of the Greek Phaeton and Typhon legends, both evidently dealing with the cometary events of the Exodus.

Ask what elements are missing from the legend that should be there, and why so? By any ordinary standards, twelve springs of water are insufficient to draw water for 20,000, much less two million people. But so the Bible says, a few days out of Egypt, at Elim, this happened [26]. Until 1930, Tehran, Iran, with 200,000 people, gathered all of its water supply from twelve wells above the town which discharged 800 liters (212 gallons) per second [27]. What is available now at Elim is not binding upon our judgement. The behavior of giant bodies of water in catastrophes is an encyclopaedia of the amazing; the Mississippi River reversed itself for several hours in the New Madrid (U.S.A., Missouri) earthquakes of 1811-2 [28]. A single verse on the volume of flow of the springs would have helped, but then who would accept the Bible generally and

APPENDIX 387

doubt this fact?

Grant the legend a generous quota of exaggerations, time lapses, and contradictions. I have addressed the problem of the numbers in the Exodus in this spirit. The problem of the great ages of Moses and others by modern standards continues to baffle one. One possibility is some electrical and/or atmospheric effect upon life duration. Another possibility is the calculation of ages by a different calendar, perhaps one of 260 days such as obtained in earliest times among the Mayans and other Meso-Americans and persisted as a sacred calendar after they knew and practiced a contemporary calendar. Then at 120 years of age, Moses would have lived 31,200 days. Measured on the year base of 365 days, he would be 85 years old. I prefer this solution.

There is much rhetorical exaggeration in the Bible, which is in part a panegyric for the Jews. Still I doubt whether the promise of Yahweh to multiply his chosen people to the number of stars and sands of the seashore exceeds in optimism the promises contained in the typical annual State of the Union Address of the President to the American people. Nor does it exceed the optimism with which the President views the heights achieved in the American standard of living, inviting now a comparison, too, with Moses' haranguing the Jews on their fine diet of quail (poisoned) and manna bread (wormy). Nor should one forego comparison between an American speaker describing the history of the U.S.A. on the Fourth of July and Moses in *Deuteronomy*, reciting the history of Israel since the Exodus.

Another rule is to *seek particular truths in a legend which is false as a whole, and seek truth as a whole in a legend which contains false particulars.* Thus, by rule number two of this list, we do not see a real Yahweh addressing Moses in the episode of the Burning bush. But the electrical environment and effects, and the reactions of Moses' character are such as to make the event believable and significant.

In converse, the Plagues of Egypt are convincing as a whole set of interconnected events that should not be dismissed because of perplexities in connection with the death of the Egyptian first-born, and because of repeated statements that the Hebrews in Goshen were exempted from them. Wishful thinking usually exaggerates the pains of one's antagonists and would create out of a quantitative difference between the sufferings of Goshen and Memphis a qualitative difference.

An explanation of all events should be attempted, within the limits of time and space available. It is not only irritating, but also and more importantly unscientific, to interpret only those events for which plausible explanations are available, while avoiding others more obscure and contradictory. One should not explain manna without conjecture upon the strange dew that fell with it. Further, a Bible critic cannot be both an historian and a faithful believer. He cannot pick and choose, preserving his reputation as now one and then again the other.

One may not say, as has Daiches, that normal natural conditions prevailed at Sinai during the handing down of the Ten Commandments, and that perhaps "the Kenites, who were desert smiths and would therefore carry fire about with them and whom the biblical story associates closely with Moses, were able to produce smoke and fire which came to be looked on and remembered as some kind of divine

APPENDIX 389

sign."[29] For then, after this incredible reductionism, he blandly finishes his book on Moses without twanging the nerves of even a moderate believer by tucking in a few words where he "concludes" that it would be "too crude" to say that "Moses thought that he might get people to obey him by getting them to believe in Yahweh [30]." Too crude, but he will let it slip off his tongue anyhow. The most significant actions are denied to Yahweh, but he will not address the question of whether Yahweh exists only through Moses or even whether Moses manipulates Yahweh.

Sigmund Freud's paraphernalia of psychiatry is simply abandoned when he writes about Moses as a person. Velikovsky evades arguments that may antagonize, whether nationalistically or religiously, Jews or fundamentalist Christians. Eliade, while including all other religions within his generalizations of historical cyclism, finds that Christianity is donated a particular linear course of history, leaving us with the uneasy question whether he is postulating an indefinitely long, perhaps eternal, course for Christianity; at any rate, it is made an exception to various generalizations by this method.

It is helpful to *check out the common psychological mechanisms in legends* to see how they are operative: wishful thinking (Freud's omnipotence of thought and James' will to believe); the fear of loss of control of the self and the world; hierocentrism, ethnocentrism, and self-centrism; reification of nature and objects; and the projection of feelings of guilt, blame and punishment onto the legendary characters and actions. Whose wish for what control over what fear is evident in what animated beings, and in the plot of their behavior?

Nor are the rules of *historiographical criticism* to be overlooked. One needs to look for signs of repeated confirmations of an event, of the implied presences of eyewitnesses, and even of expert witnesses, and of chronological sequences making logical sense. The Bible is heavily historical in its approach to events; the chains of interconnections among events are many and strong. Unlike practically all legendary material, it carries details of chronology.

With the later help of Christians and Moslems, the Jews were able to assert the authenticity of the Old Testament and benefit from a general approbation of its contents. The pagan world was not so benevolent, lacking the same spiritual investment, whereupon it occurs to us to check whether pagan sources provide some contrary renditions of our subject and supply an alternative theory. We find in the negative.

The opinions of the pagan writers of the Hellenistic and early Christian periods about Moses and the Jews are generally stereotyped. Almost none are in depth, whether friendly or unfriendly. On the basis of John Gager's research [31], the pagan stereotype can be depicted in an understandable form: Moses was an Egyptian, possibly a Heliopolitan scientist, said Apion; Moses led "numerous reasonable men" out of Egypt (Strabo). Moses and Yahweh, his god, brought plagues upon Egypt. The plagues "disfigured bodies", said Tacitus (radiation diseases?) The Jews were carriers of the plagues. They were expelled because they were lepers and forever resented their treatment. They were iconoclasts and destroyed all gods wherever they went; they were atheists, in this sense. The

APPENDIX 391

Jews were aloof, aversive to contacts with other peoples, suspicious and misanthropic. "Having been appointed leader of the exiles, he [Moses] secretly took the holy objects of the Egyptians. In trying to recover these objects with force, the Egyptians were forced by storms to return home" (Pompeius Trogus, 1st century A.D.).

It is remarkable that this caricature, assembled from numerous fragments, can be applied to the scenario of the book here. Every element in it, no matter how distorted, can be associated with corresponding realities of Moses and the Exodus. Like an elaborate rumor, it has a certain probative value, in that its parts can be traced to reality, while it contains no fundamental contradictions of it. However, without full historical understanding, the stereotype leads directly down the road to modern anti-semitism.

It is useful also to *apply certain rules about rumor mongering* to legendary materials directly. This is to disassemble artificial conglomerations and reveal the underlying reality. In solving for the original event, one recognizes a heavy simplification occurring initially over time: single causes eject multiple causality; a leader replaces a group of leaders; one reason is given for a complex of reasons. The simplifying process lends an air of stupidity to legends; however, it is a way of buying temporal endurance at the cost of realism.

There is also an invariable *stereotyping,* such as we have found in historiography as well. Again the Bible as legend veers towards history because of its frequent insistence upon the uniqueness of events and personalities. Aaron is, like Moses, authentic psychologically and yet not stereotyped. Even Miriam is not, though less is said of her.

Joshua, of whom almost no characterization is given, can be put together into a convincing personage.

Events, too. When it is said of the plague of frogs that the animals came onto the beds and into the ovens, this actually happens in local situations. And when there comes the "very heavy hail such as had never been in all the land of Egypt since it became a nation,"[32] the superlative is precise amid a context of precision, and is validated by this, and within the natural realm of events, and within the context of the total set of disasters. We know what pride the ancient Egyptians possessed in their knowledge of their own history; Plato tells of how Solon of Athens was lectured by the Egyptian seers on this point. The usage is stereotyped; the validity of the fact conveyed is not.

One watches, too, on all sides for the inevitable *distortions* that accompany the memory of events, bearing in mind, when observing the distortions, the inevitable hints of their cause which they contain. The repeated references to the Egyptian people as complaisant in lending and giving their valuables to the departing Hebrews hardly succeed in covering up the spontaneous and systematic looting that occurred in the disorganized and chaotic situation. The need to preserve for racist Yahweh a pure race of his chosen people is a continual source of distortion in the verses dealing with the character and conduct of the Hebrews in Egypt and their mingling and merging with tribes during the wanderings and in the Promised Land.

There is, too, as with rumor-mongering generally, a *vulgarization* in the account of events. What Moses does is reduced typically to the level of understanding and gullibility of the common man (though much of this may be the work

APPENDIX 393

of the priests and editors.) Legend lives by speaking to the common denominator of people; they must hear it, like it, be moved by it, and demand that it be passed on for generations without end. History reduced to miracles is the best insurance that it will live, somehow, for a long time. The Torah strives mightily to preserve history in the face of the competitive temptations and advantages of legend.

Finally, I should like to mention *the pitfalls of a simplistic anthropological approach* to the Old Testament, a matter that has arisen already on occasion in the chapters of this book. German scholars, following James Fraser, were especially impressed by the possibilities of reducing the peculiarities of the Biblical text to the commonality of comparative primitive cultural anthropology.

The bedouin primitivist school of Old Testament interpretation is well expressed in America by Julian Morgenstern who in 1929 wrote of the origins of the ark and continued in 1945 with studies of the ark, ephod, and tent [33]. Briefly summarized, he finds numerous Arab and pre-Arab mobile boxed and tented litters, carrying god images and sacred stones (or bethyls), usually on camels. These performed ark-like functions of pointing out routes, rallying tribesmen in battle, and transporting and exhibiting the deity. He concludes that the Ark of the Covenant was of this ilk and not much more - even less, since it would not, at least later on, have carried the image of Yahweh. Further, he claims that to the Ephraimites' tribe belonged the first ark, which then diffused among the confederation.

Against this line of arguments two major thrusts can be directed. One, represented by Roland de Vaux, is historical. The Ark and the Tent, says this authority, were present and together from the very beginning of the wanderings [34]. Lacking here the justification and space for an extended comparative analysis of the two propositions, of which I favor that of de Vaux, I can move to a second mode of rebuttal, which is logical and provides at the least a stalemate.

In the history of artifacts and institutions, there frequently occurs that these possibilities exist: that the historical actuality, form, and function of the central concept evolves, stagnates, or devolves. Thus "an ark" at any point of time, say between 2000 B.C. and 2000 A.D., may exist, but its form and functions may be significantly different. One might find among the bedouins of North Africa, following World War II, artillery shell cases of 105 mm caliber. Judging by their form and function, carrying nuts or valuables on camels, they are of the species of mobile storage jars. In a brief prior period they carried high explosives and were associated with a complex propelling machine and military organization. They have devolved, or evolved, depending on the "ideal" function assigned them. This is an extreme example of what occurs with all artifacts and institutions over time.

Another example is to be found in the Ark of the Torah, the standard chest that contains the Law in Jewish temples. Its design was traced by Joseph Jacobs. Its original was clearly a Roman desk constructed to hold scrolls [35].

Whatever arks and ephods and tenting may have been before and since the Ark of the Covenant and Tabernacle, and even elsewhere at the same time, the problem of the particular Ark of Moses remains. Logically, not only can it be all that we said it is (and for our purposes the Biblical description is as justifiable as any other design), but also it is to be expected that the Ark, like all inventions, was built upon prior artifacts and institutions and was part of the inheritance of subsequent peoples who changed its form and function, keeping its "spiritual" functions, say, and depressing its physical construction, and forgetting (partly because of changed meteorological and social circumstances) its illuminating divine occupancy.

If thus, historically and logically, we can substantiate our position respecting the actuality and functions of the ark, we may proceed to a third point, a counter-allegation. This is directed against bedouin primitivist thinking in general, which is a learned and potent kind of reductionism of the Bible. Once the catastrophic setting of Exodus is dismissed as exaggeration and falsehood, and most that we know of Moses is regarded as merely a fanciful hero's tale, then the door is opened wide to a new history of the Jews as an escaped slave remnant finding haven among an undisturbed nomadic tribe, and, in gratitude or by necessity, adopting their local volcano-god. But once the natural conditions of Exodus and the character of Moses and his cohorts are established, there can be assigned to bedouin primitivism only the limited role that I have already granted it in this book.

ENDNOTES

Foreword:

1. Ernst Sellin, *Mose und seine Bedeutung für die Israelitisch-Jüdische Religionsgeschichte* (1922).

Chapter 1: Plagues and Comets

1. Generally this plague is said to be of flies, not of beasts as in this rabbinical tra- dition. I also here prefer the reading of "lice" to "mosquitoes," as some writers say.
2. Louis Ginzberg, *Legends of the Jews,* Philadelphia, 1909, vol. II, 3423. (Hereafter this is cited as e.g. II G 3423.)
3. These and others are collected and quoted in Velikovsky's *Worlds in Collision* (New York: Doubleday, 1950). Additional sources will be cited below.
4. For example, Claude Schaeffer, *Stratigraphie Comparée et Chronologie de l'Asie Occidentale* (London: Oxford U. Press, 1948), and Dorothy B. Vitaliano, *Legends of the Earth: Their Geologic Origins,* (Indiana University Press, 1973), 179-271. The reader's attention is called also to a book by two British Astronomers, V. Clube and W. Napier, *Cosmic Serpent,* who assign a comet to the Exodus days. See appendix below, section 1.
5. These giants are of certain tribes, well distinguished by Bimson (see below, 1977), of very large stature, who were never numerous or organized well enough to become a major nation, and were finally extinguished; Goliath, fighting with the Philistines and killed by David's slingshot, was one

of the last such types.

6. John J. Bimson, "Rockenbach's De Cometis' and the Identity of Typhon," I *Society for Interdisciplinary Studies Review* (hereafter cited as *SISR*), 4 (Spring 1977), 9-10. F.H. Baker, 189 Living Age (1891) 818-23, gives Halepo (Da Aleppo, Halep) credit in connecting the comet with the Exodus and the destruction of the Egyptian army.

7. *Deut.* 4:37, Unless noted, Biblical citations are of the *Oxford Bible,* Revised Stan dard Version. Annotated. Martin Buber's transliteration (155) in his *Moses.*

8. *Ex.* 13:1.

9. *Num.* 24:17. To the Biblical scholar, Hyam Maccoby. I owe the suggestion that Suthites may be read "Se'thites" ("wicked people") and the embracing phrase may mean in effect "the whole human race."

10. Quoted by Z. Rix to the author in an unpublished manuscript "King Shepherds or Moloch Sheperds?" 2, 1976; Gemser, "Der Stern aus Jacob," 45 *Zeitsch. für Alttestament. Wissen.* (1925) 301 ff; and also quoting W. Staerk, "Die Jüdisch Gemeinde des neuen Bundes in Damascus," in 27 *Beitr. Zur Förederung christ. Theo.* 65 (1922).

11. *Natural History,* II, ch. XXII, 89-91.

12. *Ex.* 12:42b (Douay tr.)

13. *Deut.* 4:34-6.

14. 1 *Kg* 6:1.

15. *Ages in Chaos* (1952); *Peoples of the Sea* (1977); *Ramses II and His Time* (1978); John J. Bimson, *Reading the Exodus and Conquest, Sheffield,* 1978; Donovan Courville, *The Exodus Problem and Its Ramifications,* Loma Linda: Calif., 1971, 2v. 16. N.-A. Boulanger, *L'Antiquité Devoilée par ses Usages,* 4 v., Amsterdam, 1766, was the first major scientific writer on the

social effects of cometary encounters. More recently, see Nahum Ravel, ed. *From Past to Prophesy,* Bronfman Centre, Montreal, 1975; Earl Milton, *Velikovsky and Cultural Amnesia,* Lethbridge U. Press, 1978; A. de Grazia, ed., *The Velikovsky Affair,* 3rd ed., London; Sphere Books, 1979. 17. *The Kuzari* (ca 1140 A. D.), intro. by H. Slonimsky, New York: Schocken Books. 18. "Comets," in Lynch, ed., *Astrophysics,* New York: McGraw-Hill, 1951) 19. A.O. Kelly and F. Dachille, *Target : Earth, The Role of Large Meteors in Earth Science,* Carlsbad, Calif., 1953.
20. "Of Eating of Flesh," in *Morals,* quoted by Velikovsky in *W. in C.,* p. 12; cf. 85ff:
21. Thoum is a name of the Pharaoh of the Exodus as reconstructed by Velikovsky (see *Ages in Chaos,* New York; Doubleday, 1952, p. 40). I do not support the theory that Ramses II or other famed kings, were the Exodus pharaoh. J. Bimson, "Israel in Egypt, "IV *SISR* 2 (1979), 15, identifies the place, not far form Memphis.
22. *Natural History,* II, ch. XXII, 90, Rackham trans., 1938.
23. Hugo Gressmann, *Mose und Seine Zeit,* Göttingen, 1913, pp. 97-108. 24. I. p. 96 He was of the generation of Jesus. 25. II *Gen.* 341.
26. The royal courts and public were excited by the revival of electricity at the hands of early eighteenth century European and American scientists. One experi menter (Wall) fashioned a kind of cane of amber, which could collect and hold charges, would give cracking sounds and "infinite flashes of light," and puff and explode. It would attract to itself smoke and then give it off "like a small cloud."(Joseph Priestley, I *History and Present State of Electricity, with Original Experiments,* London, 1767, 12-4.)

27. John Zeleny, "Rumbling Clouds and Luminous Clouds, "75 *Science,* (15 Jan. 1932), 80-1.
28. Rupert Furneaux, *Krakatoa,* Englewood Cliffs: Prentice Hall, 1964, 69,74.
29. David Daiches, *Moses,* New York; Praeger, 1975, 60; Ex. 14:24.
30. Fred Hoyle and Chandra Wickramasinghe, "Does Epidemic Disease come from Space?" *New Scientist,* Nov. 11, 1977.
31. H.V. Gill, 63 Nineteenth Century (Jan. 1908), 144-150, in W. Corliss, comp., *Earthquake Phenomena,* G2-151 (GOE030).
32. II *Gen.* 352-3. Significant, in view of our later discussion of the origins of the Israelites, is the added statement that the plague of beasts came "as a punishment for desiring to force the seed of Abraham to amalgamate with the other nations." This may refer to a considerable assimilation of the Hebrew, Egyptian, and other peoples during the sojourn in Egypt.
33. II *Gen.* 354.
34. II *Gen.* 354. The air-exploding Tunguska meteor of 1908, apart from knocking down some eighty million tress, radiated the surviving trees, caused vegetables to increase in size, and induced mysterious scabs among the reindeer of the region in that year. (Vera Rich, "The 70-Year-Old Mystery of Siberia's Big Bang, "274 *Nature* (1978), 207).
35. I *Kings* 8:51, as derived from the pen of the second Deuteronomist again much later.
36. I. Donnelly, Ragnarök, New York, Appleton, 1883, ch. 2.
37. II *Gen.* 356.
38. II *Gen.* 358.
39. *Ex.* 10:4.

40. II *Gen.* 359.
41. *Ex.* 10:28-29.
42. *Ex.* 10:23.
43. II *Gen.* 345; see also 14.
44. II *Gen.* 369.
45. *Mose und Seine Zeit*, 103.
46. *Ex.* 12:12.
47. *Ex.* 4:22ff.
48. I. Michelson, IV *Pensée* n°2 (1974) 20, 18, estimates a force of 1024 ergs is required for a 180° (North to South) reversal of the geographical poles; and to bring the Earth to a stop, a trillion times more. We are speaking of incomparably smaller changes in rotational velocity. More recently, Warlow has shown that "to turn the Earth upside-down, with all the attendant havoc such an action can produce,... a mere three-hundreth of the Earth's rotational energy will suffice - and that is only borrowed for half a day." "Geomagnetic reversals?" *J. Physics,* Oct. 1978 repr. in III. *S.I.S.R.* 4 (1979); cf. IV *S.I.S.R.* 2-3 (1979-1980) 8ff.
49. The *Admonitions of an Egyptian Sage from a Hieratic Papyrus in Leiden,* Alan H. Gardiner, trans., Leipzig, 1909; Velikovsky, W. in C., p. 18-24; L. Greenberg, "The Papyrus Ipuwer," III Pensée (Winter 1973), p.36-7; anon., "A Concordance of Disaster, "I *Kronos* 2 (1975), 16-22.
50. J. Van Seters, 50 *J. Egypt. Arch.* (1964), 13; W.F. Albright, 179 *Bull. Amer. Sch. Orient. Res.* (1965), 41-2. Malcolm Lowery, "Dating the 'Admonitions': Advance Report" II *S.I.S.R.* 3 (1977-8), 54-7, gives the most useful lines of Ipuwer's Lament, and affirms that "the Admonitions offer us an eye-witness report of the events at the end of the M. K." (57).

51. See Velikovsky, *A. in C.,* 39-45.

Chapter 2: The Scenario of Exodus

1. Buber, 67.
2. The Philosophy of Magic, quote by Blavatsky, *Isis Unveiled* (1887), I 528.
3. *Ex.* 1:9-10.
4. Brevard S. Childs, *Exodus,* London: SCM Press, 1974, pp. 142-3.
5. Ibid. p. 149.
6. Ibid., pp. 170ff.
7. Buber, p. 64.
8. Ibid., p. 61.
9. Ibid., p. 68.
10. III *Gen.* 12.
11. II *Gen.* 365.
12. II *Gen.* 366.
13. Velikovsky, *W. in C.,* 59.
14. Cf. II *Gen.* 345 where Yahweh does this slaying.
15. Velikovsky, *W. in C.,* 4, from Eusebius, Preparation for the Gospels (transl. 1903), IX, ch. 27.
16. Ibid., 66.
17. *Ex.* 14:5.
18. III *Gen.* 11.
19. J.L. Heilbron, *Electricity in the Seventeenth and Eighteenth Centuries* (Berkeley: U. of California Press, 1979), 98.
20. That is, Moses had dwelt on the borderlands of Arabia, whence came the Hyksos.
21. Velikovsky, *A. in C.,* 57ff.

22. It is noteworthy that Worth Smith a century ago was able to charge a Leyden Jar with extraordinary success by carrying it to the top of the Great Pyramid. (See Peter Tompkins, *Secrets of the Great Pyramid*, New York: Harper and Row, 1971.)
23. III *Gen.* 157. See below III, 3a.
24. II *Gen.* 248.
25. III *Gen.* 286.
26. Hyam Maccoby, "Freud and Moses," Midstream (February, 1980), 9-15
27. III *Gen.* 15.
28. III *Gen.* 56-7. An alternative explanation is that the Amalekites extracted this information from captured Jews.
29. *Ex.* 14:12.
30. *Ex.* 14:11.
31. III *Gen.* 20.
32. See p. 225 in 2 *Ency. Brit.* (1973), "Astronomical Maps."
33. Tompkins, pp. 159ff, for instance, incorrectly explained, I think, as following changes in positions of fixed stars, an old theory of Lockyer. cf. K. Mohlenbrink, *Der Tempel Salomons*, Stuttgart: Kohlhammer, 1932, 79-85.
34. My source is an unpublished study by René Roussel, Albon, France.
35. III *Gen.* 21; *Ex.* 14:20.
36. *Oxford Annotated Bible*, 85, note p.
37. III *Gen.* 20.
38. III *Gen.* 26-8.
39. III *Gen.* 27. Re pre-Hyksos Chariots cf. J. Bimson, "Israel in Egypt," IV *SISR* 2 (1979), 17-8.
40. E.M. Shepard, 13 *J. Geology* (Feb. 1905), 45, in Corliss, comp. *Strange Phenomena*, G2-GQE-026, 147.

41. Granted the passing body, there would be no question that the tides would be elevated as well as moved horizontally (See Velikovsky, *W. in C.* p. 86). Priestley in his famous History and Present State of Electricity with *Original Experiments* (2v. London, 1767) describes (73) Grey's simple experiment with a bowl of water. He passed an electrically charged object over the bowl, which drew up the water into a "hill;" at the point of nearest encounter, a spark was exchanged, and the "hill" collapsed, sending out waves.
42. *Ex.* 15:14-16.
43. III *Gen.* 73-74.
44. *Ex.* 6:9.
45. *Ex.* 14:24-5 The Douay translation indicates the head of the comet is Yahweh: "The Lord cast through the columns of the fiery cloud upon the Egyptian force a glance that threw it into panic."
46. Bimson. "Israel in Egypt," IV *SISR,* no 1, (Aug. 1979), 15.

Chapter 3: Catastrophe and Divine Fires

1. III *Gen.* 13-4.
2. III *Gen.* 17.
3. Velikovsky, *W. in C.,* 156.
4. If 430 years (not 400) are divided by 86, and the dividend is 5; then Uzza could have been calculating in some cycles of 86 years, but the legend is mute about the further meaning and I know of no such cycle. I mention later that the years of Moses, some patriarch, and other events before 1440 B. C. may have been calculated on a sacred year of 260 days,

perhaps the work of Amon-Jupiter or Thoth- Hermes.
5. III *Gen.* 126. For other references to the great celestial light over Exodus, cf. II *Gen.* 37, III *Gen.* 133. 6. II *Gen.* 373. Earlier, in contradiction thereof, we spoke of Moses' last meeting with the Pharaoh being in heavy darkness.
7. *Is.* 9:2; *W. in C.,* 175.
8. B. Feldman, in a letter to VI *Kronos,* 2(1981) 92, reporting from G. Scholem's "Sabbatai Sevi: The Mystical Messiah" (trans. Werblowsky), Princeton U. Press, 1973.
9. *Num.* 21:9.
10. Velikovsky, *W. in C.,* 176.
11. II *Gen.* 316-7.
12. *Ex.* 13:21-2. Cf. 14:19-20.
13. Translated as "On comets, comet-like Luminous Apparitions and Meteors," VII *Kronos* 4(1982).
14. III *Gen.* 26.
15. G.A. Wainright, "Jacob's Bethel." *Report. Pales. Explor. Fund,* 1934, 32.
16. *Ex.* 26:49.
17. VII *Reallexikon fur Antike and Christentum,* p. 376, citing a Midrash.
18. III *Gen.* 150-1.
19. Velikovsky, *W. in C.,* 107.
20. *Ps.* 68:7-8.
21. III *Gen.* 151.
22. Ibid., 165.
23. Ibid., 231-8, with each of these four were grouped two others, making four groups of three. The Levites, not a tribe, were centered around the sacred area in the middle of the roughly nine square miles of residential area.
24. E.C. Baity, "Archaeoastronomy and Ethnoastronomy

Thus Far, "14 *Current Anthropology* 4(Oct. 1973), 389.
25. Giorgio de Santillana and Hertha von Dechand, *Hamlet's Mill*, Boston : Gambit, 1969, 239.
26. Ibid., 239-40.
27. *Oxford Annotated Bible*, fn. *Ex.* 25:40, citing also *Ex.* 25:9; 26:30; 27:8.
28. III *Gen.* 123.
29. It is called a "bull" on occassion in Jewish legend.
30. Umberto Cassuto, *A Commentary on the book of Exodus* (tr. I. Abrahams) Jerusalem: Magnes Press, Hebrew U., 1967, 412.
31. Cœ. Henri Breuil, "Le bison et le taureau céleste chaldéen, "XIII *Revue Archeologique*, series IV, Mar-Ap 1909, 250-4.
32. Velikovsky, *W. in C.* 181, quoting Nechre-Wahibre.
33. Unpubl. letter to author.
34. *Ex.* 15:14-16.
35. Velikovsky, *A. in C.*, 62, quoting Arab sources.
36. David Neev and G. M. Friedman, "Late Holocene Tectonic Activity Along the Margins of the Sinai Subplate,"202 *Science* (27 Oct. 1978) 427-9.
37. "The catastrophe Finale of the middle Age," *Proceedings, IX Int'l Congress Prehist.and Protohist.*, Nice, France, 1976.
38. W.F. Petrie, *Egyptian Archaeology*, p. 67.
39. G.L. Possehl, "The Mohenjo-daro Floods…" 69 *Amer. Anthro.*, n°1, 1967, 32-40.
40. R.M. Adams, "From sites of patterns," 68 *U. of Chicago Mag.*, winter, 1975, 19- 20.
41. Alex. Kondratov, *The Riddles of Three Oceans*, Moscow, U.S.S.R, 1974, 164.
42. William Mullen, "The Mesoamerican Record," 4 *Pensée*, 4

Fall 1974, 34-44.
43. "China's Dragon," 4 *Pensée,* 1 (1973-4), 47-50.
44. *Reallexikon fur Antike and Christentum* (Anton Hiersemann, Stuttgart,1969) 366.
45. Ibid., 362-6.
46. Zvi Rix, unpubl. mss., quoting K.B. Stark, *Gaza und die Philistäische Küste* (1852), s. 268.
47. *Reallexikon for Antike and Christentum.*
48. Rix, quoting E. Lefebure, "Le Sacrifice Humain d'après les rites de Busiris et d'Abydos," III *Sphinx* (Upsala), 1900, 143.
49. *Reallexikon,* 368.
50. Ibid., 372.
51. Ibid., 374.
52. *New Scientist* (20 Oct. 1977), 150.
53. B.A. Smith et. al., 204 *Science* (1979), 961.
54. Thomas Gold, "Electrical Origin of the Outburst on Io" 206 *Science* (1979), 1072.
55. "The Natural History of Lightning," *Proceedings,* III Tall Timbers Fire Ecology Conference, Tallahasse, Fla., 1964, 150.
56. Velikovsky, *W. in C.,* 56-57.
57. *Gen.* 11:1-9.
58. E. A. Von Fange, "Strange Fires on Earth," 12 *Creation R.Q.* (Dec. 1975), 132.
59. A. de Grazia, "Paleo-Calcinology: Destruction by fire in Prehistory and Ancient Times," I *Kronos* 4 (1976) 25-36; II *Kronos* (1976),63-71.
60. Cf. *Oxford Annot. Bible,* Ex. 3:2 fn; 19:9; 33:9; 40:34-8; 1 Kings 8:10-11.
61. *Ex.* 19:16-19.

62. *The Mosaic Tradition,* 74 and 71ff. Pythian-Adams is cited as first to suggest, in his *Call of Israel,* that all Sinai reference were Post-Exilic while the reference to Horeb are older and original.
63. *Num.* 11:1-3.
64. III *Gen.* 244.
65. III *Gen.* 245.
66. Cf. W. Corliss, comp., *Strange Phenomena,* 2 v. (1974) GLB series for recent cases.
67. The plasmoid may be distinguished from ball lightning by its more volatile and heavy explosive quality. Cf. R. Juergens, "Of the Moon and Mars," IV *Pensée* 4 (1974), 21.
68. Contradicting this, V. Manoilov, *Electricity and Man,* Moscow: Mir, 1978, 54, sets the Earth's charge at 50 million coulombs, granting that the charge is continually changing globally and locally.
69. Ibid., 55.
70. Cf. W. Corliss, comp., *Strange Phenomena,* 2 v. 1974, GE-GQE-029, 030, et passim.
71. Eric Crew, "Electricity in Astronomy," II *SISR* 4(1977), 24.
72. *U.S. Geological Survey,* "Earthquake Lights," (July 3, 1977, Wash. D.C.)
73. The space available here does not permit citation of the numerous scientific articles on electrical effects of earthquakes such as would have been experienced during the Exodus and in the wilderness. A number of useful reports are cited and partially reprinted in Corliss, compiler, op. cit. (GQE series, *Sourcebooks,* 1974f).
74. David Finkelstein and James Powell, 228 *Nature* (Nov. 21, 1970) 759-760.

75. Op. cit., 131.
76. D. Vitaliano, op. cit., ch. 8ff.
77. I. Isaacson, "Some preliminary Remarks..." I *Kronos* 2 (1975), 93-9.
78. M.R. Rampino, S. Self, R. Fairbridge, "Can Rapid Climatic Change Cause Volcanic Eruptions," 206 *Science,* 16 Nov. 1979, 826, citing J. Keller et al.
79. Velikovsky, *A. in C.* 79, ff. The cause may have been an isostatic adjustment or a cometary revisit.
80. Richard A. Kerr, "When Disaster Rains..." 206 *Science* (16 Nov. 1979), 803-4.
81. John A. Eddy, "Case of Missing Sunspots," 236 *Sci. Amer.* (May 1977), 80-92; Earl s. Milton, "The Not So Stable Sun," V *Kronos* 1 (1979), 64-78.

Chapter 4: The Ark in Action

1. Paul F. Mottelay, *Bibliographical History of Electricity and Magnetism,* London:Griffin, 1922, 235. Mason's advertisement is the earliest explicit mention that I have found of the idea that the organization and motions of the solar system can be explained on the principles of electrical forces.
2. T.A. Hankins, 206 *Science* (30 nov. 1979),1066. cf. J.L. Heilbron, op. cit. ; Bernard Cohen, Franklin and Newton, 1956.
3. *Ex.* 33:9.
4. Buber, 161.
5. *Ps.* 132:2;5.
6. Tompkins, 278.
7. Heilbron, op. cit., 340.

8. John J. O'Neill, *Prodigal Genius,* 1944, 91 et passim. Kenneth M. Swezey, *Science* (May 16, 1958). Tesla lived 1856-1943.
9. Ibid., 188, 182.
10. Heilbron, op. cit., 327ff.
11. *Ex.* 31:23-5.
12. Cassuto, 383.
13. Jotham Johnson, ed., *The New Century Classical Handbook,* New York: Appleton-Century-Crafts (1962), 411.
14. Priestley I, 140.
15. V. Grigoryev and G. Myakishev, *The Forces of Nature* (MIR Publ. Moscow, 1971).
16. *Deut.* 10:3.
17. Cassuto, 328.
18. From page 62a of *Egypt and Israel.*
19. Priestley, II,154.
20. Zvi Rix, "The Androgynous comet," I SISR 5 (1977),17.
21. Worth Smith is cited by P. Tomkins, *Secrets of the Great Pyramid,* New York, 1975, p. 278, to the effect that the unlidded open box or coffer of the Kings Chamber inside the Great Pyramid of Cheops had "exactly the same cubic capacity as the Ark of the Covenant." This is almost surely incorrect. The coffer holds 8 cubic royal cubits by Livio Stecchini's computations. The volume of the Ark would be roughly 5.625 cubic royal cubits. Further, the coffer could readily have been a sarcophagus because of its 78" length, the Ark at about 45" not at all. And the coffer is of a single piece of granite. See also Stecchini, in Tomkins, pp. 322-6. Stecchini identifies three different cubits in Egypt. Piazzi Smyth held that the "sacred cubit" used in the Great Pyramid was the same as the one used by Moses for the design of the

Holy Tabernacle (25. 025 Br. inches), Ibid. p. 77.
22. A systematic exposition of what the ancients knew about electricity, and a refutation of the liberal position that they knew very much, is contained in T.H. Martin's *La Foudre, l'Electricité, et le Magnétisme chez les Ancients,* Paris: Didier, 1866.
23. G.E. Wright, *Biblical Archaeology,* London, 1957, 65.
24. Ibid.
25. The legend says faces of boys. III G 158.
26. II. Gressmann, *Altorientalische Texte und Bilder zum Alten Testamente,* Tubingen: Siebeck, 1909, plate 106.) The goddesses are probably Isis and Nephthys.
27. Ibid., 158-9.
28. I *Sam.* 4:4; Cassuto, p.333;also I Chron. 13:6 and Ps 80:1.
29. II *Sam.* 6:2.
30. Cassuto, 336, translating Ex. 25:22.
31. Cassuto, 330, rendering *Ps.* 132:7; see also *Ps.* 99:5; I *Chron.* 28:2.
32. Buber,157,159.
33. Ibid., 150.
34. Ibid., 151.
35. For instance, 12.
36. *Ex.* 25 and 37.
37. *Ex.* 25:19; cf. 37:8.
38. II Priestley, 150.
39. Ziegler, *YHWH,* Princeton, N. J. : Metron Pubns., 1977., 10.
40. Manoilov, 120; Jellinek, *Elektrische Unfälle,* Vienna, 1925.
41. Ibid., 150.
42. *Lev.* 10:1-2. A parallel occurred in Roman history: Tullus Hostilius was a prince "who found in the Book of Numa instructions on the secret sacrifices offered to Jupiter Elicius,

made a mistake, and, in consequence of it, 'he was struck by lightning and consumed in his own palace.'" (H. Blavatsky, *Isis Unveiled,* 1877, 527, quoting here Livy, *Rom. Hist.* I, ch.31 and also Piso and Pliny.
43. III *Gen.* 187.
44. *The Pentateuch and Haftoras,* London: Soncino Press, 1938, 480.
45. Velikovsky thinks (*W. in C.* p. 56) that the "strange fire" was petroleum.
46. *Levit.* 10:1-7.
47. *Levit.* 16:2.
48. Ziegler, 27.
49. Mottelay, 204.
50. *Gen.* III 228-9.
51. *Ex.* 23;28 (New World Trans.)
52. Gressmann, *Die Lade Jahves,* 3-6, is baffled at the idea of the Ark being a direction-finder (see next page) and thinks it was hitched behind animals who were "given their own heads" with the Israelites trailing along behind.
53. Footnote to *Ex.* 25:10-22, p.99.
54. *Num.* 10:33.
55. III *Gen.* 235-6.
56. Ziegler, 23.
57. *Num.* 10:35-6.
58. Ziegler, 24.
59. II Priestley, "The Musical Tone of Various Discharges."
60. E.R. Dodds, *The Greeks and the Irrational,* Berkeley: U. of Calif. Press, 1968, 298.
61. Ibid., 299.
62. *Lev.* 25:9ff. Cf. Velikovsky, *W. in C.,* 155.
63. *W. in C.* 153-154.

64. *Num.* 14:40-5.
65. Ziegler, 28.
66. K.M. Kenyon, *Digging up Jericho,* London, 1957, 43.
67. Chaim Herzog and Mordecai Gichon, *Battles of the Bible,* New York: Random House, 1978,
28. Although these military men are psychologically insightful, the several pages that they consign to the Exodus and the Battle of Jericho suffer from "the four sins of modern biblicism": confused chronology; reductionism; primitivism; and uniformitarianism.
68. I think that Herzog and Gichon perceive correctly that the present word "harlot" was originally a "victualler" or "hostess of an inn", 27.
69. I *SISR* 3 (1976),2-7 and II *SISR* (1977) 16, 19.
70. Ibid. and K. M. Kenyon, *Archaeology in the Holy Land,* 3rd ed. London (1970), 197.
71. Kenyon, p. 254-5.
72. "The Conquest of Canaan and the Revised Chronology," I *Interdiscip. Bible Scholar* 1 (Aug. 1979), 43.
73. *Joshua* 3; *Num.* 33:48-9; 25.
74. "Notes on the Bronze Age Tombs of Jericho," *PEQ,* 1955, 128, discussed by Bimson (1979).
75. *Gen.* III 330-1.
76. When in Vietnam in 1967 the American leader urged a broader approach to the problems of pacification, a Marine general was widely quoted for saying: "Grab them by the balls and their hearts and minds will come along behind."
77. *Jud.* 17:3.
78. Theodor H. Gaster, *Myth, Legends, and Customs in the Old Testament,* New York, Harper and Row, 451-3.
79. Ziegler, 107-8.

80. Ziegler, 107 and cf. Josephus, II *Works,* Ch. 9:6, 120.
81. Manoilov, pp. 60-1, 72; Fred Soyka, *The Ion Effect,* New York: Dutton, 1977.
82. *The Oxford English Dictionary,.*
83. I *Chron.* 13:6.
84. II *Sam.* 6:1-7.
85. I *Kings* 3:1-2.
86. I *Chron.* 21:15-22, 26.
87. Ziegler, 229; *Matt.* 3:11.
88. 2 *Sam.* 24:18-24.
89. *Die Lade Jahves,* 17.
90. Cf. R.T. Omond, 40 *Nature* 102, May 30, 1889 for a description of the enhancement of St. Elmo's fire by water.
91. II *Sam.* 24:16-25; I *Chron.* 21:15-22,26.
92. I *Kings* 6:18.
93. II *Chron.* 4:6.
94. Josephus the Historian, *Jewish Wars,* bk V, ch.5; Motteley, *Biblio. Hist.,* p.10.
95. *Magazine Scientifique de Göttingen* (1783), no.5: quoted by H. Blavatsky. *Isis Unveiled,* I, 528.
96. Ibid., 527-8.
97. I *Kings* 8:28.
98. II *Chron.* 7:1-2.
99. II *Chron.* 12:9.
100. Velikovsky, *Ages in Chaos,* ch. 4, Eva Danelius, "Did Thutmose III Despoil the Temple in Jerusalem?" II *SISR* 3 (1977-8), 64-79.
101. The rod destroyed by Hezekiah was most likely an imitation of the original.
102. Cf. Eva Danelius, (discussing Velikovsky, *A. in C.,* ch. 3),"Identification..," I *Kronos* n°3 (1975), 3.

103. *New York Times,* May 4, 1941, pp. 1, B12. Hans Goedicke associates the tablet with the Exodus, and the tidal wave of Exodus with the explosion of the volcano of Thera-Santorini to the north. But Hatshepsut came in Solomon's time (948-927 B. C., see Geoffrey Gammon, "A Chronology for the Eighteenth Dynasty," II *S.I.S.R.* no. 3, 1977-8, 90-4); the Exodus occurred around 1440 B.C., by Biblical reckoning, as developed by Velikovsky in *Ages in Chaos;* and Thera, or Thira, exploded bout 1000 B.C. (see my *Chaos and Creation,* 1981, following Isaacson).

104. Since the Ark is no longer mentioned until the 7th century B.C. (R.H. Kennett, "Ark," I *Ency. Rel. and Ethics,* p. 791), and three possible arks are pictured on the bas-reliefs of Thutmoses' booty, and no ark is mentioned in Nebuchadnezzar's booty from Jerusalem, Velikovsky's reliance upon legendary source for believing the Ark was not taken (*A. in C.,* p.158) may be misplaced. Cf. III G. p.158. But Velikovsky in *A. in C.* p.210, fn. 14, reports in contradiction an Abyssinian legend that Menelik, a son of Solomon and one who may be the Queen of Sheba [Hatshepsut] stole the Ark. In a booklet published by a fundamentalist sect, the British Israelites, and reported to me by Hyam Maccoby, the thesis that Shishak looted the Ark is asserted.

105. The first letter of the Second Book of *Maccabees.*

106. 2 *Ma.* 1:31-6.
Perhaps a search for the pit of Naphtha might locate a source of badly needed oil for Israel.

107. Ziegler, 72, citing *Tosefta Sotah,* xiii, 52.

108. *Works,* III, 9, 194.

109. Ziegler, ch. 19.

110. 10 *EB*, "Julian the Apostate," 333.
111. X *EB* 786.

Chapter 5: Legends and Miracles

1. *Ex.* 19:8.
2. *Ex.* 20:18.
3. Cf. *Ps* 97:4-5: "hills melted like wax;" "the mountains melted, even that Sinai" *Jg* 5:4-5.
4. *Ex.* 24:9, 10.
5. *Ex.* 24:15-18.
6. *Gen.* III 137.
7. *Moses,* 243.
8. Berkeley: U. of Calif. Press, 1970, p.138-139.
9. *Gen.* III 92-3.
10. Mellinkoff, *op. cit.,* plate II.
11. Hugo Gressmann, *Mose und Seine Zeit,* Göttingen, 1913; cf. Cassuto, 448-51.
12. Wayne A. Meeks ("Moses as God and King," 254-71 in Jacob Neusner ed., *Religions in Antiquity,* Leiden: Brill, 1970, 370-1) writes that "in very diverse sources there persist the remnants of an elaborate cluster of traditions in Moses' heavenly enthronement at the time of the Sinai theophany."
13. *Gen.* III 190.
14. *Gen.* III 213.
15. P. 198; Cf. *Num.* 11:35; 12:1-15.
16. Ziegler, 45-7.
17. *Is.* 3:17; cf. 7:20; 3;24.
18. In II *SISR* 2(1977), letters, cf. comments on both famine

and depilation in 3 pp. 101-2, and B. O' Gheoghan in II *SISR* I (1977), pp. 2-3, where radiation disease is discussed as causing abrupt stoppage of childbirth at time of Exodus in Egypt.
19. Francis II. Baker, "Comet Lord," 189 *Living Age* (June 27, 1891). pp.818-23, repr. in W. Corliss, comp., *Strange Universe,* A2-ALC-001.
20. See also their book *Lifecloud,* Harper's and Row, New York, 1978.
21. *Ex.* 33.
22. VII *Encycl. Britannica* 1964, hereafter referred to as *EB.*
23. VII *EB* p.962.
24. Ibid.
25. (1975), 136, citing George E. Mendenhall, *The Tenth Generation,* Baltimore: John Hopkins U. Press, 1973, 43,109.
26. Num. 11:9.
27. p.80.
28. M.J. Teesdale, "The Manna of the Israelites, "3 *Science Gossip* (1897) 229-33.
29. *Ex.* 16:14-15,21,31; *Num.* 11:7-8.
30. Reade, "Manna as a Confection," I *SISR* 2 (1977), 9.
31. *Joshua* 6:12.
32. Reade, p.10.
33. Ibid., p.12.
34. Reade believes that the tent was pitched high at the center to let out fumes. Though logical, this view conflicts with the ordinary reading, which results in a construction as depicted in figure 13.
35. Commentary on Virgil: XII, 200; cf. *Eclogue* VI, 42, quoted by Blavatsky, I, 526.
36. *Ex.* 20:24-5.

37. *Ex.* 40:24-5.
38. *Ex.* 27:1-8.
39. III *Gen.* 184.
40. III *Gen.* 162.
41. Cassuto, 362-3.
42. *Lev.* 1-9; 10;23.
43. III *Kings* 18.
44. *Gen.* III 162.
45. Hare, R.; *Journal of the Franklin Institute,* 54 (1852) 28-39.
46. Velikovsky, *A. in C.,* 60; 55-6. Ex. 17:8.
47. *Num.* 21:4-9.
48. Before the Haicheng (China) earthquake of Feb. 4, 1975, "there were a multitude of warnings, local changes in the earth's magnetism and snakes coming out of their lairs in the frozen ground." *NY Times,* Oct. 1, 1979, 60.
49. Manoilov, 81.
50. *Natural History,* II, ch. XXII, 91.
51. Mottelay, 216.
52. *Ex.* 28:15-3; see Cassuto 372-87. 53. Cassuto, 380.
54. Ibid.
55. III *Gen.* 172-3.
56. I *Sam.* 14:37-38.
57. III *Gen.* 172.
58. I *Sam.* 14:45.

Chapter 6: The Charisma of Moses

1. New York: Knopf, 1939, 3.
2. *Life of Moses,* 5.

3. III *Gen.*
4. The tribe of Simeon was quite lost to history, either assimilated to Judah or lost with the people of the tribes of Northern Israel.
5. *Gen.* 49:7.
6. II *Gen.* 269.
7. II *Gen.* 262.
8. Auerbach, Moses, 17, and others.
9. Buber, 35.
10. "Die Mosessagen und die Leviten," xxxi *Sitzungsberichte der koniglich-preussischen Akademie der Wissenschaften* (1905), 640, quoted in Rank, fn. 83.
11. *Gen.* II 277-8.
12. *Gen.* II 275.
13. Ibid.
14. Sebastian de Grazia, "Mahatma Gandhi, Son of his mother," 19 *Polit. Q.* 4 (1948), 336-48.
15. A legend says that Joshua had already a vocation as an executioner before joining Moses on the Exodus. (My source here was I. Velikovsky in a conversation in Oct. 1979; the passage is in Ginzberg's Legends.)
16. The relevant verses are listed in James Strong's *Exhaustive Concordance of the Bible,* Nashville: Abingdon, 1963, based upon the Authorized Version.
17. *Moses,* 243.
18. *Ex.* 30:11-6.
19. Azazel was also a fallen star or Lucifer and called also Azzael, Azza and Uzza. Uzza we have found is the star angel of Hyksos Egypt, and was thrown into the sea during Exodus; al-Uzza is the planet Venus in Arabic, to which human sacrifices were once made. (see Velikovsky, *W. in C.,*

157-8.
20. *Ex.* 32:30.
21. *Ex.* 32:33-5;33:12-16;34:6-10.
22. *Il Principe e Discorsi,* Milan: Feltrinelli, 1960, p. 468.
23. Neher, 79.
24. Buber, p. 167-8; Cf. Philo Judaeus, *On the life of Moses,* 5.
25. *Ex.* 3:4; Ex. 19:3; Lev. 1:1.
26. *Ex.* 2:12.
27. *Gen.* II 281.
28. Philo, 11.
29. Auerbach, 25.
30. II *Gen.* 290-1.
31. *Gen.* II 293. 32. Cf. W. Hosford, "Extraordinary Case of Electrical Excitement....," 1:33 *Am. J. Sci.* (1838), 394-8, about a woman with such a faculty, unexpected and unwanted.
33. He would not be the only Hebrew dowser, but the only one with authority to whom attention was due. At this writing, on the Island of Naxos, Greece (pop. 15000), anyone may dowse, but only one dowser, Aristoteles, is hired to dowse.
34. H.S. Burr and F.S.C. Northrup, "The Electrodynamic Theory of Life, "19 *Q.J. Biol.* (1935), 323-33.
35. Probably he sent them back to Midian when the crisis deepened, for they were with Jethro when finally Moses returned to Midian after the Exodus. *Ex.* 18:5-6.
36. *Ex.* 5:24-6.
37. Freud's statement is supported by Gressmann, *Altorientalische Texte,* op. cit., 126, plate 254, which depicts an Egyptian circumcision operation.
38. *Ex.* 4:10-6.

39. *Ex.* 7:1.
40. II *Gen.* 316.
41. I find myself having to criticize Freud for his neglect of the unconscious again. He lays Moses' speech impediment to his inability to speak Hebrew properly! Even then, his reasoning is illogical, because Moses complains of his affliction as an impediment to persuading also the Pharaoh, who presumably spoke Egyptian. Arthur Koestler once pointed out that the Greeks called stutterers and foreigners by the same name, "barbarous" (IX *Ency. Britannica* 9). Here is a hint of support for Freud. We cannot eliminate the possibility that Moses confronted his speech problem by employing a special or stilted form of Hebrew.
42. Philo Judaeus, 7.
43. III *Gen.* 256.
44. Philo Judaeus, Ibid.
45. Rix,"The Great Terror," I *Kronos* n°1 (Spring ;1975) 5164 and "Note on the Androgynous Comet," I *SISR* 5 (1977), 179; cf. P. Tompkins, *The Eunuch and the Virgin,* New York: Potter, 1962.
46. *Moses,* 6.
47. John Gager, *Moses in Greco-Roman Paganism,* Nashville, Abingdon Press, 1972.
48. *Moses,* 41. 208.
49. 10 *Encycl Brit.,* 193.
50. Ziegler, 105ff.
51. *Moses,* 67.
52. III *Gen.* 260.
53. *Deut.* 17:2-5.
54. II *Gen.* 362.
55. Velikovsky, *W. in C.,* 124.

56. M. Coe, "Native Astronomy in Mesoamerica," in A.F. Aveni, ed., *Archaeoastronomy in Pre-Columbian America*, Austin, U. of Texas, 1975.
57. *Ex.* 17:14.
58. *Ex.* 32:33.
59. Neher, 62-3, citing signs sculpted upon a statue at Serbit-el-Hadim.
60. Ernest Sellin, *Introduction to the Old testament* (tr. London, 1923), 13-14.
61. Barry Page, "A Palaeography of Biblical Israel," I *Inter-disc. Bib. Scholar* 1 (1979), 26.
62. Max Weber credits Moses with inventing the Convenant with the deity, p. 78, *Ancient Judaism,* Glencoe: Free Press, 1952. The Covenant codes of Ex, 20:22-3; 33; 34:11-6. cf. M. Greenberg, "History of Judaism," 10 *Encycl. Brit.* 304.
63. *Ex.* 20;24; *Deut.* 5.
64. Winnett, 30ff.
65. *The Ritual Decalogue* (Ex.20:23-6; 23:10-9) is assembled by Winnett, 192-3.
66. Weber, 121.
67. Julian Jaynes, *The Origins of Consciousness in the Breakdown of the Bicameral Mind,* Boston: Houghton Mifflin, 1976, 87.
68. Furneaux, *Krakatoa,* 219.
69. *Num.* 9:89.
70. *Num.* 11:17-25. The exceptions prove the rule. The spirit of Yahweh changed the false prophet Balaam into an absurd but true one (Num. 24:2). Jephthah, with the "spirit of the Lord" upon him sacrificed his daughter (Jg. 11:29). Elijah the Prophet, transfers his spirit to Elisha before he is carried to heaven by a chariot of fire (2 Kg., 2:9-10).
71. *Mose and Seine Zeit,* 441.

72. Actually, scorching heat, leprosy and boils, in legend. II G 266.
73. Buber, 168-9.
74. *Num.* 11:10-25.
75. *Ex.* 18:13ff.
76. III *Gen.* 68-72.
77. R.G. Hoskins, *The Biology of Schizophrenia,* New York: Norton, 1946, pp.82-9.
78. Buber, 50.
79. Paul E. Meehl, "Schizotaxy, Schizotypy, Schizophrenia," A. and E. Buss, eds., *Theories of Schizophrenia,* New York, Atherton, 1969.
21. 80. *Ex.* 15:20-1.
81. Ziegler, 33-7.
82. 85
83. Carl G. Jung, *Psychology of Dementia Praecox* (1906, tr. Hull, Princeton U. Press, 1974). 181.
84. Breasted, *The Dawn of Conscience* (1934), 334.

Chapter 7: The Levites and the Revolts

1. Bimson (1979), 16.
2. A.S. Yahuda, *The Language of the Pentateuch in Its Relation to Egyptian,* vol. 1, London: Oxford U. Press, (1933), 294.
3. Some say that Jacob (Israel) and his twelve sons and families (Gen. 46:37) totaling 170 persons in Egypt could not in 430 years grow to 2 millions. They could have grown to 10 or 100 millions or more, theoretically, by the exponentials of population theory. Daiches (p. 82) estimates 2000 to 6000 marched in Exodus, on no evidence. Cf. Ginzberg II, p. 375;

600,000 heads of families plus five children each on horseback, plus a mixed multitude, "exceeding greatly the Hebrews in number." The "mixed multitude" referred to in Ex. 12:38 in some translations is termed "persons of mixed ancestry" in the Douay (R.C.) translation and a fn. p.89 defines the term as "half-Hebrew and half-Egyptian." Sir Flinders Petrie (Egypt and Israel, p.67) offered an ingenious explanation of the numbers... Instead of translating the Hebrew word for "thousand" as a numeral, he would translate it as "family" or "tent." Thus the number in the tribe of Manasseh in the first census at the Holy Mountain, 32, 200, would really mean 32 tents for 200 people, at six people per tent or family. The total number in Exodus would be 5-6000 people. This attractive hypothesis is not accepted by experts in the Hebrew language. G. Mendenhall, 77 *J Bib Lit* (1958) 52-6, says the same word may mean "military units."
4. A legend (IV G fn, 806) claims that only one in fifty Hebrews believed in Yahweh and left Egypt. (Cf. Pseudo-Philo, 14:156)
5. *Psalm* 68:22 speaks of the people lost in the depths of the Sea of Passage and promises them redemption and revenge.
6. See also *Ex.* 1:9-10; *Ex.* 4:3-4; *Ex.* 16:22, all indicating an organized movement. But they are not tight tribal groups, more an insurrectionary movement like the Long March of Mao and the Chinese communists. "The human groups whom he proposes to lead out are only loosely associated with one another; their traditions have grown faint, their customs degenerate, their religious associations insecure." (Buber, 69).
7. *Ex.* 17:8-14.
8. VI *EB* 180-1 Cf. Buber, p. 218-9; fn 284, on theory and

literature of Levite origins.

9. Freud, 46, and curiously, several XIII Dynasty Pharaohs possessed semitic names (Bimson, 17 fn. 50).

10. III *Gen.* 248.

11. III *Gen.* 194.

12. IV *EB* 180-1.

13. *Deut.* 33:8-11.

14. On Levite functions, cf inter alia *Num.* 4:4-15; ch.18; 6:22-7.

15. III *Gen.* 224, 228.

16. *Num.* 3:11-13.

17. *Num.* 3:40-51.

18. *Ex.* 17:1-7; *Num.* 20:2-13.

19. III *Gen.* 272.

20. IV *Gen.* 3; (cf. IV G 353-4)

21. IV *Gen.* 3 fn2.

22. *Num.* 11:1-3.

23. *Ex.* 14:13.

24. *Ex.* 15:25.

25. *Ex.* 16:7-8.

26. Buber's term, pp.102-3; 108.

27. Winnett offers a close discussion of the murmurings. For mnemonic purposes, the Biblical editors sought to contain the number at ten. Winnett establishes the important point: the editors labored to change the insurrectionism against Moses into tests of Yahweh.

28. III *Gen.*, p.36-7.

29. *Ps.* 78:31; cf. *Ps.* 106:13-15; *Ex.* 16:12-13; *Num.* 11:20, 31-2, 33.

30. Ziegler, p. 47.

31. III *Gen.* 243ff.

32. *Num.* 14:1-4; cf. III *Gen.* 172.
33. III *Gen.* 277.
34. III *Gen.* 333ff.
35. Buber, 202.
36. *Joshua,* 5:2-8.
37. *Deut.* 9:24.
38. III *Gen.* 122-3.
39. *Ex.* 32. 22.
40. *Ex.* 32:35.
41. 2 *Kg.* 17.
42. Velikovsky, *W. in C.,* 297.
43. Gunnar Heinsohn ltr. II *SISR* I(1977), 3.
44. III *Gen.* 123.
45. *Ex.* 27:2.
46. III *Gen.* 132.
47. III *Gen.* 130.
48. *Num.* 16.
49. Daiches, 183.
50. Ziegler, 15.
51. *Num.* 16:8-11.
52. In the early years of modern electrostatics, experimenters used animals and human subjects repeatedly. Grey, in 1731, electrified a boy and suspended him from a rope; he suspended a second boy, unelectrified; then he connected them with a wire and observed with satisfaction that the "fire" (charge) passed to the second boy. (Cf. Priestley, pp. 52-3.) Only rarely did someone die; Moses would probaly have no qualms about "putting the heat" on prisoners; it would be an easier death than others then in vogue.
53. "Lightning" 10 *EB* 967.
54. Manoilov, 133.

55. 16 *EB* 698, "Electrical shock."
56. Corliss, op. cit. cf. Manoilov, 152.
57. Priestley. 122.
58. Ibid., 125-6.
59. Ibid., II 151-2.
60. Ibid., II 152.
61. Joseph Bozolus, an Italian priest and professor, proposed in 1767 to lay two wires underground connecting with a Leyden Jar at one end and close enough at their other ends to let sparks jump in coordination with coded messages sent at the Leyden Jar end. This was one of the first schemes for a telegraph. (Stottely, pp. 226-9.) Heilbron recalls (320) that Le Monnier "passed the shock through a mile of long-suffering Carthusians joined together by grounded iron wires. In fact moist ground may offer a discharge path as good as a human chain."
62. In Galvani's classic discovery of the neural response to electroshock, the scalpel that discharged to the frog's nerve and caused the leg muscle to contract had been charged accidentally by ionized air emanating from an idle electrostatic machine that happened to be nearby.
63. This follows the New World translation; some Bibles view the "blinding" as a metaphor, e.g. "Do you expect these people to be blind?" *(Jerusalem Bible.)*
64. *Num.* 16:35. The number seems impossibly large, like the number of those leaving Egypt and other numbers. There may at one time have been a formula for inflating biblical numbers, but no one has yet been able to break the code. Decimal numbers and numbers to the base of 60 are preferred. Here a clue that about 50 might be involved is available in the melting of the censers into an altar plate sub-

sequently (see below, VI-40). The altar would not hold a plate, even a thick one, made up of the bronze of more than fifty melted censers.
65. II *Gen.* p.303.
66. Martin Buber rather believes (309-10) that Korah and the Rebels were doused with oil, burned, and cast into a pit, than that they were electrocuted by a powerful battery, as Fisher had suggested (in *Beiträge zur Urgeschichte der Physik in Schweigger's Sinne,* 1833, pp 4 ff), My position would be that such a "voltaic pile" was not beyond Moses' capabilities but was unneccessary, since the electrical turbulence of those times in effect provided continuous "batteries" of nature for electrostatic devices and procedures. As for Martin's theory, it wanders too far from the story, which is obviously attempting to be historical. Velikovsky's similar solution (*W. in C.* p. 56) is similarly mistaken; furthermore, he generally interprets electrical fires as petroleum fires.
67. Num. 5:16-31.
68. Num. 16:5.
69. I Priestley. 125.
70. Ibid., 102-4.
71. Ibid. 125.
72. Heilbron, 320.
73. I Priestley, 122.
74. Num. 36:37.
75. III G 303.
76. Num. 18:46.
77. III G 310-2.
78. Jones, (1 vol. ed.) 246. Cf. I. Velikovsky, *Oedipus and Akhnaton* (1960) 196-202.
79. Velikovsky, *A. in C.* 329 et passim, where Akhnaton is

made contemporary of Ahab.
80. The literary sources of this paragraph are extensive. Cf. de Grazia et al. (1978), and Society for Interdisciplinary Studies, *A revised Chronology for the Ancient Near East,* Cleveland (Eng.), 1977.
81. *Num.* 25:1 ff. "Peor" says a legend, is a second name for an Angel of Death that Moses had once scared away for excessive vindictiveness against the Jews, and by facing Peor, he would continue to frighten the angel away from this same task.
82. *Num.* 25:3 Baal Peor, it is suggested, is the god or lord of fire. Mendenhall noted there is no satisfactory semitic etymology for the word Peor, but the meaning now seems clear. Peor is the Hittite word for fire. It is the base of the Greek word, Pyr, meaning fire, and of course the English word "fire." (Von Fange, 136.)
83. *Num.* 31.
84. *Deut.* 31:1-2. "The lord spoke to Moses, saying, Avenge the Israelite people on the Midianites; then you shall be gathered to your kin."
85. Ernst Sellin, *Mose and seine Bedeutung für die Israelitisch-Judische Religiongeschichte,* Leipzig (1922).
86. Sellin, 81-113, based mostly on a study of Deutero-Isaiah. See also Sellin, *Introduction to the New Testament,* 142-4. The second original sin is rendered below for Hosea, 9:10.
87. *Ex.* 32:32.
88. Sellin, 49.
89. *Hosea,* 5:2. The accursed Shittim was the point of entry into the Promised Land (*Num.* 33:49; *Joshua* 3:1; *Ex.* 33:1-6; *Hosea* 6:4-6).
90. *Hosea,* 9:7-14.

91. *Hosea*, 12:14-13:1.
92. *Hosea*, 9:10.
93. Citing *Num.* 25:6-15.
94. *Five Biblical Portraits,* South Bend, Ind. : U. of Notre Dame Press, 1981.
95. IV Gen. fn 904.
96. *Joshua* 5:2 (New world tr.).
97. *Joshua* 5:8.
98. *Joshua* 5:5. 99. *Ancient Judaism,* 443 fn. 2:92.
100. *Deut.* 34:7.

Chapter 8: The Electric God

1. III *Gen.* 431.
2. *The Origin of Consciousness in the Breakdown of the Bicameral Mind,* Boston: Houghton Mifflin,1976.
3. *The Palaetiology of Homo Sapiens Schizotypicalis,* Princeton: Quiddity Press, 1976. See, now, *Homo Schizo* volumes I and II, Princeton, N.J.: Metron Publns., 1983.
4. William J. Broad, "Syria Said to Suppress Archaelogical Data." 205 *Science* (31 August 1979), 878-1, 880.
5. *Gen.* 49:18; Buber, 50.
6. Winnett, 20-4.
7. Ziegler, 98.
8. III *Gen.* 94.
9. *Ex.* 4:14-15.
10. II *Gen.* 318-9.
11. Auerbach, 189.
12. Buber, 113-4.
13. Ziegler, 14.

14. Ibid., 72. See A. de Grazia, *Chaos and Creation,* Princeton, N.J.: Metron Publns, 1981, where a setting of the skies is said to begin at this time.
15. See also *Lev.* 19:12 against swearing falsely and profaning the name. *Lev.* 24:15 sets the death penalty by community stoning for cursing the Lord or blaspheming his name. Weber writes (p. 447, fn. 23), "The abuse of the name of Yahweh finds its correspondence in the sanction of blinding." Why? So that they may not ever see Yahweh upon the Ark speaking his name? Cf. Gaster, nos. 187, 72; Erman, *SBAW* (1911) pp. 1098 ff.
16. Ziegler, 13.
17. Cassuto, 243-4.
18. Ibid., 334.
19. III *Ency. Relig. and Ethics,* 510.
20. *Moses and Monotheism,* 144.
21. Jaynes, 89ff.
22. Ex.7:3-4. See also here in chapter I, where it is shown that this "hardening" theme is owing to the comet's implacability.
23. *Is.* 45:7; Cf. Buber, 58.
24. *Ezek.* 20:26. See *Ex.* 13:1-2; 34:19-20; 23-29; *Lev.* 27:26-7; *Num.* 3:13; 8-17-8; 18-15. Cf. *Gen.* 22:1-19; I *Kg.* 16:34; II *Kg.* 16:3; *Mic.* 6:7.
25. M. Eliade, *Traité d'Histoire des Religions* (1964, 1974), 88.
26. 2 *Sam.* 22:9.
27. George E. Mendenhall, *The Tenth Generation: The Origins of the Biblical Tradition,* Baltimore: John Hopkins U. Press, 1973.
28. *Psychopathology and Politics* (Chicago: U. of Chicago Press, 1930.
29. This sharp statistical distinction between the religion of

Genesis and the other Books of Moses supports the argument made elsewhere in this book, that Moses invented Yahweh and that Yahweh is unconnected with Elohim in actuality.

30. *Jer.* 2:6.
31. Daiches, 154.
32. *Ex.* 32:9-10.
33. *Ezek.* 20:13-14 (New World transl.)
34. Buber, p.117; *Ezek.* 1:26.
35. *Ex.* 3:6.
36. *Ex.* 6:2.
37. Buber, 44.
38. *Mose and seine Zeit,* p.433.
39. Max Weber, 49, citing *Gen.* 13:8f.
40. "Judaism," 10 *EB* (1980) 304. Also Cassuto (27) and Sellin are unusual in stressing that Moses was a Messiah and Savior.
41. Buber, 105.
42. *Amos* 9:7-10.
43. Jacob is Israel.
44. *Deut.* 32:8-12; *Oxford Bible,* fn 256-7 says "sons of god" means "the divine beings who belong to the heavenly court."
45. Cf. *Gen.* 1:26; *Ps.* 29:1; 1 *Kg.* 22:19; *Job* 1:6; *Is.* 6:8.
46. Andrew Jukes, *The Names of God,* London: Kregel, 1888.
47. Contained as pp.129-31 in G.A. Tuttle, ed., *Bible and Near Eastern Studies,* Grand Rapids, Eerdmans.
48. Weber, 128-130.
49. Ibid. I Sam. 14:15; Is. 2:21f, 46:6.
50. Ibid. *Gen.* 19:24; *Ex.* 19:11f; *Psalm* 46:6.
51. Ibid. *Is.* 30:27.
52. Ibid. *Zech.* -:14.

53. Ibid. *Psalm* 18:14.
54. *Mose and seine Zeit,* 443.
55. J. Van Seters, *The Hyksos* (1966), 99 quoted by Bimson, I *SISR* 4 (1977) 9.
56. Larousse *Encycl. of Mythology,* "Thoth." 57. Tomkins, 169.
58. Mircea Eliade, *Myth of the Eternal Return,* 22.
59. See G.A. Wainwright, "The Relationship of Amun to Zeus and His Connection with Meteorites," XVI *J. Egypt. Archaeo.* (1930), 35-8.

Conclusion

1. *Ex.* 3:3.
2. *The Religion of Ancient Israel* (London: Lutterworth Press, 1967), citing N. Soderblom, P. Volz and J. Pedersen.

Appendix

1. I examine the Homeric origins in a 1968 manuscript on **The Disastrous Love Affair of Moon and Mars,** published in 1983, but Velikovsky, in part II of *W. in C.* presents the original case.
2. Cassuto, 2.
3. Ibid., 27-8, et passim.
4. *Num.* 33:1-49.
5. "Biblical Literature," 2 *EB* 882.
6. Winnett, op. cit.
7. Ibid., p. 132.
8. 1969, p. 476.
9. Tr. Israel Abrahams (1959), Hebrew U., Jerusalem, 26-7.

10. 69 *Zeitschrift fur Alttestament. Wiss.* (1957), 84-103 and 70 *ZAW* (1958), 48-59.
11. Op. cit.
12. This approach is also used by A.G. Galanopoulos and E. Bacon, *Atlantis,* Bobbs-Merril Co.: Indianapolis, 1969, 192-9.
13. Hort, p. 59.
14. 66.
15. 67-8.
16. 69-73.
17. 144-5.
18. 77.
19. 74.
20. 111.
21. 79.
22. 256.
23. J.G. Galway and J.T. Schaefer, "Fowl Play," 32 *Weatherwise* (1979) 116-8.
24. *The Sirius Mystery,* London: Sidgwick and Jackson, 1976.
25. Von Fange, 131.
26. *Ex.* 15:27.
27. 17 *EB* 519.
28. James Perrick, Jr., *The New Madrid Earthquakes of 1811-1812,* (1976)
29. Daiches, 90.
30. Ibid., 237.
31. *Moses in Greco-Roman Paganism,* Nashville: Abingdon Press, 1972.
32. *Ex.* 10:24.
33. *The Ark, the Ephod, and the "Tent of Meeting,"* Cincinnati: Hebrew Union CP, 1945.

34. *The Bible and the Ancient Near East,* New York: Doubleday, 1967, ch. 8, 136-51. 35. "Earliest Representation of the Ark of the Law," 14 *JQR* (1902), 737-9.

INDEX

(Denoting prominent passages on names, places and subjects. The abbreviation e.p. Stands for *et passim,* when other mentions are present in the work.)

Aaron: 25-6, 42, 68, 90, 102, 116, 119, 122, 132, 137-140, 145, 153, 164, 167-8, 171, 173, 179, 185, 187-8, 199, 201, 205, 212, 217-8, 228, 239, 242, 246, 263, 266, 268-274, 278-282, 286-8, 294, 296-8, 306, 313, 344, 359, 364,, 371, 385 *e.p.*
altars: 54-5, 80-1, 96, 102, 136-7, 160, 164, 182-7, 222, 231, 245, 268-9, 281, 285, 288, 295-6, 310, 316, 326, 426-7
alphabet: 124, 194, 227-9
Amalekites: 51,57, 69, 87-8, 147, 189, 226, 246, 262, 277, 385, 402
angel: 16-24, 48-9, 61-2, 73-7, 79, 107, 194, 217, 234, 277, 322, 357, 384, 418, 428 *e.p.*
Apollo: 154-5
Ark: 15, 53-5, 77, 82, 112-166, 188, 204, 223, 239, 245, 247-8, 254, 268, 272, 284, 288, 292-3, 295, 313, 316, 322-5, 360, 370, 372, 393-4, 409, 411, 414, 430 *e.p.*
Ark of the Covenant: 54, 82, 113, 118-9, 121, 126, 141, 147, 161, 209, 247, 254, 284, 322, 360, 393-4, 409
Ark of the Torah: 394

Baal: 31, 80-2, 91, 157, 186-7, 206-7, 283, 304-6, 309-311, 333, 350, 428
Balaam: 19, 217, 421
Beth Peor: 152, 205, 280, 304-314, 341
Bible: see Appendix, *e.p.*
Brazen Serpent: 162, 187-193, 224, 355
Buber, Martin: 42, 48, 127, 129, 180, 203, 210, 214, 221-2, 319, 334, 348, 376-9, 397
Burning Bush: 15, 25, 46, 56, 66, 75, 208, 211-3, 217-8, 220, 240, 273, 320-1, 348, 388

burnt offering: 160, 164, 182-7

capacitor: 114, 122, 142, 191
Cassuto: 116, 185, 324-5, 363, 373
charisma: 58-9, 84, 197, 198-258, 284, 328
circumcision: 214-221, 245, 253, 280, 299, 314
cherubim: 55, 79, 113, 121, 125-133, 144-5, 148, 157-8, 161, 191, 239, 288, 293, 325
comet: 10, 15-40, 59, 62, 71-5, 81-2, 84-6, 90, 92, 97, 105-7, 109-111, 144, 146, 148, 152, 164, 170, 175-6, 191, 206, 220, 282-5, 349, 353, 359, 386, 398, 403

Daiches, David: 207, 214, 334, 376, 378-9, 388
darkness: 17, 24, 28, 32-3, 39, 48-9, 61, 74, 78, 87, 167, 175, 180, 276, 374, 379, 385, 404
David: 150-1, 157-160, 194-5, 202, 275, 280, 396
Decalogue: 226, 229-233, 320, 342, 365, 372, 377
dew: 177, 179-180, 212, 269, 388
dowser: 187, 211, 419

Earth, motion changed: 36-7, 49, 59, 61, 78, 94, 101, 225, 352
earthquake: 16, 28-9, 34-6, 48-50, 61-3, 78-9, 87-9, 99, 104-7, 146, 149-150, 152, 352, 386
Egypt: 9, 15-6, 18-27, 29-40, 41-45, 48-53, 55-70, -4, 82, 87, 90-4, 978, 102, 106, 108-111, 116, 119-128, 131, 144, 154-5, 157-8, 162-3, 171, 174-180, 184, 187, 197-218, 221-2, 224-230, 233-7, 240, 242-4, 246-251, 255, 259-296, 298-300, 303-4, 320-2, 333, 340, 347-355, 360, 363, 373-376, 385-6, 390-2, *e.p.*
El Arish: 87
electricity: 10, 42, 51-3, 81, 96, 105, 108, 112-6, 122-5, 134, 139, 143-4, 147, 150, 154-5, 159, 163, 170, 176-7, 185, 189, 192-5, 211-3, 249, 251, 272, 290, 295, 316, *e.p.*
electrochemistry: 107, 179, 239
electrocution: 101, 114, 118, 134-140, 158, 166, 168, 208, 268, 289, 294, 313, 427
Elohim: 134, 166, 232-3, 318-321, 348-9, 352-5, 368, 431
Ephraim: 79, 201, 271, 307, 309-311, 393

ENDNOTES, INDEX 437

Eusebius: 17, 49

fire: 18-21, 25, 29-32, 36, 38-9, 50-4, 62, 70, 71-111, 112-5, 121, 124-5, 127, 133, 137-139, 142, 145-6, 149-150, 156, 159-160, 163-6, 167-8, 170-1, 175, 177, 182-7, 192, 212, 217, 221, 229, 232, 244, 249, 267, 272-3, 278, 284-5, 290, 296, 320, 328, 351-2, 360, 374, 380-1, 388

first-born: 17, 30, 32-35, 62, 74, 207, 247, 269-272, 328, 340, 374-5, 388

Freud, Sigmund: 68, 100, 197-8, 201, 204, 214, 298-304, 307, 326, 379, 389

Gaster: 372-3, 375-6
Gentiles during Exodus: 86-92, 276
God's Fire: see Electricity
Golden Calf: 74, 80-2, 129, 168-9, 173, 199, 205, 207, 209, 231, 278, 281-5, 309, 325, 345, 350, 369-371, 386
Goshen: 34, 37, 42-3, 74, 189, 204, 259-260, 263, 265, 276, 298, 385, 388
guilt: 208, 285, 295, 299-302, 307-310, 314, 324, 334-6, 341, 368, 389

hallucination: 16, 208, 234, 237-8, 250, 252, 258, 316-8, 327, 329, 331, 337, 355, 359, 382, 384
Heaven, design of: 77-86
Heilbron: 50, 293
hemorrhoids: 155-6
historiography: 226, 229, 364, 390-1
Holy Mountain: 101, 167-8, 171, 208-9, 226, 243, 260, 369, 423
horns: 81, 101, 149, 169-172, 183-4
Hosea: 305, 307-310, 333
Hoskins: 250, 255
Hyksos: 40, 51, 57, 69, 73, 82, 87, 90, 93-4, 109, 122, 225, 228, 265, 277, 353-4, 378

immortality: 248, 342, 344-5
inventions: 119-122, 228-233, 253, 257, 316, 319, 322, 332, 395
invisible deity: 85, 113, 118, 128-9, 168, 253, 292, 325, 347, 360, 371
Ipuwer: 37-39, 78, 87, 174

Israelites, attitudes to Moses: 243

Jethro: 67, 211-é, 233, 262, 279, 419
Jericho, battle of: 145-152, 159, 181, 313
Joshua: 147-151, 153, 164, 168, 183, 194, 205, 216, 226, 228, 240, 246, 262-3, 271-2, 279-280, 288, 294, 302, 307,311-3, 344, 392
Judaism: 22, 46, 282, 301, 307, 326, 349, 368-9
Jung, Carl: 247, 302

Kohatites: 139-140, 286
Korah: 56, 102, 223, 255, 280, 286-298, 427

legends, analysis: appendix, *e.p.*
Levites: 42, 50-1, 56, 62, 68, 123, 139-143, 148, 158, 186, 201, 207, 209, 216, 220, 247-8, 259-314, 340, 364, 368, 404
Leyden Jar: 53-5, 113-5, 117-8, 296, 402
lightning: 62, 76, 94-7, 101-2, 104, 106-7, 115, 123, 136-7, 143, 160, 162, 167, 188, 213, 220, 289, 320, 352, 356

manna: 15, 81, 85, 107, 152, 174, 177, 180-2, 224, , 241, 244, 246, 249, 252, 273, 278, 328, 384-5, 387-8
matzos: 49
Micah: 153
Middle Bronze Age: 78, 88, 150, 152, 227, 258-9, 385
Midianites: 63, 67, 124, 173, 201, 210, 215, 237, 243-4, 262, 279, 299, 304-6, 319
"mixed multitude:" 67, 199-200, 243, 278, 423
monotheism: 70, 197, 214, 258, 298-300, 303, 339, 347-358
Moses: *passim*
mouse: 154-5
murder of Moses: 298-314
murmuring: see rebellion
mythology, rules: appendix, *e.p.*

negotiations: 10, 24, 41-5, 48, 189, 238, 249, 375
numbers of Exodus: 67-8, 260-6

ENDNOTES, INDEX 439

oracles: 96, 116, 141, 143-5, 147, 165-6, 223
organization: 22, 57, 67, 232, 238, 245, 258, 262, 339, 394
Ovid: 17, 91

Passover: 33, 35, 48, 91, 225, 229, 377-8
pharaoh: 10, 16, 24–7, 29-37, 39, 41-8, 50-8, 63, 68, 73, 93-4, 109, 162,
    189, 197, 199-3, 210, 215, 217-8, 234-5, 244, 258, 263, 2656,
    276, 286, 298, 303, 321, 327, 348, 359, 374, 376-7, 385, 398
Philistines: 87, 153, 155-7
phosphorus: 177-8, 212, 224, 249, 263, 273, 297
piezoelectricity: 106-8
plagues: 10, 15-40, 44-9, 58, 62, 67, 87-8, 91-3, 106, 108, 144, 152, 156-7,
    173, 175, 179, 222, 244, 249, 269, 272, 276, 279, 282, 285-6, 297,
    305-6, 311, 349, 352-3, 372-7, 388, 390-2
Pliny: 17-9, 24, 86, 89, 191
Plutarch: 17, 24, 93, 165
Pouch of Judgement: 193-6
pragmatics of legend:
Promised Land: 18, 35, 66-8, 211, 230, 258, 260, 267, 271, 279-280, 302,
    304, 307, 313, 339, 343, 392
pursuit, in Exodus: 10, 32, 50-6, 68, 70, 265, 377
Pyramid: 31, 36, 52-5, 88-9, 97-8, 102, 134, 162-3, 210, 224, 250, 322,
    339, 402

quail: 241, 244, 246, 252, 273, 278, 381-3, 385, 387

radiation: 26, 39, 113, 156, 171-5, 177-8, 180, 224, 269, 278, 390, 416
rebellion: 16, 48, 70, 276, 286-298, 299-300, 385
red, horror of: 92-4, 179
report of the spies: 271-2, 279-280, 286
revolt: see rebellion
Rockenbach: 18, 21
rods: 18, 25-6, 114, 124, 132-3, 139, 155-6, 160-2, 187-191, 196, 224, 244,
    263, 266, 273, 278, 288, 290, 292-3, 297-8, 385

scientist, science: 9, 21-2, 24, 26, 28, 42, 45, 50-4, 66, 70, 94-5, 112-5, 119,
    121-5, 131, 138-9, 143-4, 153, 157, 175–6, 179, 182, 186, 187,

192, 195, 200, 204, 211, 214, 216, 221-233, 244, 248-259, 275, 284-5, 289-292, 300, 304, 315-7, 330-2, 337, 342, 356, 358-361, 364, 373, 375, 383-4, 390, 397
schizophrenia: 198, 217, 249-256, 317, 327, 341
Sellin, Ernst: 9, 227, 299, 305, 307, 309-311
Sennacherib: 154
sin: 73, 172, 200, 207, 226, 232, 252, 274, 277, 294, 301, 309-310, 324, 331-343, 347, 353, 361
speech disorders: 201, 213-221, 228, 248, 250, 253, 420
stereotyping: 390-2
sun: 28, 50, 61, 74, 76, 89-2, 103, 105, 109-111, 112, 145, 153, 164, 177, 221, 224-5, 263, 297-8, 306, 315, 338

Tabernacle: 77-81, 100, 102, 135, 172, 175, 178-9, 181-2, 184-5, 188, 208, 233, 238, 257, 267-8, 284, 286, 288, 298, 306, 325, 394
Temple of Solomon: 21, 82, 158, 160-1, 166, 283, 322, 325,   394
Tesla, Nicola: 115, 163-4
Thera: 108-9, 375, 414
Thoth: 35, 45, 52, 55, 82, 96, 126, 155, 187, 203, 221-2, 250, 316, 354-8,

Thoum, Pharaoh Thaoi: 24, 39, 41, 43-4, 163, 189, 398
Thut-Moses III: 162-3
tongues, speaking in: 145, 244
Typhon: 18, 89-90, 93-4, 111, 121, 191, 378, 386, 397

Urim and Thummim: 193-6, 194-5, 227
Uzza: 73
Uzzah: 139, 158, 372

Vitaliano, Dorothy: 375
Velikovsky: 21, 23, 28, 34, 37, 73-4, 87, 89, 91, 111, 146, 163, 225, 303-4, 389

warfare: 248, 280
waters, movement of: 15, 25, 59-66, 68-9, 265, 277, 375, 403
wire conductors: 114, 123-5, 133, 140, 164, 229, 286, 290-3, 295-6

Yahweh: 15-6, 18-21, 25, 29, 32, 34-5, 42-9, 52, 56, 59, 66-70, 74-8, 80, 82, 84-5, 96, 100-3, 113, 116, 118, 121, 126-133, 137-141, 143-5, 147, 149, 157-8, 160, 162, 164, 166-173, 175-178, 182-190, 194, 196, 199, 204-9, 213-223, 226, 228-233, 237, 239-248, 252-8, 262, 266, 268-288, 292-314, 315-358, 360, 364-5, 367-371, 377, 381-390, 392-3 *e.p.*

Ziegler, Jerry: 114, 128, 134, 143, 147, 154, 165, 191, 254, 323

www.ingramcontent.com/pod-product-compliance
Lightning Source LLC
Chambersburg PA
CBHW022056150426
43195CB00008B/154